European and Global Governance: Laws and Rights

European and Global Governance: Laws and Rights

Edited by Jameson Kemp

MURPHY & MOORE
www.murphy-moorepublishing.com

Murphy & Moore Publishing,
1 Rockefeller Plaza,
New York City, NY 10020, USA

ISBN: 978-1-63987-217-6

Cataloging-in-Publication Data

European and global governance : laws and rights /
edited by Jameson Kemp.
p. cm.
Includes bibliographical references and index.
ISBN 978-1-63987-217-6
1. European Union. 2. International cooperation. 3. Administrative law--European Union countries. 4. Law--European Union countries. 5. Public administration.
I. Kemp, Jameson.

KJE947 .E875 2022
341.242 2--dc23

For information on all Murphy & Moore Publications
visit our website at www.murphy-moorepublishing.com

MURPHY & MOORE

Contents

Preface

The term European governance refers to the set of rules, practices and procedures which are related to the exercising of powers in the European Union. It aims to strengthen democracy across Europe and improve the relationship between the citizens and European institutions. The key objectives of European governance are to increase the transparency in European Union institutions, formulate well-managed policies, and develop a predictable and stable framework for growth. It also attempts to study the challenges related to democratic control, judicial review and accountability in a global context. The book presents researches and studies performed by experts across the globe. It traces the progress of this field and highlights some of its key concepts and applications. This book is a vital tool for all researching or studying the laws and rights related to European and global governance.

After months of intensive research and writing, this book is the end result of all who devoted their time and efforts in the initiation and progress of this book. It will surely be a source of reference in enhancing the required knowledge of the new developments in the area. During the course of developing this book, certain measures such as accuracy, authenticity and research focused analytical studies were given preference in order to produce a comprehensive book in the area of study.

This book would not have been possible without the efforts of the authors and the publisher. I extend my sincere thanks to them. Secondly, I express my gratitude to my family and well-wishers. And most importantly, I thank my students for constantly expressing their willingness and curiosity in enhancing their knowledge in the field, which encourages me to take up further research projects for the advancement of the area.

Editor

1

Revisiting the Role and Future of National Constitutions in European and Global Governance

Anneli Albi and Samo Bardutzky

Abstract The Introduction provides an overview of the research project 'The Role and Future of National Constitutions in European and Global Governance', which was funded by a five-year grant of 1.2 million EUR, awarded by the European Research Council (ERC). The research findings are published in the present two-volume book, containing national reports from twenty-eight EU Member States, and a twenty-ninth report – focusing on constitutional reforms related to global governance – from Switzerland. The reports are based on the project Questionnaire. The main themes are threefold: (a) constitutional amendments with a view to EU membership; (b) constitutional adjudication at the national level regarding EU measures such as the Data Retention Directive, European Arrest Warrant and ESM Treaty; and (c) novel challenges that are increasingly highlighted in the wider context of global governance (i.e. beyond the classic international treaties that advance human rights, peace and environmental protection) in relation to democratic participation, judicial review and the rule of law. Whilst in the mainstream discourse national constitutions have typically

---

Anneli Albi is Professor of European Law, University of Kent, United Kingdom. e-mail: A.Albi@kent.ac.uk.

Samo Bardutzky is Assistant Professor of Constitutional Law at the University of Ljubljana, Slovenia; at the time of writing Research Associate, University of Kent, United Kingdom. e-mail: samo.bardutzky@pf.uni-lj.si.

A. Albi (✉)
Law School, University of Kent, Canterbury, UK
e-mail: A.Albi@kent.ac.uk

S. Bardutzky
University of Ljubljana, Ljubljana, Slovenia
e-mail: samo.bardutzky@pf.uni-lj.si

been approached from a top-down perspective and with a focus on sovereignty, the present bottom-up study allows for the perspective to be broadened by looking at how EU and transnational law have affected constitutional cultures in specific areas, such as fundamental rights protection, rule of law safeguards and constitutional review. The reports are accompanied by a linked book with a Comparative Study, which divides the constitutional systems of the EU Member States into three broader constitutional cultures and identifies overarching trends, changes and processes regarding constitutionalism. The comparative research findings are briefly outlined in the Introduction, inviting discussion on what ought to be the direction of travel for national, comparative European, EU and global constitutionalism. The project and the reports explore constitutional developments up until 2014-15 and do not address the more recent illiberal trends.

Keywords Comparative constitutional law and comparative European constitutional achievements · Political, post-totalitarian and traditional legal constitutions Constitutional amendments regarding EU integration · Fundamental/constitutional rights · The rule of law and the social democratic *Rechtsstaat* · European Arrest Warrant · Data Retention Directive · ESM Treaty, euro crisis, mutualisation of debt and democracy · Autonomous EU and global constitutionalism
The governance paradigm and neofunctionalism · Changing language of constitutionalism at the transnational level · Uniformity and diversity

1 The Reasons for Revisiting the Role of the National Constitutions

We are delighted to bring to the readers what in our view is a truly fascinating book, *National Constitutions in European and Global Governance: Democracy, Rights, the Rule of Law – National Reports*, with two combined volumes containing twenty-nine national reports, and which will shortly be accompanied by a linked comparative monograph that is hereinafter referred to as the 'Comparative Study'.[1] With the important transformations in the discourse on EU and global constitutionalism over the last few decades, we consider this to be an opportune moment to take a step back and revisit what is, or ought to be, the role of national constitutions in the new transnational legal environment. Indeed, the book comes at a time when both the European Union and the broader discourse on constitutionalism are at crossroads, with many important questions about their future directions at the centre of discussions.

Before the euro crisis, on the broader level of global constitutionalism, one leading scholarly article summarised the ongoing processes – primarily in relation to democratic legitimacy – as 'the end of constitutionalism as we know it'.[2] Another book brought together leading scholars of constitutional theory to examine issues

[1] For the publication details of the Comparative Study, see below the text accompanying note 44.

[2] Kuo 2010.

relating to what in the title was rhetorically phrased as 'The twilight of constitutionalism?'[3] Some scholars have additionally noted the emergence of a thin, weak, procedural version of the rule of law, judicial review and democratic control in the context of European and global economic co-operation, with reduced opportunities for citizens to challenge public decisions.[4] Furthermore, the extent to which the vocabulary of constitutionalism may have changed emerges from a recent influential monograph, *Beyond Constitutionalism*, by Nico Krisch, who calls for breaking away from and discarding the paradigm of constitutionalism in post-national law altogether, in favour of a paradigm of pluralism.[5] Krisch has summarised what seems to be the prevailing view amongst EU and global governance lawyers: 'the prospect of domestic constitutionalism shaping global governance or controlling its impact is very limited', and the only hope would be 'to turn the clock back and begin to withdraw from regional and international structures of cooperation'.[6]

An increasing number of scholars have begun to express heightened concerns about the decline of constitutionalism in the context of the euro crisis management. For example, Agustín Menéndez has documented the breadth of the European Union's 'constitutional mutation',[7] warning that 'the breakdown of constitutional law will result in the mid- or long-run in the breakdown of the Social and Democratic *Rechtsstaat*'.[8] Gunnar Beck cautions that the recent euro crisis adjudication in the European and national courts has allowed a bending of the rules to suit the executive to the extent that 'the Rechtsstaat is effectively suspended'.[9] The prevailing theories in Italy, as summarised by Andrea Simoncini, are that the euro crisis measures have accelerated a 'decline of European constitutionalism', with constitutions 'destined to be obsolete' in 'the present age [that is] no longer the age of constitutions'.[10] A small but growing number of scholars have even expressed concern about the EU having taken an authoritarian turn in the euro crisis governance. Christian Joerges and Maria Weimer have cautioned against the entrenchment of 'authoritarian executive managerialism'[11] that 'threatens to discredit the idea of the rule of law and its intrinsic linkages to democratic rule'.[12] Alexander Somek finds that in the EU's euro crisis management, 'formal legal constraints are bent in order to accommodate necessities'; he is concerned that this has led to

[3] Dobner and Loughlin 2010, p. xi.

[4] Harlow 2006, p. 195; Galera 2010, p. 302.

[5] Krisch 2010, pp. 21, 26, 79, 303. On the changing vocabulary of constitutionalism, see Martinico 2015, pp. 5 et seq., and below notes 74 and 92, along with the accompanying text.

[6] Krisch 2010, pp. 20–21.

[7] Menéndez 2014.

[8] Menéndez 2013, pp. 522–533, quote at p. 523.

[9] Beck 2012, pp. 446–449, as cited in Bobek 2014, p. 423.

[10] Simoncini 2013, pp. 158–159, 186.

[11] Joerges and Weimer 2012.

[12] Joerges 2014, p. 26.

'authoritarian liberalism' and 'loss of political agency', with the executive branch gaining power, as the constraints on governance are economic.[13] Michael Wilkinson, also describing the EU crisis governance as 'authoritarian liberalism', has observed a process of 'de-democratisation', 'de-legalisation' and the overriding of Europe's constitutional law with market teleology.[14]

However, what has hitherto received negligible attention is the way in which European constitutionalism and the European constitutional law discourse **had already changed in the years preceding the financial crisis, during the 'state of normalcy'**. In particular, two key EU measures – the European Arrest Warrant Framework Decision[15] and the (eventually annulled) Data Retention Directive[16] – are emblematic of broader changes in fundamental rights protection, constitutional review and judicial practice. In the following paragraphs, we will bring some examples of the issues explored in the national reports in the present two-volume book and in the accompanying Comparative Study. We consider the quotes cited to be both disconcerting – as they signal an uncertain fate for some of the historical achievements of European constitutionalism – as well as motivating for lawyers and scholars who may have had concerns about strain on well-established fundamental rights and values within individual national constitutional orders but without awareness that such concerns are often more widely shared.

By way of such examples, with regard to the European Arrest Warrant (EAW), the Italian report poignantly documents the way in which the national legislature was caught between criticism regarding infringements of fundamental rights in the context of the EAW and pressure from the European Commission, which was relentless in its calls for a faithful and complete implementation of the controversial Framework Decision. The report summarises concerns articulated by governmental committees and numerous legal scholars in Italy. Among the latter, the eminent constitutionalist Cesare Pinelli characterised the EAW as 'the first serious threat of disablement of the constitutional guarantees to the right of liberty'.[17] In Ireland, the automaticity involved in giving effect to foreign prosecutorial and judicial decisions has been a constant source of concern for the Irish courts, which the Irish report extensively documents with examples from case law.[18] In Slovenia, scholarship has

---

[13] Somek 2014, pp. 23–24.

[14] Wilkinson 2016, pp. 29 et seq.

[15] Council Framework Decision of 13 June 2002 on the European arrest warrant and the surrender procedures between Member States (2002/584/JHA), [2002] OJ L 190/1.

[16] Directive 2006/24/EC of the European Parliament and of the Council of 15 March 2006 on the retention of data generated or processed in connection with the provision of publicly available electronic communications services or of public communications networks and amending Directive 2002/58/EC, [2006] OJ L 105/54.

[17] Pinelli 2012, p. 2399, as cited in the report on Italy by Martinico, Guastaferro and Pollicino in this book [The Constitution of Italy: Axiological Continuity Between the Domestic and International Levels of Governance?], Sect. 2.3.5.1.

[18] The report on Ireland by Hogan in this book [Ireland: The Constitution of Ireland and EU Law: The Complex Constitutional Debates of a Small Country], Sects. 2.3.1.1 and 2.3.6.

warned that the 'uncritical application of the principle of mutual recognition bears the danger of transforming the judge into a kind of a "ticking box" automaton checking only pre-established criteria and neglecting his/her duty of a critical assessment and safeguarding fundamental (constitutional) rights to the defendant'.[19] From the Netherlands, concerns expressed by Judge Rob Blekxtoon from the District Court of Amsterdam are summarised in the accompanying Comparative Study. Judge Blekxtoon has written that his 'quiet life was disturbed' and he 'began writing critical articles on the European Arrest Warrant in various journals and law reviews', and that he even took the initiative in 2005 to publish the *Handbook on the European Arrest Warrant* in his effort to save 'the well-established principles of extradition law which serve to safeguard the interests of the requested persons'.[20] Judge Blekxtoon additionally wrote that he was 'very disappointed', as he had been 'told by people closely following the drafting of the EAW Framework Decision that the officials responsible for the outcome did not really want to listen to the experts present at the negotiations who knew what they were talking about'. It had been 'more important to speed up matters for political reasons'.[21]

Turning to the Data Retention Directive, the Austrian report spells out a concern that also implicitly arises from several other reports – that a 'taboo' has been 'broken':

> ... Austrian society and the state did everything to escape this unconstitutional situation and finally succeeded. The damage, however, was already done. The taboo was broken and since [... the annulment of the Directive], Austrian police authorities have increased political pressure for re-implementation.[22]

The Slovenian report notes that if the Data Retention Directive

> had been a purely domestic legislative project, it would have probably met insurmountable constitutional and democratic obstacles. But as it originated in the EU, it became part of the law in a very different atmosphere.[23]

Along with the above measures, the present edited volume predominantly focuses on the constitutional impact of the pre-financial crisis developments and the question of **what is, or ought to be, the normal state of affairs in European constitutionalism**.

It should be noted early on that the project and the reports explore constitutional developments up until 2014-15 and do not address Brexit or the more recent illiberal trends. The timeline of the project is explained below in Sect. 5.

---

[19] Erbežnik 2014, p. 131, as cited in the report on Slovenia by Bardutzky in this book [The Future Mandate of the Constitution of Slovenia: A Potent Tradition Under Strain], Sect. 2.3.5.3.

[20] Blekxtoon 2009, p. V.

[21] Ibid., p. V.

[22] The report on Austria by Lachmayer in this book [The Constitution of Austria in International Constitutional Networks: Pluralism, Dialogues and Diversity], Sect. 2.12.

[23] The report on Slovenia by Bardutzky in this book [The Future Mandate of the Constitution of Slovenia: A Potent Tradition Under Strain], Sect. 2.13.

2 Overview of the ERC-Funded Research Project 'The Role and Future of National Constitutions in European and Global Governance'

The issues explored in the previous section are at the centre of the large-scale research project 'The Role and Future of National Constitutions in European and Global Governance'. The research project was funded by a five-year grant of 1.2 million EUR, awarded by the European Research Council (ERC) (Grant Agreement No. 284316; project acronym: ConstEurGlobGov), as part of the EU's Seventh Framework Programme.

The present two-volume book contains the first main aspect of the research: the twenty-nine national reports prepared by leading constitutional law experts. The national reports were written on the basis of a Questionnaire, which was prepared by Professor Anneli Albi, the Principal Investigator of the research project, in consultation with Dr Samo Bardutzky, who worked for several years as the project's Research Associate. The two volumes are accompanied by a linked, complementary book containing a Comparative Study. These aspects of the research project will be outlined in greater detail here and in the subsequent sections.

In designing the project's Questionnaire and thereby also the general framework of the national reports, the idea was to **bring together case law, doctrine and constitutional debates from the perspective of a multitude of national constitutional systems**. We sought to provide viewpoints from national and comparative constitutional law in order to offer a fuller understanding of European constitutional law than what has prevailed in the mainstream English language European constitutional discourse, where **the starting point has typically been the autonomous nature of EU constitutional law** and its **top-down reception** in the Member States. Additionally, whilst existing comparative studies are typically based on a limited number of case studies, we committed to covering all of the twenty-eight Member States of the Union, and added a twenty-ninth report – focusing on constitutional reforms related to global governance – from Switzerland. The inclusion of smaller and what are often regarded as more peripheral countries has not only allowed the project to give a greater voice and visibility to the diverse constitutional systems, but has also unearthed numerous interesting and important broader trends, patterns and changes that warrant wider attention and discussion. Some of these will be summarised at the end of this introductory chapter.

The editors would like to express their greatest gratitude for the generous grant funding from the ERC, which has made it possible to carry out such comprehensive and systematic research on comparative constitutional law that otherwise quite possibly would never have been brought to life. The views and any errors are solely those of the editors and authors, and cannot be attributed to the European Research Council or to the European Union.

We are also pleased that this book has been published by T.M.C. Asser Press, which has a long-established tradition of publishing in the field of interaction between EU law and national legal systems. One key Asser Press book that has become part of a well-established canon in the field is the so-called 'Red Book', *The Constitutional Impact of EU Enlargement at EU and National Level*, which explores how national constitutions both in the older and new Member States have been adjusted to accommodate EU membership.[24] Another leading Asser Press publication that sparked interest in the research that follows is the above-mentioned *Handbook on the European Arrest Warrant*, edited by Judge Blekxtoon.[25]

3 The Questionnaire

The national reports have been structured and written on the basis of the above-mentioned Questionnaire, which is reproduced in the chapter in book. Questionnaire invited constitutional law experts to consider national case law, doctrine and policy documents in three main areas, and was divided into three parts.

Part 1 explored how constitutions reflect the transfer of powers from domestic to European and global institutions, and thus to what extent they provide legitimacy to the shift in the exercise of power to the transnational level and retain their social relevance. Part 2 of the Questionnaire looked beyond the question of transfer of sovereignty, which has been the predominant focus of the discourse so far, and asked for reflection on constitutional values that have a continued importance in the contemporary globalising and pluralist legal setting, such as the protection of fundamental rights, the rule of law and constitutional review.

The experts were tasked with outlining constitutional court judgments that tackle the protection of these rights and values in transnational judicial dialogues, e.g. regarding the Data Retention Directive, the European Arrest Warrant, the Treaty Establishing the European Stability Mechanism (ESM Treaty) and European Commission and International Monetary Fund (IMF) economic crisis/austerity measures. The Questionnaire also invited assessment of the responsiveness of the European Court of Justice (CJEU) with regard to these rights and values, as well as assessment of the standard of protection at supranational level. Finally, Part 3 sought to explore the novel challenges that are increasingly highlighted in the wider context of global governance (i.e. beyond the classic international treaties that advance human rights, peace and environmental protection) in relation to legitimacy, democratic control, accountability and the rule of law.

It should be noted that the Questionnaire was prepared in 2013–2014 when critical scholarly and public discussion about EU and transnational governance was rare and very limited.

---

[24] Kellermann et al. 2001.

[25] Blekxtoon 2005; cf. also Blekxtoon 2009, p. V, supra n. 20 and the accompanying text.

4 The Constitutional Law Experts

The constitutional experts from whom the reports were commissioned are leading scholars in the field of constitutional law or European constitutional law, with an extensive record of publications in the field of interaction between national and EU constitutional law (in English, given the overall nature of the book, which inevitably had to take priority over our commitment to bring other voices and languages to the fore). In some countries, two experts were invited as joint experts, while in other cases, the main constitutional expert opted to invite one or more research collaborators, given the extensive scope of the Questionnaire. In particular, we are pleased that several scholars specialising in the field of criminal law kindly joined the project to cover the questions relating to the European Arrest Warrant. The main constitutional experts are listed in the Preface. We are honoured that a number of distinguished, current and former judges of constitutional courts and other highest courts have joined us here as scholarly colleagues. In the intervening years, we were honoured to observe that several colleagues were subsequently appointed as Judge or Advocate General to the European Court of Justice. The editors are delighted to be able to present the full, collected reports which, thanks to countless hours of thorough, patient and perceptive research by more than sixty colleagues, make for rich and thought-provoking reading.

In the framework of the project, the Network of Constitutional Experts was established in the hope that it would provide a more long-term structure and forum for deliberating perspectives from comparative constitutional law in the context of transnational governance.

The project questions and draft reports were discussed at a work-in-progress seminar 'Assessing the Responsiveness of the EU to Constitutional Rights: Data Retention, Arrest Warrants and Beyond', held at the University of Kent on 28–29 August 2014. In addition to contributions from project experts, we were honoured to have presentations from a number of guest speakers who are distinguished judges and/or scholars working in related areas. The themes covered included: cases regarding the EU Data Retention Directive (Brun-Otto Bryde, Jiři Zemanek and Gerard Hogan); case law on social rights affected by the IMF austerity measures (Kristīne Krūma); the EU's democratic responsiveness (Damian Chalmers); the shift towards authoritarian executive managerialism in euro crisis governance (Christian Joerges); rights protection issues in the context of the European Arrest Warrant (Valsamis Mitsilegas, Esther Herlin-Karnell); and the constitutional issues surrounding the Trans-Atlantic Trade and Investment Partnership (TTIP) (Harm Schepel).

5 The National Reports and the Timeline of the Project

The structure of the national reports follows the three parts of the Questionnaire.[26] In principle, the authors were expected to follow the numbering of the questions from the Questionnaire, so that the reader would be able to compare the situation in a number of jurisdictions regarding a particular issue. To a great extent, this is indeed the case. Nevertheless, as the accounts of the individual constitutional systems differ, the editors did not insist on the numbering and, in many instances, the answers to questions have been merged. In the editorial process, we aimed to ensure that the reports would, as far as possible, be written in a way that would allow for them to be read independently without reference to the Questionnaire.

Whilst the reports are relatively lengthy – in the range of 19,000–23,000 words – they are also simultaneously not long enough, as they essentially provide but a glimpse of both the constitutional culture as well as of the constitutional doctrine and debates in the individual areas explored. Experts were not expected to answer all of the questions in an equal level of detail; they were invited to focus on issues of particular relevance for the Member State in question. Where the national discussions were considered particularly to be of broader, Europe-wide interest, an editorial decision was made to accommodate a longer report (e.g. Germany, Cyprus and Estonia).

In terms of the timeline, it should be noted that the majority of the reports were submitted during 2015, with some having been received in 2014 and some later in 2016. The Comparative Study was written in 2016–2019. The publication of the national reports was delayed, as the comparative analysis was initially meant to take the form of a shorter comparative report to be included in the present volumes. However, as the analysis grew in length, depth and breadth, it was eventually decided that it would be published as a separate but linked book.

It is important to note that the **aim of the project was to take stock of and identify the challenges posed to the Member States' constitutional law up until 2014–2015**; the reports and the Comparative Study **do not include more recent developments**. This book therefore does not cover the Brexit referendum (although a brief post scriptum note has been added to the British report), France's state of emergency regime after the November 2015 terrorist attacks in Paris or the developments in Poland from autumn 2015 that prompted the European Commission to act under the EU rule of law framework. The book also does not explore the recent, more wide-spread turn towards illiberal constitutional trends, at least beyond the national report on Hungary.

Instead, **the project explores the deeper comparative European constitutional culture and the approach to the rule of law as it had been consolidated before the financial crisis** and before the other more recent crises and illiberal developments. The project examines the common and diverse elements in the comparative European constitutional landscape, and how these have been affected

[26] With the exception of the report on Switzerland (see below).

or changed by the ongoing transition to autonomous EU constitutional law and global governance. In the accompanying Comparative Study, the comparative European constitutional achievements prior to the recent illiberal turn are collated and documented in greater detail, **in the hope that these will serve as guidance for a quest to restore the values of European constitutionalism** that have been eroded, and help shield the values that remain.

6 The Structure of the Two-Volume Book: The Categorisation and Typology of Europe's National Constitutional Cultures

The national reports are structured in the present two-volume book on the basis of a somewhat revised typology of Europe's national constitutions, which is developed and explained in greater detail in the linked Comparative Study. As was once remarked by Dieter Grimm, former judge of the German Federal Constitutional Court and one of the national constitutional experts for Germany, '[t]ypologies are not ends in themselves. They help to answer questions' depending on the 'research interests that a scholar of constitutionalism pursues'.[27] The basis for the typology that underlies the structure of the present book is the dichotomy between **historical constitutions** on the one hand and **revolutionary constitutions** on the other, as developed by Leonard Besselink and outlined in the Questionnaire.[28] A similar division of Europe's national constitutions has also been suggested by other scholars, at times with somewhat different terminology. For example, Cesare Pinelli writes about 'evolutionary' or incrementally evolving constitutions, 'artificial' constitutionalism that prevailed on the European continent since the 1789 Revolution, and the more recent formation of a constitutional tradition in continental Europe that was based on the collapse of totalitarian regimes.[29] Within the present research project, the categorisation of the constitutional systems became somewhat more nuanced as the national reports were gradually received and as the broad and diverse landscape of national constitutions in Europe began to reveal itself to the editors of the book. As will be explained briefly in this introductory chapter, the categorisation of the constitutional systems is closely linked to the essence of the research question pursued by this project, which is **how EU law and global governance have affected the different national constitutional cultures**. Whilst in the mainstream EU discourse, national constitutions have typically been approached as a relatively monolith set of instruments that primarily protect

[27] Grimm 2012, pp. 98–99.

[28] See Besselink 2006, p. 113 et seq., and as summarised in the Questionnaire [Questionnaire for the Constitutional Law Experts of the Research Project 'The Role and Future of National Constitutions in European and Global Governance'], Sect. 1.1.1 in this book.

[29] Pinelli 2016, p. 258 and, on the same page, footnotes 4 and 5, with references.

sovereignty, the present bottom-up study allows for the perspective to be broadened by looking at the effects of EU law in specific areas of constitutional culture, such as fundamental rights protection, rule of law safeguards and constitutional review.

Following the above revised typology, in the first category, as explained in greater detail in the accompanying Comparative Study, are the **political or historical constitutions**. These constitutional systems are characterised by the predominance of parliament and the absence of or a weak role for a constitutional court, and by a generic bill of rights that in some cases is historically older or based on the European Convention on Human Rights (ECHR). Additionally, the broader orientation of these constitutions is to incrementally incorporate changes *ex post facto* rather than to pre-determine the acceptable margins of behaviour for institutions in advance. In this category, we have placed the United Kingdom, Malta, the Netherlands, Luxembourg, and the Nordic countries Sweden, Denmark and Finland. Emblematically, the national report on the Netherlands is entitled 'The Pragmatics of a Flexible, Europeanised Constitution'. It emerges from the report that the Constitution, which dates back to 1814–15, bans constitutional review of Acts of Parliament, and constitutional rights are not justiciable upon the judicial review of Acts, with the ECHR and the EU Charter being applied instead.[30] The national reports on these constitutional cultures are placed in the opening part of the book after the introductory chapter.
Constitution of Switzerland, which is explored in a separate chapter, also belongs to this type of constitutional culture.

This category is followed by what in Besselink's dichotomy are referred to as 'revolutionary' constitutions, which have a strongly legal character and are enforceable by courts (Parts III–V of the book). In general constitutional theory, this type are also referred to as 'legal' constitutions. The majority of the constitutions of the Member States of the European Union can be considered as 'legal' or 'revolutionary' in character. However, as explained in greater detail in the Comparative Study, in this project the category of 'legal' or 'revolutionary' constitutions is divided into two sub-categories, which would seem more expressive in terms of conveying the constitutional impact of the EU constitutional order on the different constitutional cultures. The new proposed sub-categories are:

(1) post-totalitarian or post-authoritarian constitutions; and
(2) traditional or hybrid legal constitutions, which have strict elements combined with historical or flexible, less prescriptive aspects.[31]

The central features of the constitutions in the first of these sub-categories – **the post-totalitarian or post-authoritarian constitutions** – stand in clearest contrast to the features that characterise the political or historical constitutions. In the post-totalitarian constitutional cultures, which embody **the 'Never again' ethos**, constitutional review

[30] The report on The Netherlands by Besselink and Claes in this book [The Netherlands: The Pragmatics of a Flexible, Europeanised Constitution].

[31] For an explanation of this categorisation, see a brief explanation below in this section, and a fuller explanation with references to literature in the accompanying Comparative Study.

by constitutional courts plays a central role, the constitutions contain extensive and detailed bills of rights, and the constitutions and constitutional courts pre-determine the margins of constitutionally acceptable political behaviour. The post-totalitarian or post-authoritarian constitutions are presented in two groups, and are referred to hereinafter as the 'post-totalitarian' constitutions; the differences between totalitarian and authoritarian regimes will be explained in greater detail in the Comparative Study. The first group of post-totalitarian constitutions are those adopted after the atrocities of the Second World War in Germany and Italy, and those adopted after the end of the dictatorships of the 1970s in Spain, Portugal and Greece.

Second group are the post-communist constitutions of Central and Eastern Europe, adopted or brought back to life in the 1990s in the aftermath of the fall of the Berlin Wall in 1989. Here we study the constitutions of the countries that became the 'new' Member States: Poland, the Czech Republic, Slovakia, Slovenia, Estonia, Latvia, Lithuania, Romania, Bulgaria and Croatia.

A history of arbitrary exercise of power under socialist and communist regimes. Accordingly, their constitutions have entrenched strict constitutional safeguards as a reaction to the human rights violations and abuses of public power experienced by the people living under the pre-1990s regimes.[32]

In fact, the eminent constitutionalist Cesare Pinelli regards the above constitutions as representing a broader continental European constitutional tradition, for the understanding of which the collapse of the totalitarian regimes in these countries is essential.[33] Prompted by a sense that the understanding of this tradition is fading in the mainstream English language EU constitutional discourse and that its classic elements are often brushed aside as representative of old-fashioned protection of sovereignty or of idiosyncratic national constitutional identity, the accompanying Comparative Study embarks on identifying **a list of twelve distinctive features of the post-totalitarian type of constitution**. These features include the following. Whereas in the political or historical type of constitutions parliament is supreme as an expression of the people's will in line with the influences of the Enlightenment and the French Revolution, in the countries that experienced totalitarianism, the constitutional design had to go further. Here the constitutional design proceeds from the understanding that democracy is not always capable of ensuring rights and the rule of law, and thus they have been removed from the realm of politics and are ensured by constitutional courts.[34] Furthermore, some core provisions (typically regarding the democratic, social state governed by the rule of law; core fundamental

---

[32] The historical background and the central tenets of the post-communist constitutionalism are explained in particular in the report on the Czech Republic by Kühn with reference to the respective judgments of the Czech Constitutional Court [The Czech Republic: From a Euro-Friendly Approach of the Constitutional Court to Proclaiming a Court of Justice Judgment Ultra Vires], Sects. 1.1.1 and 2.1.3, and in the report on Poland (pre-2016) by Biernat and Kawczyńska [The Role of the Polish Constitution (Pre-2016): Development of a Liberal Democracy in the European and International Context], Sects. 1.1.1–1.1.2, in this book.

[33] Pinelli 2016, p. 258.

[34] See e.g. Pinelli 2016, pp. 264–266, and Somek 2014, pp. 15 et seq., 84–85 and 90–95.

rights) are unamendable or subject to a special, stringent amendment procedure, often involving a referendum. With the exception of Greece, the constitutional systems of all post-totalitarian countries feature a strong, centralised constitutional court,[35] and constitutional review is typically rigorous, with a statistically high rate of annulment of legislation, in particular in cases of so-called abstract review. These courts often follow the intellectual leadership of the German Constitutional Court, and have cemented the legal character of the constitutional safeguards provided in the bills of rights and the clauses protecting the *Rechtsstaat* or *stato di diritto*, i.e. 'the state governed by the rule of law'. Crucially, these constitutions embody a value order centred on fundamental rights and based on human dignity; they typically start with extensive, detailed, directly applicable and justiciable chapters on fundamental rights and rule of law safeguards. Indeed, the editors were surprised to find that the respective constitutional provisions – especially as regards safeguards for deprivation of liberty, access to courts and the protection of the home, privacy and secrecy of communications – are often worded in a way that is notably more stringent and/or offers more extensive protection than the relatively generic provisions set out in the ECHR and the EU Charter of Fundamental Rights. The respective provisions are written out in the national reports for ease of reference. These constitutions typically also include extensive provisions on social rights and/or the social state, which form part of the concept of human dignity. This reflects the recognition that a life lived in dignity and with freedom of choice requires that a basic level of material needs is met; based on historical lessons, the social state dimension aims to avoid the root causes of the emergence of authoritarian regimes, which are economic insecurity and dependence.[36] The overall aim of the constitutional design was to avoid 'a social situation that would [give] rise to mass support for another militant, anti-democratic, populist movement'.[37] The Comparative Study additionally documents the extensive and often constitutionally codified protection of the rule of law and its different sub-principles (e.g. parliamentary reservation of law; rules on publication of laws; the rules governing the limitation of rights; the principles of legal certainty; legitimate expectations and non-retroactivity) in this constitutional tradition.

The second sub-category of 'legal' or 'revolutionary' constitutions was – after considerable reflection – designated as **'traditional or hybrid legal constitutions'**, and these are placed in a separate part of the book (Part V). The reference to 'legal' constitutions aims to signify that these constitutions have a legal character, are binding in nature and enforceable in courts, and set the broad, constitutionally acceptable margins for the political institutions and civil servants *in advance*. However, they also contain more historical, political, or otherwise flexible or less prescriptive elements. The constitutional systems placed in this category are those of France, Belgium, Ireland, Austria and Cyprus. The constitutions of the first four of these countries have historical bills of rights with limited justiciability (e.g.

[35] In Estonia, this function is carried out by the Constitutional Review Chamber of the Supreme Court.

[36] For historical background, see e.g. Somek 2014, pp. 10–13, 85–86 and 155.

[37] Somek 2014, pp. 85–86.

France's 1789 Declaration of the Rights of Man and of the Citizen, and Austria's 1867 Basic Law on the General Rights of Nationals), and the protection of fundamental rights is predominantly reliant on the ECHR. In France and Belgium, the mandate for constitutional review was initially confined to guaranteeing respect for the constitutional separation of powers scheme,[38] and thus full human rights based review is more recent.[39] In France and Ireland, the approach to judicial review is regarded as deferent to the governing institutions, as observed in the respective national reports. The constitutions date back to the pre-World War II period in Belgium (1831), Austria (1920) and Ireland (1937). The Cypriot Constitution is described in the Cyprus report as 'a hybrid model' due to special circumstances in the country.[40] The ways in which these constitutional systems are less strict and extensive in protection than the post-totalitarian constitutions are outlined in greater detail in the Comparative Study.

Hungary has been placed in a separate part of the book (Part VI), and an editorial note has been added to the report. In the recent past, Hungary's Constitution was in the category of post-totalitarian constitutions, and its Constitutional Court was widely acclaimed for its activist approach to constitutional review and the protection of fundamental rights and rule of law safeguards. The changes that have occurred since 2010 and which have been widely described as a turn to illiberal constitutionalism are explored in the national report, entitled 'Constitutional (R) evolution or Regression?'.[41]

The national report on Poland, a country which has recently followed the trend of illiberal constitutional reforms started by Hungary, was completed before these developments began to unfold. For the purposes of this study, therefore, the Polish Constitution is considered to be in the category of post-totalitarian constitutions in the 'new' Member States. It is notable that based on the case law of the Polish Constitutional Tribunal cited in the Polish report,[42] it is evident that at least up until

---

[38] De Visser 2014, p. 7.

[39] In France, fundamental rights did not become justiciable for individuals until 2010, following a constitutional amendment of 2008 whereby *ex post* control of constitutionality was introduced into French constitutional law, allowing individuals to challenge the constitutionality of legislative provisions that violate their rights. The Belgian Constitutional Court was established relatively lately, in the 1980s – first as the 'Court of Arbitration' – with the task of adjudicating federal competences. Fundamental rights review of legislation was formally introduced in 2003. See, respectively, the report on France by Burgorgue-Larsen, Astresses and Bruck [The Constitution of France in the Context of EU and Transnational Law: An Ongoing Adjustment and Dialogue to Be Improved], and the report on Belgium by Popelier and Van de Heyning [The Belgian Constitution: The Efficacy Approach to European and Global Governance], in this book.

[40] See the report on Cyprus by Kombos and Laulhé Shaelou in this book [The Cypriot Constitution Under the Impact of EU Law: An Asymmetrical Formation].

[41] The report on Hungary by Chronowski, Varju, Bárd and Sulyok in this book [Hungary: Constitutional (R)evolution or Regression?].

[42] See the report on Poland by Biernat and Kawczyńska in this book [The Role of the Polish Constitution (Pre-2016): Development of a Liberal Democracy in the European and International Context].

that time (autumn 2015), the Polish Constitutional Tribunal had taken one of the most stringent approaches to the protection of the post-totalitarian understanding of constitutionalism and the rule of law, including in the context of EU law. This deserves wider awareness, as in the mainstream European constitutional discourse, many of the respective cases of the Polish Constitutional Tribunal (pre-2016) have in a somewhat reductionist and even unfair manner been portrayed as representative of a Eurosceptic and sovereignty-protective approach.

The final part of the book (Part VII) contains the report from Switzerland, which is the only country covered by this research project that is not a member of the EU. Experts from Switzerland were invited to participate because of the **important constitutional reforms adopted in Switzerland to guarantee parliamentary participation in global governance issues** as well as a role for direct democracy in these matters.[43] It emerges from the other reports that the Swiss reforms, by and large and comparably speaking, can be considered both pioneering as well as extensive. In other countries, international law has traditionally remained a matter of one-way reception. It is thus hoped that the Swiss experience will be of considerable wider interest, and will foster thinking and discussion elsewhere.

7 The Comparative Study: Outlining the Broader Trends and Processes Emerging from the National Reports

The wealth of material collated in the national reports is synthesised in a comparative monograph written by the Principal Investigator of the project, Anneli Albi. This will be published as an accompanying, linked book entitled *National Constitutions in European and Global Governance: Democracy, Rights, the Rule of Law. A Comparative Study* (T.M.C. Asser Press, 2019), and is referred to in the present book as the 'Comparative Study'.[44] The Comparative Study outlines a number of important issues and challenges that are shared by a significant (but not always overlapping) range of Member States. Furthermore, **it identifies broader, overarching trends and processes** that at times surprised the editors and in our view warrant wider attention.

By way of examples, these include **the shift in a large number of Member States from the rule of parliamentary reservation of law to the use of governmental decrees** when implementing EU law, including – somewhat strikingly – when limiting fundamental rights and imposing sanctions.

[43] See the report on Switzerland by Kunz and Peters in this book [Constitutionalisation and Democratisation of Foreign Affairs: The Case of Switzerland].

[44] Readers writing a book review are kindly asked to obtain a copy of both books – the two-volume book with the national reports as well as the Comparative Study – from the publisher, and to review these together.

The existence of **a wider, endemic strain on constitutional values** emerged most clearly in relation to **the near-automatic process of extraditions under the European Arrest Warrant system**. Numerous ombudspersons, NGOs and associations of defence lawyers, courts and especially lower instance courts, a considerable number of dissenting judges in the highest national courts, as well as other institutions and scholars – especially scholars in the field of criminal law – in a large number of Member States have expressed significant concerns about the presumption of innocence and other defence rights, and about the absence of judicial review in extradition cases. Judicial review is not allowed even in cases where serious fundamental rights concerns have been expressed in the context of deprivation of personal liberty. Strikingly, in several reports it was observed that the European Commission, in its critical evaluation reports, has required constitutional and legislative amendments to remove protective provisions in the Member States (see especially the accounts in the reports on Cyprus, Croatia, Ireland and Italy).

Regarding the **EU Data Retention Directive**, whilst in the mainstream European discourse the constitutional challenges have widely been portrayed as cases representing national constitutional identity, it emerged that **privacy** and **protection of home and correspondence** have **'deep roots' in the continental European constitutional tradition**.[45] They have especially been subjected to **heightened protection and safeguards in the post-totalitarian constitutions**, given the historical experience of these countries with pervasive state surveillance. Although the Directive was eventually annulled by the CJEU on the second round, the far-reaching consequences have been difficult to undo. A 'taboo' was broken, as observed above in the Austrian report. As with the EAW, there has been a **spillover** from the originally intended use for serious crime into other areas. Additionally, in a development representative of a wider trend, a uniform, autonomous, self-referential standard was set by the CJEU in *Digital Rights Ireland*[46] on the basis of Arts. 7 (privacy) and 8 (data protection) of the EU Charter combined with the principle of proportionality. The more stringent approach and the diversity of the rights protected under many national constitutions and by many national constitutional courts were by and large displaced.

By way of examples from other areas, in the approach to **the rules on publication of laws**, for post-totalitarian constitutional systems there has been a shift through CJEU case law from the rule that an unpublished law is void and non-existent *ab initio/ex tunc* to the 'valid but not enforceable against individuals' approach that applies in France and Belgium. Similarly, with regard to the post-totalitarian constitutional systems, the Comparative Study documents significant changes in the approach to **limitation of fundamental rights** and in the interpretation of the principles of **legitimate expectations** and **non-retroactivity** as

---

[45] Hogan 2014, pp. 162–164. See also the report on Ireland by Hogan in this book [Ireland: The Constitution of Ireland and EU Law: The Complex Constitutional Debates of a Small Country], Sect. 2.10.1.

[46] Joined cases C-293/12 and C-594/12 *Digital Rights Ireland and Seitlinger and Others* [2014] ECLI:EU:C:2014:238.

well as **the principle of proportionality** through CJEU case law. Additionally, several national reports mentioned **strains on legal certainty** and on the clarity and **'quality of law'**.[47] A further host of profound changes emerged in a chapter exploring the **'relocation' of judicial review from constitutional courts to the European Court of Justice** in increasingly wide areas of law. These changes are discussed in the Comparative Study in the light of emerging literature where concerns have been expressed about the displacement or exclusion of constitutional courts and national highest courts, along with their well-established case law.[48]

Another area where widespread disquiet emerged concerns **the severe and prolonged erosion of the social state dimension of Europe's post-totalitarian and some traditional legal constitutions through the EU and/or IMF euro crisis measures**, e.g. by **curtailing social rights** (as well as funding for social benefits by redirecting state funds e.g. to the ESM) and reducing the protection of workers.[49] The strain on the social state is most clearly evident in the reports on Portugal, Greece, Latvia, Romania and Spain.[50] The euro crisis developments are further explored from the perspective of constitutionalisation as constitutional entrenchment – through the Treaties – of a certain economic order. As part of this broader theme, the Comparative Study explores constitutional issues relating to the

---

[47] This issue is explored report on Finland by Ojanen and Salminen [Finland: European Integration and International Human Rights Treaties as Sources of Domestic Constitutional Change and Dynamism], the report on Cyprus by Kombos and Laulhé Shaelou [The Cypriot Constitution Under the Impact of EU Law: An Asymmetrical Formation] and the report on Denmark by Krunke and Baumbach [The Role of the Danish Constitution in European and Transnational Governance] in this book. For specific guidance that implementation of EU law ought not to weaken the 'quality of law', see the work of the Finnish Parliament's Constitutional Law Committee, as outlined in the report on Finland by Ojanen and Salminen in this book [Finland: European Integration and International Human Rights Treaties as Sources of Domestic Constitutional Change and Dynamism], Sect. 2.3.6.

[48] See e.g. Komárek 2014, pp. 16 et seq.

[49] Whilst the observations regarding the social welfare dimension are also relevant e.g. with regard to the Nordic countries, in the political type of constitutions, social rights tend to be regulated at the legislative level rather than being entrenched through the text of the constitution. As it was seen above (see the text accompanying links to n. 36 and 37 respectively), historically, in the case of Germany and subsequently other post-totalitarian constitutions, protection of the social state was prompted by the lessons that the root causes of the rise of authoritarian and totalitarian governments are economic insecurity and dependence. This historical observation would seem to have significant contemporary relevance, but has perhaps been unduly neglected in the prevailing discourse where recent illiberal developments have predominantly been attributed somewhat generically to populism and nationalism.

[50] See the report on Portugal by Pereira Coutinho and Piçarra [Portugal: The Impact of European Integration and the Economic Crisis on the Identity of the Constitution], the report on Greece by Contiades, Papacharalambous and Papastylianos [The Constitution of Greece: EU Membership Perspectives], the report on Latvia by Krūma and Statkus [The Constitution of Latvia – A Bridge Between Traditions and Modernity], the report on Romania by Iancu [Romania – The Vagaries of International Grafts on Unsettled Constitutions], and the report on Spain by Solanes Mullor and Torres Pérez [The Constitution of Spain: The Challenges for the Constitutional Order Under European and Global Governance] in this book.

privatisation of public services and the entrenchment of independent regulatory agencies in the process of market liberalisation, which are mentioned in several national reports.[51]

The revised typology of constitutional systems that was briefly outlined in the preceding section is relevant for the understanding of the **broader patterns that emerge in the Comparative Study in terms of whether EU law has given rise to constitutional conflicts in individual Member States**. It should be noted that the study here does not concern areas where rights have been advanced – typically in an activist manner – in fields of EU law such as free movement, non-discrimination, gender equality and consumer protection, which have been extensively researched in the existing literature.[52] In general terms – with of course exceptions – a pattern can be discerned whereby EU law has strengthened the protection of fundamental rights and the general principles of law and has expanded judicial review in countries with a political or historical constitutional system. However, this strengthening has often come at the cost of a reduction in the priority of parliamentary and democratic processes. These developments are perhaps most evocatively captured in the titles of the national reports from the UK ('Europe's Gift to the United Kingdom's Unwritten Constitution – Juridification'[53]) and Sweden ('The Constitution of Sweden and European Influences: The Changing Balance between Democratic and Judicial Power'[54]). At the same time, EU law has caused strain with regard to the standards previously established by the constitutional courts in the Member States with a post-totalitarian constitutional culture, both in

[51] See the report on Spain by Solanes Mullor and Torres Pérez [The Constitution of Spain: The Challenges for the Constitutional Order Under European and Global Governance], the report on Portugal by Pereira Coutinho and Piçarra [Portugal: The Impact of European Integration and the Economic Crisis on the Identity of the Constitution], the report on Belgium by Popelier and Van de Heyning [The Belgian Constitution: The Efficacy Approach to European and Global Governance], the report on Slovenia by Bardutzky [The Future Mandate of the Constitution of Slovenia: A Potent Tradition Under Strain], the report on Austria by Lachmayer [The Constitution of Austria in International Constitutional Networks: Pluralism, Dialogues and Diversity], the report on Croatia by Goldner Lang, Đurđević and Mataija [The Constitution of Croatia in the Perspective of European and Global Governance], the report on Finland by Ojanen and Salminen [Finland: European Integration and International Human Rights Treaties as Sources of Domestic Constitutional Change and Dynamism], and the report on Hungary by Chronowski, Varju, Bárd and Sulyok [Hungary: Constitutional (R)evolution or Regression?] in this book.

[52] This so-called 'double standards' issue is explained in greater detail in the Questionnaire in this book [Questionnaire for the Constitutional Law Experts of the Research Project 'The Role and Future of National Constitutions in European and Global Governance'] (Introduction to Sect. 2 and Sect. 2.6.1). See also Coppel and O'Neill 1992, pp. 670 et seq.

[53] See the report on the United Kingdom by Young, Birkinshaw, Mitsilegas and Christou in this book [Europe's Gift to the United Kingdom's Unwritten Constitution – Juridification].

[54] The report on Sweden by Nergelius in this book [The Constitution of Sweden and European Influences: The Changing Balance Between Democratic and Judicial Power].

Western Europe and in Central-Eastern Europe.[55] This is conveyed in the clearest terms in the title of the Slovenian report ('The Future Mandate of the Constitution of Slovenia: A Potent Tradition Under Strain'[56]). This finding has a further important dimension in the light of other observations in the national reports – which we initially noted with interest and subsequently with an increasing sense of unease – concerning the **numerous direct and indirect ways in which EU law and the CJEU case law have led to the uniformisation and homogenisation of the Member States' constitutional law**. This includes the transition to a uniform ECHR/EU Charter standard in increasingly wider areas of law, including where this entails downgrading national standards of protection.

Another broader pattern in terms of correlation between the type of constitution and the effects of EU law emerged in relation to **constitutional amendments regarding European integration**. In broad lines, this could be based on a distinction between an '**efficacy approach**' and a '**legitimacy approach**', which is drawn in the Belgian report on the basis of Patricia Popelier's study of EU clauses in the national constitutions.[57] As summarised in the Belgian report:

> Two main approaches can be discerned: an 'efficacy approach', which is predominantly occupied by the concern for efficient through-put of EU law, and a 'legitimacy approach', which is specifically concerned with providing legitimacy to inflowing EU law. If a legitimacy approach is adopted, ideally, (a) the transfer of powers is submitted to special procedural and/or substantive conditions, (b) the precedence of EU law over the constitution is contested and (c) constitutional or supreme courts play the role of watchdogs over the constitution, assuming the power to ultimately delineate competences. If an efficacy approach is adopted, (a) the transfer of powers to the EU is allowed without special formal conditions, (b) the precedence of EU law over national law, including the constitution, is uncontested and (c) the judicial review of EU laws and treaties is constrained.[58]

Popelier's study observes that in Belgium, the Netherlands and Luxembourg, an efficacy approach clearly dominates, with Germany being on the other side of the spectrum.[59] This research finding is confirmed in the Comparative Study.[60]

---

[55] It is important to note that these conclusions specifically concern the rights explored in the project Questionnaire. In other areas, e.g. as regards prison conditions, media pluralism, the strength of civil society and the actual level of social welfare entitlements, the countries with a political or historical constitutional culture often have some of the highest standards in Europe.

[56] The report on Slovenia by Bardutzky in this book [The Future Mandate of the Constitution of Slovenia: A Potent Tradition Under Strain].

[57] Popelier 2014, as summarised in the report on Belgium by Popelier and Van de Heyning in this book [The Belgian Constitution: The Efficacy Approach to European and Global Governance], Sect. 1.5.3.

[58] The report on Belgium by Popelier and Van de Heyning in this book [The Belgian Constitution: The Efficacy Approach to European and Global Governance], Sect. 1.5.3.

[59] Popelier 2014, p. 316.

[60] See also, for example, the extensive constitutional conditions and adjudication outlined in the report on Germany by Grimm, Wendel and Reinbacher [European Constitutionalism and the German Basic Law], and the observations about the absence of constitutional conflicts in the report

Additionally, it emerges that a solution akin to the 'efficacy' approach has also been adopted in Ireland, Cyprus and Estonia, whereas the 'legitimacy' approach prevails in most of the post-totalitarian constitutional cultures. The tensions that an 'efficacy'-based approach presents to a post-totalitarian constitution that has been influenced by the German Constitution are perhaps most evident in the Estonian report. What might appear to be the ideal solution from the perspective of the EU legal order – suspending conflicting constitutional provisions in order to ensure the full supremacy and effectiveness of EU law – has led to widespread concerns amongst Estonian lawyers about negating the hitherto binding, enforceable and rights-protective Constitution, as well as to practical difficulties in constitutional adjudication by the Supreme Court.[61]

Whilst the working title of the book was '*The Role of National Constitutions in European and Global Governance*', the above findings led us to expand the title and add '***Democracy, Fundamental Rights, the Rule of Law***'. With this subtitle, we sought to draw attention to the fact that these values have in fact been central to the national constitutions since the Enlightenment, and that these values have also provided the key, expressly worded conditions governing the transfer of powers to the supranational level, especially in the constitutions of Germany, Slovenia and Portugal, as well as in the case law of many constitutional courts. This is important to bear in mind, given that in the mainstream European constitutional discourse, the **national constitutions have primarily come to be associated** with a somewhat old-fashioned protection of **sovereignty** or, more recently, **national constitutional identity**. Sovereignty and the assessment of Euro-friendliness or Euroscepticism have also been the prevailing lens of assessment in the scholarly literature on constitutional courts, where unduly harsh and reductionist language has often been used with regard to those constitutional courts that have sought to retain some degree of constitutional review or uphold constitutional values in the context of EU law.[62] In the Comparative Study, it is submitted that many of the constitutional rights and values that have come under strain in the context of EU law are in fact **comparative European constitutional achievements,**[63] which in several aspects quite possibly represent **the most advanced constitutionally codified and judicially protected fundamental rights, social rights and rule of law safeguards in**

---

on Luxembourg by Gerkrath [The Constitution of Luxembourg in the Context of EU and International Law as 'Higher Law'], both in this book.

[61] For a summary of the discourse, see the report on Estonia by Ernits, Ginter, Laos et al. in this book [The Constitution of Estonia: The Unexpected Challenges of Unlimited Primacy of EU Law] in this book, Sects. 1.2.3, 1.2.4, 1.5.3, 1.3.4, 2.3, 2.7 and 2.8.

[62] These trends in the scholarly literature have been documented with references in Albi 2015a, Sect. I and Albi 2015b, Sect. VIII.

[63] The expression 'constitutional achievements' is borrowed from Dieter Grimm, who uses it more generally in relation to the democracy and rule of law elements in modern constitutions (Grimm 2012, p. 104). See also Somek (2014, p. 10), who regards especially the constitutions based on the German model as representing the emancipation of constitutionalism – see below n. 99 and the accompanying text.

the world. However, the understanding of these has started to fade, as will be noted below.

At this juncture, it should be underlined that throughout the project, **EU and international treaties and rules that protect human rights, ensure peace or enhance environmental protection** are regarded **as part of the constitutional achievements**. Indeed, especially the ECHR has a constitutional or semi-constitutional status in the internal legal order of a large number of the countries studied. However, the material synthesised would seem to indicate a need for **a more differentiated and nuanced approach** in discussions on the domestic constitutional reception, on the one hand, of the above type of treaties and, on the other hand, of **treaties and instruments that may have adverse effects on rights and constitutional values** or that significantly curtail democracy beyond the constitutionally entrenched values. Some examples of such adverse effects from EU law were brought earlier in this section (e.g. the European Arrest Warrant and the Data Retention Directive). Regarding some constitutionally problematic examples from international and global law, the reader is invited to take a look at the following accounts in the national reports: the cases regarding IMF and/or European Commission instruments whereby already subsistence-level pensions and social benefits were drastically cut and social rights were curtailed along with the principle of legitimate expectations (reports on Latvia, Portugal, Greece and Romania; see also more generally the report on Spain); the adjudication of international extradition treaties (reports on Poland, the UK, Cyprus, Portugal, France); issues around access to judicial review regarding measures implementing targeted sanctions against individuals under the UN anti-terrorist resolutions and blacklists (reports on Belgium, Switzerland and the UK); the question whether parliamentary ratification and/or implementation by parliamentary law is needed for international instruments such as extradition treaties, UN sanctions targeting individuals, and IMF memorandums of understanding and loan agreements (reports on Latvia, Finland, Ireland and Belgium); the role of private actors in global governance, including their unpublished but binding technical standards (reports on the Netherlands, Estonia and Austria); transparency and access to documents in the context of international co-operation (the reports on Sweden and Finland); and constitutional issues regarding the effects of international investment arbitration treaties (reports on Romania and the UK).

Regarding the material in the national reports, in addition to outlining the domestic case law and legal discussion, we also **invited the constitutional law experts to express their own views on how some of the older and more recent points of debate in the EU constitutional and judicial dialogues could be addressed**. For example, we asked for the experts' assessments relating to the provision of higher standards of protection, if hitherto so provided under the national constitution, in the context of the ongoing debate regarding Art. 53 of the EU Charter. What role do the experts see for the common constitutional traditions? Would there be value in bringing national constitutional concerns to the CJEU and other European institutions and, if so, what avenues ought to be used? And, ultimately, how do the constitutional scholars see the role of national constitutions in

European and global governance? The editors are immensely grateful to the project experts for joining us in constructively thinking about the new challenges to constitutional law posed by transnational governance. Their key observations are summarised in the Comparative Study, along with some specific policy recommendations.

The Comparative Study concludes with broader observations about an ongoing, gradual **process of transition from the paradigm of (comparative) constitutional and public law to the paradigm of governance that prevails in EU law and large parts of transnational law.**[64] The governance paradigm is predicated on a different underlying logic, which in the main seems to have emanated from the neofunctionalist thinking that underlies much of the European integration and transnationalisation processes and discourses. Other underlying theoretical constructs of the governance paradigm include e.g. the '[c]ontemporary delegation theory, with its emphasis on principal, agents, and dilemmas of agency control', which 'is an adaptation of concepts of contract law to the political world', including concepts from fiduciary constitutionalism, the law of trusts and other private law concepts.[65] It is not easy to reconcile these theories and classic constitutionalism. For example, the core tenets of neofunctionalism that drive supranational governance are integration-through-law, spillover, 'never let a good crisis go to waste', and the mobilisation of and instrumental use of law, of courts, institutions, political, bureaucratic and business elites, scholarship, as well as individuals and their rights towards a gradual shift of law, authority and loyalty from the national to the supranational level.[66] Whilst this has led to many progressive developments with lasting, beneficial changes, **there is a structural flaw in neofunctionalist constitutionalism**, in that it views national constitutional law as inherently inferior for the simple reason that it is national and based on a sovereign state. There has been a blind spot to and fading understanding of the comparative European constitutional achievements, which in many respects may quite possibly be the most advanced in

---

[64] Some aspects of such a paradigm change from constitutional and public law to governance have been identified by the following scholars: Joana Mendes (with regard to transnational technical regulatory regimes with norms that acquire the status of EU legal acts and also acquire supremacy through incorporation into EU law without traditional avenues for participation (Mendes 2014, p. 371)); Alexander Somek (in EU governance, constraints on public power have become economic (Somek 2014, pp. 23–24; see also above n. 13 and the accompanying text)) and Agustín Menéndez (conceptual innovation in legal research (Menéndez 2014, p. 140; see below n. 85 and the accompanying text)).

[65] Cf. e.g. Sweet and Brunell 2013, p. 67, with further references, including the influential writings of Giandomenico Majone.

[66] For an overview of the core tenets of neofunctionalism, see e.g. De Búrca 2005, pp. 316 et seq. and Sweet 2012. The Principal Investigator would like to acknowledge that the draft chapters of Maris Moks' Ph.D thesis 'Guardianship of the Constitution versus the Expectations of the European Integration: Judicial Review of the Euro-crisis Management' (Hertie School of Governance in Berlin), which contained an extensive literature review, greatly helped her to formulate the broader observation about a change from the constitutional law mindset to a neofunctionalist mindset, especially as regards the changing role of courts towards agents of integration in the neofunctionalist theory.

the world, as noted above. A good example to illustrate the difference between the neofunctionalist and the comparative European constitutional thinking is the commentary on the *Pupino* case.[67] Lawyers specialising in EU law widely regard it as a milestone 'constitutional' case, as it extended indirect effect, effectiveness and loyal co-operation to the then third pillar. Lawyers specialising in the field of constitutional law and criminal law, however, point out that the case concerned application in the field of criminal trials of a framework decision that had not yet been implemented in national law and that had furthermore been adopted at the ministerial level by the EU Council. These aspects raise profound concerns from the point of view of the classic values protected in Europe's national constitutions, such as the principles of the rule of law, including maximum certainty in criminal law, clearly determined provisions and democratic legitimisation by parliamentary law.[68]

A tentative **list of foundational changes** in the transition from the classic constitutional law paradigm to the governance paradigm is compiled in the Comparative Study. Examples of such foundational changes include: a broader shift from constitutions to the Treaties as the normative point of reference and thereby to a market-oriented order or – in the euro crisis governance – to the exercise of public power simply on the basis of general economic exigencies; a shift from constitutional and rule of law requirements to the prioritisation of effectiveness, policy objectives and functionality; a changing understanding of the role of courts and constitutional courts in the neofunctionalist literature and in practice; a change away from the liberal separation of powers to a new autonomous system; an approach to fundamental rights whereby fundamental rights are treated as restrictions to economic freedoms and are ultimately subordinated to them as well as to the imperatives of uniformity and effectiveness; a changing understanding of the rule of law; the disappearance of constitutional law as higher law; and the manifold changes at the EU and national level towards executive governance, especially the gradual phasing out of national level democracy and the chain of legitimacy between public power and a territorial community of people. The severe curtailment of parliamentary democracy and control over the budget due to the very large financial liabilities undertaken by virtue of the ESM Treaty have been subject to particularly acute constitutional debates and challenges in Germany, Estonia, Ireland, Austria, Poland and to some extent in Lithuania, as documented in the respective national reports. In addition, the issue of parliamentary control over large-scale state guarantees was also at stake in the EFSF (European Financial Stability Facility) case before the Slovenian Constitutional Court.

[67] Case C-105/03 *Pupino* [2005] ECR I-05285.

[68] For a critical assessment of the constitutional significance of *Pupino* for EU law, see Herlin-Karnell 2007, pp. 1151 and 1154. More generally on the uneasy fit between EU criminal law and classic values in European criminal law and constitutional law, see the concerns of fourteen scholars in the 'Manifesto on the European Criminal Policy' (2009) *Zeitschrift für Internationale Strafrechtsdogmatik*, Issue 12, 70–716, at 715, available online at http://www.crimpol.eu/; Schünemann 2007, p. 227; Walsh 2009, pp. 5–34.

A more general foundational change may be, as a number of leading political scientists have observed, that the governance model is 'post-political' or 'unpolitical', and in fact oriented towards constraining dissent.[69] The picture that emerges from the national reports does little to alleviate this concern. For one, there is a near-absence of formal structures for invoking national constitutional grounds at the EU level, at least beyond the subsidiarity and proportionality arguments for national parliaments and for the national constitutional identity ground in judicial proceedings. Indeed, the Maltese expert makes the very commendable suggestion to extend the *ex ante* yellow card mechanism of national parliaments to a fuller monitoring procedure, which would include essential constitutional concerns beyond subsidiarity and proportionality.[70] The severely constrained scope for national level democratic protest or even for constitutional review by constitutional courts is perhaps most compellingly evident in the proceedings in which the European Commission threatened or imposed fines on Sweden and Germany for delays in implementing the Data Retention Directive, explored in the respective national reports. The scope for demonstrations and protest has been further reduced in different ways by CJEU rulings in cases such as *Schmidberger*, *Viking Line* and *Laval*,[71] as well as by the European Commission and IMF economic conditionality measures that require the curtailing of trade union rights.[72] In general, we observed a **near-absence of debate in a considerable number of countries**[73] regarding EU measures that in many other Member States had raised heightened concerns and extensive discussion about deficiencies in rights protection.

The Comparative Study further explores the corresponding **changes in constitutional thinking and constitutional vocabulary,** which have increasingly become the default, new baseline for constitutionalism, especially for the younger generations of scholars and lawyers. Indeed, one point of added value of the national reports is that many of them contain detailed documentation of the clashes between the classic constitutional thinking and the governance-oriented mindset.

---

[69] For references to literature, see Bouza Garcia 2017, pp. 348, 349, 340.

[70] The report on Malta by Xuereb in this book [The Constitution of Malta: Reflections on New Mechanisms for Synchrony of Values in Different Levels of Governance], Sects. 2.12.3 and 2.13.4.

[71] Case C-112/00 *Schmidberger* [2003] ECR I-05659; Case C-438/05 *The International Transport Workers' Federation and The Finnish Seamen's Union* [2007] ECR I-10779; Case C-341/05 *Laval un Partneri* [2007] ECR I-11767.

[72] On the latter, see especially report on Spain by Solanes Mullor and Torres Pérez [The Constitution of Spain: The Challenges for the Constitutional Order Under European and Global Governance], and the report on Greece by Contiades, Papacharalambous and Papastylianos [The Constitution of Greece: EU Membership Perspectives], in this book.

[73] The absence of debate is in particular mentioned in the report on Lithuania by Jarukaitis and Švedas [The Constitutional Experience of Lithuania in the Context of European and Global Governance Challenges], the report on Slovakia by Vikarská and Bobek [Slovakia: Between Euro-Optimism and Euro-Concerns], and the report on Bulgaria by Tanchev and Belov [The Bulgarian Constitutional Order, Supranational Constitutionalism and European Governance] in this book.

A careful reader may well observe that the former tends to remain on the dissenting or losing side (e.g. the grounds and arguments used by dissenting judges, traditional constitutional litigants such as ombudspersons, defence lawyers' associations and minority groups of MPs). Different aspects of the changes in the constitutional language in the transnational context are more specifically explored in the reports on Italy, Romania and Germany.[74] On a more general level, the fact that **the language of constitutionalism in transnational law has little in common with the world of comparative constitutional law** has perceptively been explained on the basis of an extensive literature review by Peer Zumbansen.[75] Transnational constitutionalisation depicts the dynamic forces of constantly newly emerging functional and specialised fora of law-making.[76] The risk, according to Zumbansen, is that the focus on limiting or placing constraints on governmental power, which is the central tenet of 'traditional constitutionalism', has been displaced.[77] The focus is on the autonomy of the emerging global legal order from claims from the nation state, and there has been 'erosion of institutionalized, accountable exercises' of political power.[78]

Whilst scholarly research has hitherto predominantly focused on the benefits of EU and transnational constitutionalism, the present study looks at the risks arising from the way these ongoing processes have changed the application of the classic European understanding of constitutionalism and of the concept of the rule of law. It seeks to invite discussion on the shift to the governance paradigm, along with the merits and demerits of the gradual transition to autonomous EU constitutional law, and on the optimal balance between striving toward uniformisation and retaining the diversity of the national constitutional cultures. Discussion on the profound changes would also seem particularly timely, as the EU is moving towards the mutualisation of debt and ultimately to the EU raising its own revenue that would in the last resort be backed by the Member States,[79] and whereby individual Member

---

[74] See the report on Italy by Martinico, Guastaferro and Pollicino [The Constitution of Italy: Axiological Continuity Between the Domestic and International Levels of Governance?], the report on Romania by Iancu [Romania – The Vagaries of International Grafts on Unsettled Constitutions], and the report on Germany by Grimm, Wendel and Reinbacher [European Constitutionalism and the German Basic Law], in this book. See also notes 5 and 92 and the accompanying text. The report on Romania [Romania – The Vagaries of International Grafts on Unsettled Constitutions], additionally, makes perceptive observations about the change of the constitutional language in the quasi-constitutionalisation of the EU anti-corruption conditionality in Romania.

[75] Zumbansen 2012, p. 47, see also pp. 31 and 38.

[76] Ibid., p. 47, with further references.

[77] Zumbansen 2012, p. 38, with further references.

[78] Ibid., p. 47.

[79] The European Commission sees 'a step-by-step, policy-by-policy basis' advancement towards the latter as the ultimate goal according to its Communication 'A blueprint for a deep and genuine monetary union. Launching a European Debate' (COM 2012 777 final/2 30.11.2012, http://ec.europa.eu/archives/commission_2010-2014/president/news/archives/2012/11/pdf/blueprint_en.pdf). According to the Commission Blueprint, if the guarantee is claimed by creditors, accountability through national parliaments is no longer relevant and shifts to the European Parliament.

States and their parliaments would no longer be in control of their financial liabilities. This may well mark a significant transformative turning point – and one of no return – for classic European constitutionalism.

8 The Broader Importance of the Project for the Future Direction of Travel for National, Comparative European, EU and Global Constitutionalism

We hope that the readers will come to agree that such thinking and discussion about the future direction of travel for European constitutionalism is of real and pressing importance. In the past, EU law has been developed primarily in a top-down, autonomous, self-referential manner from the perspective of the needs and priorities of the EU legal order. On the one hand, European integration has brought **important, lasting benefits, which include peace and stability, relative prosperity, freedom of movement** and the **broadening of important opportunities for individuals** for greater self-realisation and enriched horizons. Indeed, **all of the national reports in the present book strongly emphasise the beneficial changes and impacts resulting from EU law**, as well as the importance of Euro-friendly interpretation of EU law by courts and of the (now predominantly extensive) national constitutional provisions that ensure openness to European and international law. European integration also entails valuable external mechanisms of control vis-à-vis national institutions, the need for which has been illustrated clearly e.g. by the developments towards an illiberal regime in Hungary and, since autumn 2015, in Poland. On the other hand, the increasing concerns with regard to governance at the EU level as well as the maturing of the EU legal order in general, make it the right time to consider a greater inclusion of perspectives that are more accommodating of national and comparative constitutional values and concerns, in a two-way[80] or multi-directional, pluralist process. The national reports in the present book are an essential precondition for such a multi-directional process, as they provide a wider audience with an overview of national case law and constitutional debates, of which there has typically been little awareness in the mainstream English language European constitutional discourse. Indeed, a recent BBC article raised the question '[a]re we "losing knowledge" because of the growing dominance of English as the language of higher education and research?'[81]

One could add that indirect mutualisation of debt liabilities through asset purchases by the European Central Bank programme and the need for a continued chain of democratic legitimacy between the people and the exercise of public power were also the underlying issues in the *OMT* case from the German Constitutional Court, BVerfG, case 2 BvR 2728/13 et al., *OMT*, order of 14 Jan. 2014, BVerfGE 134, 366.

[80] Mutanen 2015, pp. 387, 392–393.

[81] Pickles, M. (20 January 2016) Could the dominance of English harm global scholarship? BBC News. http://www.bbc.co.uk/news/business-35282235.

Upon reading the national reports, the editors developed a sense that this concern is of direct relevance to constitutional law in terms of losing constitutional knowledge more generally. We even had a sense that perhaps national constitutions and national constitutional law are being displaced and written out of mainstream English language European constitutional narratives. Historical accounts have documented the considerable investment by the European Commission in founding specialised EU law journals and university centres, with the aim of shifting EU studies away from a comparative analysis of national laws (which would aim to identify common principles) to the study of the 'specificity' of EU law, focusing on the relationships between EU law (and the CJEU) and national law (and courts).[82] On a broader level, Anne Lise Kjaer has raised a concern about the far-reaching impact of the changes in the discourse:

> [W]hat will happen to the mutually divergent national languages and cultures of law when independency and autonomy of a common European law are presumed by an increasing number of European lawyers; when they accept the European Courts as legitimate interpreters of a supranational and transnational European law and involve themselves in an increasingly self-referential European legal discourse with lawyers from other European countries; and when communicating about law and speaking the law are no longer conducted in divergent national legal languages, but ***in a Europeanized legal language with no reference to the domestic laws of the Member States*** [emphasis added].[83]

Sharing the broader concern expressed by Kjaer with regard to the disappearance of comparative law, the editors more specifically have a sense that in the quest for new epistemic communities to build the autonomous, self-referential and new constitutional order of the European Union,[84] there is a substantial risk that some of the distinctively and uniquely valuable comparative European achievements in constitutionalism are being left behind and lost. Whilst this general impression had been based on reading mainstream English language European constitutional law literature, the Principal Investigator, since having started to write and present papers on the above topics, has been struck by the significant and growing number of researchers, doctoral students and even eminent, agenda-setting EU law scholars who have informally mentioned that they have never heard of what Pinelli above described as a continental European constitutional tradition that is predicated on post-totalitarian constitutional safeguards.

Thus, when taking a look at the national reports, the reader is invited to consider the broader question of **what ought to be the direction of travel for national, comparative European, EU and global constitutionalism**. Whilst 'EU', 'global' and 'post-national' constitutionalism may sound inherently more progressive, advanced and appealing, on a closer look they also entail an element of vagueness and even hollowness if compared e.g. to the post-totalitarian constitutional tradition

---

[82] Vauchez 2009, pp. 20–21.

[83] Kjaer 2015, p. 98.

[84] The shift from comparative European constitutional law to the autonomous EU constitutional law in the mainstream discourse has been explored and documented in greater detail in Albi 2015b, Sect. VIII.

in continental Europe noted above, at the essence of which are extensive, precise, constitutionally codified and judicially protected fundamental rights and rule of law safeguards. There is a danger of conflating European constitutional law with EU constitutional law, which is in fact very different. The distinction, however, has increasingly become muddled and blurred. Indeed, in the large volume of books and articles written in this field, one can discern that the expression 'European Constitutional Law' has already predominantly come to denote EU constitutional law, often with no mention of Europe's national constitutions. Similarly, the term 'Europeanisation' has predominantly come to denote transition to autonomous EU law and to the EU governance model, rather than referring to the classic comparative European constitutional values.

The difference between EU constitutional law and continental European constitutional law has also been observed by a growing number of scholars. For example, Agustín Menéndez has pointed out that 'European legal studies have been very keen … on conceptual innovation', which includes a switch to 'governance' amongst other concepts. He finds that it may be a suitable time to 'reconstruct European constitutional law with the help of "classical" democratic constitutional theory, as developed for decades in national Social and Democratic *Rechtsstaats*'.[85] Menéndez regards '**the collective of national democratic constitutions**' in Europe as '**[t]he deep constitution of the European Union**, the ultimate normative foundation of the whole edifice of the Union', rather than the EU Treaties. He finds that '[w]hen integration starts going against the key normative content of the national constitutions, it is time to start using such constitutions … as the ultimate source of the yardstick of European constitutionality'.[86] Nicola Lupo and Giovanni Piccirilli note the 'progressive decline of the formal categories that dominated the public law literature in the past two centuries' in the context of CJEU as well as ECHR case law. They highlight the risks to democracy, fundamental rights and to the legality principle, and express concern that there has been a shift towards the 'lowest common denominator' of the legality principle.[87] Lupo and Piccirilli have put forward a plea that the parliamentary process in the first instance, and the ordinary and constitutional courts as a second step in the process, ought to promote and protect fundamental rights 'in order to restore the legality principle to its proper place'.[88] In a similar vein, the Principal Investigator has elsewhere outlined the procedural, formal, thin nature of EU constitutionalism where the keywords are supremacy, uniformity, direct effect, autonomy, effectiveness and trust. She has propounded the concept of 'substantive co-operative constitutionalism', in which the aim would be to uphold the established standard of protection of fundamental rights, the rule of law and other constitutional values, and also to retain the

[85] Menéndez 2014, p. 140.
[86] Menéndez 2013, pp. 525–526 (references omitted). Emphasis added.
[87] Lupo and Piccirilli 2015, pp. 55–56.
[88] Lupo and Piccirilli 2015, pp. 76–77.

diversity of national constitutional orders.[89] Jan Komárek has cautioned against transition to autonomous EU fundamental rights protection, especially in the Area of Freedom, Security and Justice, as EU constitutional law rests on the foundations of a market integration project and not on the post-war liberal constitutionalism that underlies Europe's national constitutions.[90] Susana Galera has written that 'Europeans share a well-defined doctrine about the European understanding of rule-of-law requirements, initiated in 1949 by the Council of Europe', whereas in the EU context, 'persistent gaps in the EU judicial review system and the different understanding of what judicial independence or division of powers means … represent a serious divergence affecting values and principles that have been applied for a long time on the European institutional scene'.[91] Amongst the national reports, the Italian report points out that the idea of constitutionalism propounded by leading international scholars 'does not readily correspond to what constitutional lawyers mean by the same word', and is 'conceived as an autonomous concept of international law rather than a concept derived by analogy from the domestic conception of constitutionalism'.[92] The report underlines the importance of parallelism and axiological continuity between the values inspiring the domestic activity of the Italian Republic and those inspiring the external dimension (cf. the title 'The Constitution of Italy: Axiological Continuity between the Domestic and International Levels of Governance?').

It should be noted that another extensive part of the discourse associates European constitutionalism with the **ECHR**. Although the ECHR is beyond the scope of the present study, it is important to underline that the ECHR is regarded here, as explained above, as **part of the well-established achievements of constitutionalism at the international level**. Indeed, it emerges from the reports that the ECHR (and other international human rights treaties) has a constitutional status in the internal legal order in a large number of the countries studied, it is extensively and routinely referred to by the constitutional courts and other national courts, and the judgments of the European Court of Human Rights in Strasbourg (ECtHR) have widely had extensive rights-advancing, transformative effects. However, what is often overlooked is that **the ECHR sets the minimum floor of protection** for forty-seven countries in the wider European area, and the ECtHR grants the states a considerable **margin of appreciation**. Whilst the ECHR is the main domestic instrument of fundamental rights protection especially in several political/historical and traditional legal constitutional systems, in many others – especially among the post-totalitarian constitutional systems – the text of the constitution and the constitutional court have provided a higher and more extensive level of protection, also simply to a much greater range of fundamental

[89] Albi 2015b, Sect. VIII ff.

[90] Komárek 2014, pp. 12–13, with references to further literature.

[91] Galera 2010, p. 302.

[92] The report on Italy by Martinico, Guastaferro and Pollicino in this book [The Constitution of Italy: Axiological Continuity Between the Domestic and International Levels of Governance?], Sect. 3.1.4, some references omitted. The changing vocabulary of constitutionalism is further explored in Martinico 2015. On this, see also references to national reports and literature supra in notes 5, 74 and 75. and the accompanying text.

rights than those listed in the ECHR. By way of some typical examples, unlike most continental European systems, the ECHR does not require the adoption of a parliamentary statute for the limitation of fundamental rights, and it does not contain a list of social rights. Through EU law, however, the ECHR standard has in many areas become the maximum standard rather than the minimum floor.

In this context, the Comparative Study also seeks to draw attention to **the centre-periphery dimension** in the mainstream English language EU and transnational constitutional discourse. That is, the leading, influential, agenda-setting scholars and experts often come from what in terms of the scholarly discourse could be regarded as the 'centre' countries, many of which – especially the Netherlands, Belgium, the UK and Ireland – have a political/historical or traditional legal type of constitutional system, where fundamental rights protection is mainly based on the ECHR and the constitutional system is regarded as more pragmatic or 'efficacy'-oriented, as seen above. Additionally, considerable influence is held by US constitutional scholarship. Notably, in the euro crisis management, studies by economic actors have expressly called for political reform in '**political systems around the periphery**' – especially Portugal, Spain, Italy and Greece – where the 'shortcomings' of the political and constitutional legacy include 'weak executives', 'constitutional protection of labour rights' and 'the right to protest'.[93]

Whilst one limitation of the present book is its Euro-centric approach, the above questions are also more broadly relevant to what might be described as '**global constitutionalism**' and '**global rule of law reform**'. One of their elements is the above-mentioned **shift to autonomous transnational and global standards and rules**, with displacement of institutional accountability mechanisms as well as of standards of fundamental rights protection and constitutional review that have been established in traditional, state-based constitutionalism.

There is a further influence on the direction of travel that is relevant to global constitutionalism and global rule of law reform: **the constitutional law of and constitutional thinking in the United States**. The differences between the US and European (comparative) constitutionalism have been explored by leading comparative law scholars in a book edited by Georg Nolte under the auspices of the Venice Commission (the Council of Europe's Commission for Democracy through Law).[94] Nolte observes that while focus during the Cold War era was on the similarities between US and European constitutional thought, in the present-day processes of globalisation and European constitutionalism – in the meaning of EU integration – attention on their differences has gained in importance. EU constitutionalism, as Nolte notes, 'seems to embody something which is both **more removed from the "people"** and **more vague** than national constitutional law', with clear-cut differences starting to

[93] Mackie et al. 2013, pp. 12–13. Emphasis added.

[94] Nolte 2003a.

disappear and 'characteristic constitutionalisms' being transformed.[95] Some concrete, profound differences between US and continental European constitutionalism include the following: the minimalistic approach to the role of the state and to fundamental and social rights in the US; the continuing debate in the US over the legitimacy of judicial review of legislation, which is known as the 'counter-majoritarian difficulty'; and the different approach to separation of powers, e.g. as regards the extensive role of independent agencies.[96] Profound differences between the continental European tradition and US constitutionalism are found in the approach to courts and defence rights in criminal law and the understanding of human dignity, liberty, and the rule of law in this context. The continental European approach to constitutionalism and the rule of law places a strong emphasis on manifold safeguards for access to courts, and on the presumption of innocence and defence rights. By contrast, in the US, about 95% of criminal cases are resolved by the system of plea-bargaining, which entails out-of-court negotiations where there is no trial at all. This system has been explored in greater detail by Fair Trials International, which has expressed concern that the US has promoted the global spread of out-of-court plea-bargaining as part of the global rule of law reform.[97]

An understanding of the differences in the US constitutional system is crucial to the future direction of travel for European countries because the United States has become the main point of comparison for the EU constitutional order, and this has also impacted substantive European constitutional law. For example, in the Comparative Study, concern is expressed that through the EU mutual recognition system, the direction of travel has been towards removing judicial review in the country of residence in cross-border criminal as well as civil and administrative cases, and generally towards a more punitive and repressive criminal law. The Comparative Study also considers the influence of US thinking about state and social rights on the IMF and European Commission conditionality and austerity programmes. More broadly, we share the concern of Matej Avbelj that the dominant constitutional narrative, which equates the constitutionalisation of the EU with US-style federalism, has been transplanted in a misconceived way that is unsuited to the European constitutional landscape and may be a cause of the present malfunctioning of European integration. Hence, we support Avbelj's call that 'work must begin' on the EU's 'own, genuine and authentic constitutional theory' that would be oriented towards a pluralist legal entity with twenty-eight autonomous legal orders.[98] Some scholars have overtly noted that the point of reference in the quality of constitutionalism today ought to be the

---

[95] Nolte 2003b, p. 10. Emphasis added.

[96] Some of these are outlined in contributions by different scholars to Nolte 2003a (especially Bognetti 2003). On the 'counter-majoritarian difficulty', see Somek 2014, pp. 15 et seq.

[97] 'Fair Trials to document the use and abuse of plea bargaining worldwide', 8 February 2016, https://www.fairtrials.org/fair-trials-to-document-the-use-and-abuse-of-plea-bargaining-worldwide/; 'What is plea bargaining? A simple guide', 9 February 2016, https://www.fairtrials.org/what-is-plea-bargaining-a-simple-guide/.

[98] Avbelj 2008, pp. 4 et seq., 15 et seq., 23, 24.

German system rather than the American model, as is discussed more in the Comparative Study, with reference to literature collated by Alexander Somek, who sees constitutionalism as a project of emancipation.[99] Further, Giovanni Bognetti, exploring human dignity, has noted a certain 'ruggedness' of the American system in comparison with the European systems, although he has observed that this ought to be balanced against other values, such as the greater individual initiative and competitiveness enabled by the US system.[100]

Against this background, **for countries beyond the European area in search of good models for developing constitutionalism, awareness about some of the main differences between the EU, the ECHR, Europe's political/historical, traditional legal and post-totalitarian constitutional cultures, and US constitutional law is of direct practical importance for shaping discussion about what models might be considered as optimal**. The present book, along with the Comparative Study, documents these differences in greater detail.

As a concluding note, we hope that the readers will appreciate the little known yet fascinating material in the national reports, which we consider to be of real practical importance, and that the edited volumes will make a contribution towards developing European constitutionalism in a way that would be better informed by comparative European constitutional law perspectives. We believe that the wealth of material, concerns and suggestions stemming from the national constitutional discourses in the Member States will prove to be a useful resource for national judges – as well as members of parliament, ombudspersons and other custodians of constitutional values – who might, in the light of the changes in the discourse described, be in doubt as to whether they should uphold the national constitution. In particular, we believe that in the dialogue with the European Court of Justice, national judges should not shy away from expounding a higher level of protection of fundamental rights or other constitutional values where these exist in national law. We hope that the wealth of bottom-up constitutionalism on display in these two volumes will give them the confidence to do so. It is our aspiration that scholars in constitutional and public law – who have a long and proud tradition in Europe as *custodes* over the exercise of public authority – will perceive this book as confirmation that their vigilance can and ought to continue when public power is transferred to new sites of authority and veiled in new legal orders. Recognition that colleagues in other Member States have similar fears about strains on constitutional values, and the solutions adopted, may provide new vigour for constitutionalism in Europe.

Last but not least, we believe that the present volumes will also be of interest to the judges of the European Court of Justice and the lawyers of the institutions of the EU. In fulfilling their mission to create, interpret and advance European Union law, we hope that they will find inspiration in this comprehensive study that brings together the research of over sixty experts from throughout the Union, highlighting

---

[99] Somek 2014, p. 10 (emancipation of constitutionalism) and pp. 85–86 footnotes 38 and 42 (summary of writings of authors comparing German and US constitutionalism).

[100] Bognetti 2003, p. 78.

the constitutional traditions common to these European states as well as important elements of diversity that derive from the historical evolution and unique equilibrium of the individual constitutional systems in Europe.

As the book is going to press, we have decided to add the following final observation. In the time after the material for the book was completed, there has been a widespread surge of illiberal and extremist, right-wing political forces across Europe and beyond, and thus the protection of the comparative European constitutional values and achievements has become more difficult. Regrettably, there is a risk that these values may be conflated with general protection of nationalism or populism and dismissed offhand. However, it is hoped that – when looking through the national reports – the reader will agree that there has been a structural oversight, in that advanced comparative European constitutional values and achievements have unduly been left out of the transnational discourse, and that it is important for this omission to be corrected by the mainstream scholarly, political and legal communities, in order to avoid it happening that the protection of these values will be misused by and/or associated with extremist movements.

References

Albi A. (2015a) Erosion of Constitutional Rights in EU Law: A Call for 'Substantive Co-Operative Constitutionalism' Part 1. Vienna J of International Constitutional L 9: 151–185. Available Open Access at http://ssrn.com/abstract=2746522.

Albi A. (2015b) Erosion of Constitutional Rights in EU Law: A Call for 'Substantive Co-Operative Constitutionalism' Part 2. Vienna J of International Constitutional L 9:291–343. Available Open Access at http://ssrn.com/abstract=2741623.

Avbelj M. (2008) The Pitfalls of (Comparative) Constitutionalism for European Integration. Eric Stein Working Paper 1/2008. http://www.ericsteinpapers.cz/.

Beck G. (2012) The Legal Reasoning of the Court of Justice of the EU. Hart, Oxford.

Besselink L. (2006) The Dutch Constitution, the European Constitution and the Referendum in the Netherlands. In Albi A., Ziller J. (eds.) The European Constitution and National Constitutions: Ratification and Beyond. Kluwer, Alphen aan den Rijn, pp. 113–123.

Blekxtoon R. (ed.) (2005) Handbook on the European Arrest Warrant. T.M.C. Asser Press, The Hague.

Blekxtoon, R. (2009) Foreword. In: Keijzer N., van Sliedregt E. (eds.) The European Arrest Warrant in Practice. T.M.C. Asser Press, The Hague, pp. V–VI.

Bobek M. (2014) The Legal Reasoning of the Court of Justice of the EU. ELR 39:418–428.

Bognetti G. (2003) The Concept of Human Dignity in European and U.S. Constitutionalism. In: Nolte G. (ed.) European and U.S. Constitutionalism. European Commission for Democracy Through Law (Venice Commission) CDL-STD(2003)037, pp. 65–80. http://www.venice.coe.int/webforms/documents/default.aspx?pdffile=CDL-STD(2003)037-e.

Bouza Garcia L. (2017) The "New Narrative Project" and the politicisation of the EU. Journal of Contemporary European Studies 25(3):340–353.

Coppel J., O'Neill A. (1992) The European Court of Justice: Taking Rights Seriously? CML Rev. 29(4):669–692.

De Búrca G. (2005) Rethinking Law in Neofunctionalist Theory. Journal of European Public Policy 12(2):310–326.

De Visser M. (2014) Constitutional Review in Europe. A Comparative Analysis. Hart Publishing, Oxford.

Dobner P., Loughlin M. (2010) Introduction. In: Dobner P., Loughlin M. (eds.) The Twilight of Constitutionalism? Oxford University Press, Oxford, pp. xi–xvi.

Erbežnik A. (2014) Mutual Recognition in EU Criminal Law and Its Effects on the Role of a National Judge. In: Peršak N. (ed.) Legitimacy and Trust in Criminal Law, Policy and Justice Norms, Procedures, Outcomes. Ashgate Publishing Limited, Farnham, pp. 131–152.

Galera S. (2010) The European Contribution to an emerging global law. In Galera S. (ed.) Judicial Review: A Comparative Analysis Inside the European Legal System. Council of Europe, Strasbourg, pp. 301–308.

Grimm, D. (2012) Types of Constitutions. In. Rosenfeld M., Sajó A. (eds.) The Oxford Handbook of Comparative Constitutional Law. OUP, Oxford, pp. 98–132.

Harlow C. (2006) Global Administrative Law: The Quest for Principles and Values. EJIL 17:187–214.

Herlin-Karnell E. (2007) In the Wake of Pupino: Advocaten voor de Wereld and dell'Orto. German Law Journal 8(12):1147–1161.

Hogan G. (2014) The Influence of the continental constitutional tradition on the drafting of the Constitution. In: Ruane B., Barniville D., O'Callaghan J. (eds.) Law and Government: A Tribute to Rory Brady. Round Hall, Dublin, pp. 162–164.

Joerges C. (2014) Three Transformations of Europe and the Search for a Way Out of its Crisis. In: Joerges C., Glinski C. (eds.) The European Crisis and the Transformation of Transnational Governance. Authoritarian Managerialism versus Democratic Governance. Hart, Oxford and Portland, pp. 25–46.

Joerges C., Weimer M. (2012) A Crisis of Executive Managerialism in the EU: No Alternative? Maastricht Working Paper 2012-7. http://www.maastrichtuniversity.nl/web/Faculties/FL/2012_maastricht_working_papers.htm.

Kjaer A. (2015) Theoretical Aspects of Legal Translation in the EU: The Paradoxical Relationship between Language, Translation and the Autonomy of EU Law. In Šarčević S. (ed.) Language and Culture in EU Law. Multidisciplinary Perspectives. Ashgate, London and New York, pp. 91–108.

Kellermann A., De Zwaan J.W., Czuczai J. (eds.) (2001) The Constitutional Impact of EU Enlargement at EU and National Level. T.M.C. Asser Press, The Hague.

Komárek J. (2014) Why National Constitutional Courts Should Not Embrace EU Fundamental Rights, LSE Law, Society and Economy Working Papers 23/2014, http://eprints.lse.ac.uk/60568/1/WPS2014-10_Komarek.pdf.

Krisch N. (2010) Beyond Constitutionalism: The Pluralist Structure of Postnational Law. Oxford University Press, Oxford.

Kuo M.-S. (2010) The end of constitutionalism as we know it? Boundaries and the State of Global Constitutional (Dis)ordering. Transnational Legal Theory 1:329–369.

Lupo N., Piccirilli G. (2015) The Relocation of the Legality Principle by the European Courts. Case Law: An Italian Perspective. EuConst 11(1):55–77.

Mackie, D., Barr M. et al. (2013) Euro Area Adjustment: About Half-way There, by J.P. Morgan Bank, Europe Economic Research 28 May 2013, http://www.europe-solidarity.eu/documents/ES1_euro-area-adjustment.pdf.

Martinico G. (2015) Constitutionalism, Resistance and Openness: Comparative Law Reflections on Constitutionalism in Global Governance. STALS (Sant'Anna Legal Studies, Pisa) Research Paper No 5/2015. http://www.stals.sssup.it/files/martinicoSTALS.pdf. A modified version published as Martinico G. (2016) Constitutionalism, Resistance, and Openness: Comparative Law Reflections on Constitutionalism in Postnational Governance. YEL 35:318–340.

Mendes J. (2014) Rule of law and participation: A Normative analysis of internationalized rulemaking as composite procedures. ICON 12(2):370–401.

Menéndez A.J. (2013) The Existential Crisis of the European Union. German Law Journal 14:453–526.

Menéndez A.J. (2014) Editorial: A European Union in Constitutional Mutation? ELJ 20:127–141.

Mutanen A. (2015) Towards A Pluralistic Constitutional Understanding of State Sovereignty in the European Union? The Concept, Regulation and Constitutional Practice of Sovereignty in Finland and Certain Other EU Member States. Ph.D. thesis, University of Helsinki.

Nolte G. (ed.) (2003a) European and U.S. Constitutionalism. European Commission for Democracy Through Law (Venice Commission) CDL-STD(2003)037. http://www.venice.coe.int/webforms/documents/default.aspx?pdffile=CDL-STD(2003)037-e; also published as Nolte G. (ed.) (2003) European and US Constitutionalism. CUP, Cambridge.

Nolte G. (2003b), Introduction – European and U.S. Constitutionalism: Comparing Essential Elements. Nolte G. (ed.) (2003) European and U.S. Constitutionalism. European Commission for Democracy Through Law (Venice Commission) CDL-STD(2003)037, pp. 9–22. http://www.venice.coe.int/webforms/documents/default.aspx?pdffile=CDL-STD(2003)037-e.

Pinelli C. (2016) The Formation of a Constitutional Tradition in Continental Europe since World War II. EPL 22:257–268.

Popelier P. (2014) Europe clauses and constitutional strategies in the face of multilevel governance. Maastricht Journal of European and Comparative Law 21:300–319.

Schünemann B. (2007) Alternative-Project for a European criminal law and procedure. Criminal Law Forum 18(2):227–251.

Simoncini A. (2013) Back to "Flexible" Constitutions? The Impact of Financial Crisis and the Decline of the European Constitutionalism. Italian Journal of Public Law 5(2):157–187.

Somek A. (2014) The Cosmopolitan Constitution. OUP, Oxford.

Sweet A.S. (2012) Neofunctionalism and Supranational Governance (unabridged version). Faculty Scholarship Series, Paper 4628, http://digitalcommons.law.yale.edu/cgi/viewcontent.cgi?article=5636&context=fss_papers.

Sweet A.S., Brunell T. (2013) Trustee Courts and the Judicialization of International Regimes: The Politics of Majoritarian Activism in the ECHR, the EU, and the WTO. Journal of Law and Courts 1(1):61–88. http://digitalcommons.law.yale.edu/fss_papers/4625/.

Vauchez A. (2009) The transnational politics of judicialization. *Van Gend en Loos* and the making of the EU polity. ELJ 16:1–28.

Walsh D.P.J. (2009) The European Arrest Warrant in Ireland: Surrendering Our Standards to a European Criminal Law Area. In: Bacik I.C., Heffernan L. (eds.) Criminal Law and Procedure: Current Issues and Emerging Trends. First Law, Dublin, pp. 5–34.

Wilkinson M. (2016) The Reconstitution of Postwar Europe: Lineages of Authoritarian Liberalism. LSE working paper 5/2016. http://www.lse.ac.uk/law/working-paper-series.

Zumbansen, P. (2012) Comparative, global and transnational constitutionalism: The emergence of a transnational legal-pluralist order. Global Constitutionalism 1(1):16–52.

2

Hungary: Constitutional (R)evolution or Regression?

Nóra Chronowski, Márton Varju, Petra Bárd and Gábor Sulyok

Abstract Since 2010, Hungarian constitutionalism has turned in a direction that has widely been regarded as illiberal and has attracted criticism from European and international organisations and other Member States. Central to the change was the adoption of the new Fundamental Law in 2011. The Hungarian report explores the post-2010 period in the context of EU and international law. Whilst the Hungarian

Nóra Chronowski is Associate Professor of Constitutional Law, National University of Public Service, and Visiting Researcher, Hungarian Academy of Sciences. email: chronowski.nora@tk.mta.hu.

Márton Varju is Senior Research Fellow at the Hungarian Academy of Sciences, Centre for Social Sciences, Head of the Lendület-HPOPs Research Group, and Senior Legal Advisor at the Curia, Hungary. email: varju.marton@tk.mta.hu.

Petra Bárd is Assistant Professor of Criminology, Eötvös Loránd University Faculty of Law, and Visiting Professor, Central European University, Budapest. email: bardp@ceu.edu.

Gábor Sulyok is Senior Research Fellow, Hungarian Academy of Sciences, and Professor of International Law, Széchenyi István University Györ, Hungary. email: sulyok.gabor@tk.mta.hu.

Nóra Chronowski wrote Sects. 1, 2.1, 2.4 and 2.12; Márton Varju wrote Sects. 2.2, 2.3.5.2–2.3.5.4, 2.5–2.11, 2.13 and 3.5; Petra Bárd wrote Sects. 2.3.1–2.3.5.1; and Gábor Sulyok wrote Sects. 3.1–3.4.

N. Chronowski (✉) · M. Varju · G. Sulyok
Hungarian Academy of Sciences, Budapest, Hungary
e-mail: chronowski.nora@tk.mta.hu

M. Varju
e-mail: varju.marton@tk.mta.hu

G. Sulyok
e-mail: sulyok.gabor@tk.mta.hu

N. Chronowski
National University of Public Service, Budapest, Hungary

Constitutional Court in 2012 affirmed the 'constitutional continuity', in that the interpretations that had been used prior to the new Fundamental Law would be applied, this was overruled by a subsequent constitutional amendment, which has reinforced concern that the governing majority is ignoring the constitutional traditions of the last two decades. Since this amendment, the Constitutional Court adds reasoning if it refers to the former case law. In the rulings related to international law and EU law, the constitutional practice did not change significantly, although it became somewhat ambiguous until 2015. An Editorial Note has been added to the country chapter to explain that before the illiberal turn in 2010 and in the aftermath of the post-communist constitutional reforms, the Hungarian constitutional system had in fact been widely acclaimed in Europe for the particularly extensive safeguards for the rule of law and human dignity established by the Constitutional Court. For instance, the Hungarian Constitutional Court during that period represented a robust approach to the principles of legal certainty and non-retroactivity as part of the doctrine of the rule of law, which was invoked frequently as the basis for annulment of legislation.

Keywords The Hungarian Fundamental Law 2012 • The Hungarian Constitutional Court • Illiberal constitutionalism • Decline in the rule of law • Venice Commission Constitutional amendments regarding EU and international co-operation European Arrest Warrant • Data Retention Directive • Privatisation of public services

1 Constitutional Amendments Regarding EU Membership

1.1 Constitutional Culture

1.1.1–1.1.2 In Hungary, no new constitution was formally approved during the change of regime (1989–1990). The Constitution of the Republic of Hungary was a derivative of Act XX of 1949, which was comprehensively revised by Act No. XXXI of 1989 (in force until 31 December 2011; hereinafter 1989 Constitution).[1] With regard to content, new acts emerged not through revolution, but via a parliamentary process of constitution-making that accompanied the regime change in 1989–1990. These proposed and approved amendments were fully compatible with the requirements of democracy and the rule of law. From then until 2011,

P. Bárd
Eötvös Loránd University Faculty of Law, Budapest, Hungary
e-mail: bardp@ceu.edu

P. Bárd
Central European University, Budapest, Hungary

G. Sulyok
Széchenyi István University, Győr, Hungary

the Constitution was under continuous revision, with several acts amending it. The most comprehensive amendment was carried out in December 2002 in connection with the anticipated accession of the country to the EU. In 2010, the parliamentary elections resulted in a two-thirds majority, which enabled the right-wing governing party alliance to write a new constitution (however, this ambition was not articulated during the campaign). The new constitution – the Fundamental Law of Hungary (FL) – was adopted in April 2011 and came into force on 1 January, 2012.[2]

In 2010, in parallel with the constant – altogether more than 10 – amendments of the 1989 Constitution reflecting ad hoc political interests, the governing parties announced the creation of a new constitution. The constitution-making procedure was criticised by the European Parliament and Venice Commission for the absence of pluralistic social debate.[3] While the FL contains the basic principles and institutional system that had become crystallised through democratic constitution-making (like the principles of rule of law, democracy, division of powers, protection of human rights), they do not fully prevail, primarily because of the rules of interpretation referring to the 'historic constitution' of the ancient Hungarian kingdom and the restriction of constitutional jurisdiction.

This is particularly true in cases where the FL itself grants exemptions from the implementation of funda-mental principles. Although the catalogue of fundamental rights in the FL is more modern in some parts than that of the 1989 Constitution, the system of fundamental rights protection as a whole represents a step backward compared to the 1989 Constitution. It is undoubtedly the greatest weakness of the FL that it does not ensure the possibility of a comprehensive review of and remedy for violation of the constitution by the legislature. This is because the FL reduces the scope of action of the Constitutional Court and maintains the procedural and material restrictions introduced in 2010 for an uncertain period. More specifically, the FL lays down that with regard to *ex post* norm control and constitutional complaint procedures, the Constitutional Court is prohibited from reviewing the content of or annulling acts on public finances, with the exception of four 'protected fields of fundamental

[1] Available at (with the amendments of 2010/11) http://www-archiv.parlament.hu/angol/act_xx_of_1949.pdf.

[2] All translations are from the official English translation of the Fundamental Law (consolidated version after the Fourth Amendment) available at http://www.mfa.gov.hu/NR/rdonlyres/8204FB28-BF22-481A-9426-D2761D10EC7C/0/FUNDAMENTALLAWOFHUNGARY\mostrecentversion01102013.pdf.

[3] See Venice Commission Opinion No. 614/2011, Strasbourg 28 March 2011, and Opinion No. 621/2011 on the new constitution of Hungary adopted by the Venice Commission at its 87th Plenary Session (Venice, 17–18 June 2011) points 29, 34. Many Hungarian scholars also criticised the tight time limits for the drafting, and the restricted possibilities for open political and social debate. See Arato et al. 2011, pp. 3–7.

rights', as long as the state debt exceeds half of the gross domestic product. A regulation adopted on 16 November 2010 that essentially corresponds to the content of Art. 37(4) of the FL which restricts the Constitutional Court's right of review and annulment, also fails to accord with the principles of European constitutional development, the traditions of Hungarian constitutionalism developed since 1989–1990 and democratic political culture. It violates the constitutional principles of the rule of law, legal security and separation of powers. As a result of the restriction of the procedure of the Constitutional Court, numerous fundamental rights (especially, for example, the right to property, social rights, the freedom of enterprise and the right to a profession) became 'defenceless'.

Parliament has modified the FL five times since 2011,[4] and has, *inter alia*, cemented the model of limited constitutional judicial review, attempted to break constitutional continuity, to restrict the exercise of the right to vote and freedom of expression and perpetuated the practice of overruling the Constitutional Court's decisions. The Constitutional Court has tried, sometimes with greater, sometimes with less determination, to protect the FL, with a varying degree of success. European bodies have followed this process with great interest: the Venice Commission of the Council of Europe continues to provide opinions on the significant amendments to the FL and on the cardinal laws,[5] and the European Parliament has adopted several resolutions as well. The sharpest criticism has been raised with regard to the fourth amendment to the FL, with which

- *lex specialis* rules were introduced in contrast to the fundamental principles of the rule of law, democracy and the protection of fundamental rights;
- regulations (e.g. relating to student contracts, the acknowledgement of churches, the concept of family) evading or bypassing Constitutional Court rulings were enacted, substantially reducing the space for constitutional protection;
- a specific procedural review and a new limit on interpretation were imposed with regard to constitutional judicial review (excluding substantial review of amendments to the FL, repealing Constitutional Court decisions adopted before the FL); and
- open infringement of EU law (limitation of election campaigns, possibility of special taxation as an indirect result of court rulings)[6] was also risked.

The European Commission has initiated several infringement proceedings as well, on the basis of which the Court of Justice of the European Union (CJEU) has issued important judgments with direct constitutional implications: one on the subject of a radical lowering of the retirement age of judges and another on the

[4] See the amendments in Sonnevend et al. 2015, pp. 45–70.

[5] Cardinal laws are Acts of Parliament that can be adopted or amended with a two-thirds majority of votes of the MPs present.

[6] As the European Commission expressed its serious concerns about the conformity with EU law of the new article on CJEU judgments entailing payment obligations, the fifth amendment repealed this rule.

subject of bringing to an end the term served by the Data Protection Supervisor. Hungary was held to have infringed EU law in both cases.[7]

The European Court of Human Rights (ECtHR) has also heard Hungarian cases which have arisen due to the elimination of the previous constitutionalism and from the arrangements based on the new FL – such as the recognition of churches, dismissal from employment without reason, lifetime imprisonment without compulsory review, premature termination of the mandate of the President of the Supreme Court and a ban on the parliamentary right of expression.[8] The ECtHR has found that the State of Hungary infringed the European Convention on Human Rights (ECHR) in every case.

There is no room here to provide a comprehensive analysis of all of the issues which have arisen and been debated at European forums;[9] however, expeditiously we can diagnose that the developments of the last 3–5 years question the commitment to liberal constitutional values such as the rule of law, democracy and individual freedom. The Constitutional Court still has some margin of appreciation on the basis of the constitutional text to safeguard the achievements of liberal constitutionalism and disregard political expectations, but the quality of reasoning and the decisive arguments of the Court have given rise to a very specific ideational framework that cannot be interpreted under liberal values of rule of law.[10]

1.2 The Amendment of the Constitution in Relation to the European Union

1.2.1 The amendment of the Hungarian Constitution related to EU accession was passed by Parliament in December 2002 (Act LXI of 2002), and introduced a new Art. 2/A into the text of the Constitution:

> By virtue of treaty, the Republic of Hungary, in its capacity as a Member State of the European Union, may exercise certain constitutional powers jointly with other Member States to the extent necessary in connection with the rights and obligations conferred by the treaties on the foundation of the European Union and the European Communities (hereinafter referred to as 'European Union'); these powers may be exercised independently and by way of the institutions of the European Union. The ratification and promulgation of the treaty referred to in subsection (1) shall be subject to a two-thirds majority vote of the Parliament.[11]

---

[7] Case C-286/12 *Commission v. Hungary* [2012] ECLI:EU:C:2012:687; Case C-288/12 *Commission v. Hungary* [2014] ECLI:EU:C:2014:237.

[8] *Magyar Keresztény Mennonita Egyház and Others v. Hungary*, nos. 70945/11, 23611/12, 26998/12, 41150/12, 41155/12, 41463/12, 41553/12, 54977/12 and 56581/12, ECHR 2014 (extracts); *K.M.C. v. Hungary*, no. 19554/11, 10 July 2012; *László Magyar v. Hungary*, no. 73593/10, 20 May 2014; *Baka v. Hungary*, no. 20261/12, 27 May 2014; *Karácsony and Others v. Hungary*, no. 42461/13, 16 September 2014.

[9] See e.g. Vörös 2014, pp. 1–20; Zeller 2013, pp. 307–325; Vincze 2013, pp. 86–97.

[10] Szente 2015, p. 185.

[11] The English translation of the former Hungarian Constitution is available at http://www-archiv.parlament.hu/angol/act_xx_of_1949.pdf.

Thus, in 2002, an authorisation was added permitting the signing of the Treaty of Accession, and a commitment to European unity was declared. Additionally, the rules on cooperation between the National Assembly and the Government in matters of EU integration were determined (for the wording see Sect. 1.4), and the constitutional definition of the National Bank of Hungary was modified. In addition, the rules on voting rights were changed in anticipation of European parliamentary and European local elections.[12] The relevant provisions provide as follows:

> Art. 32/D(1)
>
> The National Bank of Hungary shall define the country's monetary policy in accordance with the provisions of specific other legislation.
>
> Art. 70(2)
>
> All adult Hungarian citizens residing in the territory of the Republic of Hungary and all adult citizens of other Member States of the European Union who reside in the territory of the Republic of Hungary shall have the right to be elected in local ballots for the election of the representatives and mayors; they shall have the right to vote, provided that they are in the territory of the Republic of Hungary on the day of the election or referendum, and furthermore to participate in local referendums or popular initiatives.
>
> Art. 70(4)
>
> All adult Hungarian citizens residing in the territory of the Republic of Hungary and all adult citizens of other Member States of the European Union who reside in the territory of the Republic of Hungary shall have the right to be elected and the right to vote in elections for the European Parliament.

The second amendment to the 1989 Constitution in relation to EU membership took place in December 2007 before the ratification of the Lisbon Treaty (Act CLXVII of 2007). It was an embarrassing amendment and a surprise for experts, as it was not communicated by the Government and the amending process was very rapid. The aim of the amendment was to create constitutional authorisation for criminal law cooperation under the Area of Freedom, Security and Justice (AFSJ) provisions of the EU Treaty. The following text was inserted into Art. 57(4) – the *nullum crimen* rule – of the 1989 Constitution:

> No one shall be declared guilty and subjected to punishment for an offense that was not considered – at the time it was committed – a criminal offense under Hungarian law, or the laws of any country participating in the progressive establishment of an area of freedom, security and justice, and to the extent prescribed in the relevant EU legislation with a view to the mutual recognition of decisions, without any restrictions in terms of major fundamental rights.

The EU provisions in the FL broadly follow the above amendments, and are cited in Sect. 1.3.1.

1.2.2 The constitutional amendment procedure is provided in Art. S) of the FL. An amendment may be initiated by the President of the Republic, the Government, any parliamentary committee or any Member of the National Assembly. The adoption

[12] Chronowski 2005, pp. 190–199.

of a new FL or the amendment of the FL requires the votes of two-thirds of all the Members of the National Assembly. The amendment has to be signed by the President, who may refer the matter to the Constitutional Court if the President finds that any procedural requirement laid down in the FL with respect to adoption of the FL or amendment of the FL has not been met.

In the 1989 Constitution the rules were the same except for the possibility of *ex ante* constitutional review.

1.2.3 The Constitutional Court played a significant role in the wording of the 2002 amendments. The Constitutional Court proclaimed its jurisdiction for posterior review of the constitutionality of statutes (and other legal instruments implementing international treaties) in a decision in 1997.[13] In that decision the Court declared that a statute implementing an international treaty – and the international treaty – may be subjected to subsequent constitutional review. The reasoning of the Court is noteworthy:

> The Constitutional Court emphasizes that the constitutional review of international treaties forms part of the practice of the constitutional courts of countries applying the dualistic-transformational system as a general rule, also in respect of international treaties becoming part of the domestic law by this technique. For instance, Article 59 of the German Basic Law prescribes the dualistic-transformational system. The German Federal Constitutional Court, despite its lack of jurisdiction for preventive norm control, has extended its practice to the control of international treaties prior to their ratification. … It becomes clear from these decisions that in addition to 'naturally' exercising the competence concerning posterior norm control, the German Constitutional Court cannot fail in performing all parts of its duty to safeguard the constitution – especially in respect of the European Union treaties. … On this ground, the [Hungarian] Constitutional Court keeps the subordination to Community law under its continuous supervision – besides examining the implementing acts.[14]

Thus, in 1997, the Court was ready to examine the constitutionality of Community law. In this respect, Decision 30/1998 (VI. 25.),[15] assessing the constitutionality of a provision of Act I of 1994 on the Implementation of the Europe Agreement, is equally notable. Here, the Court treated the agreement as a traditional international treaty. In theory, it was correct in doing so, as Hungary was not then an EU Member State, although the agreement also had some supranational features. The decision declared that the Hungarian Parliament – in the absence of constitutional authorisation – is not entitled to act beyond the principle of territoriality in fields of law within the scope of the exclusive jurisdiction of state authority, nor may it amend the Constitution in a disguised manner by adopting and promulgating an international treaty. Thus, Decision 30/1998 had a significant impact on the drafting of the 2002 authorising provision (Art. 2/A, the so-called 'Europe Clause') of the Hungarian Constitution.

---

[13] Constitutional Court Decision (hereinafter CC Decision) 4/1997 (I. 22.) AB.

[14] Ibid.

[15] CC Decision 30/1998 (VI. 25.) AB.

1.3 Conceptualising Sovereignty and the Limits to the Transfer of Powers

1.3.1 Article E(1) as the basis of European and Union cooperation essentially follows word by word the Art. 6(4) of the 1989 Constitution. Thus, the frame of interpretation remains unchanged;[16] this objective expresses the commitment to European (international or supranational) cooperation. FL Art. E) provides as follows:

> (1) In order to enhance the liberty, well-being and security of the people of Europe, Hungary shall contribute to the creation of European unity.
> (2) With a view to participating in the European Union as a Member State and on the basis of an international treaty, Hungary may, to the extent necessary to exercise the rights and fulfil the obligations deriving from the Founding Treaties, exercise some of its competences set out in the Fundamental Law jointly with other Member States, through the institutions of the European Union.
> (3) The law of the European Union may, within the framework set out in Paragraph (2), lay down generally binding rules of conduct.
> (4) For the authorisation to recognise the binding force of an international treaty referred to in Paragraph (2), the votes of two-thirds of the Members of the National Assembly shall be required.

Article E) paras. (2) and (4), with some simplification, adopts the rules of Art. 2/A of the 1989 Constitution; however, the formulation differs in one aspect. The difference is that the two distinct clauses of Art. 2/A(1) ['exercise certain constitutional powers jointly with other member states ...; these powers may be exercised independently and by way of the institutions of the European Union'] have been merged in Art. E(2) ['jointly with other Member States, through the institutions of the European Union']. However, according to the legal understanding, the Member States do not exercise their competences 'jointly' in the Union legislative processes, rather these are exercised by the institutions. Art. 2/A defined the 'way of institutions' as one form of joint exercise of powers in the EU. Yet in Art. E) of the FL, the exercise of powers 'through the institutions' is referred to as a joint exercise. While the Lisbon Treaty abolished the so-called pillar system and created a single institutional system, the supranational (i.e. Community) method has not become automatically dominant. The Lisbon Treaty intended to integrate the perspectives of supranational and intergovernmental methods, e.g. by respecting the constitutional identity of the Member States, the effective involvement of national parliaments and the consolidation of Member States' initiative in respect of some competences. Strictly speaking, the joint exercise of powers is not the same as exercise through the institutions.[17]

---

[16] See also Bragyova 2012, pp. 335–338; Blutman and Chronowski 2011, p. 329; Bárd 2013, p. 457.

[17] The Constitutional Court has also respected the relevance of the difference of exercising powers jointly and by the way of institutions. See CC Decision 143/2010. (VII. 14.) AB on the Act promulgating the Lisbon Treaty; press release is available at http://www.mkab.hu/letoltesek/en_0143_2010.pdf.

Article E) contained originally only one new rule compared to Art. 2/A of the 1989 Constitution. In its para. (3) it states that '[t]he law of the European Union may … lay down generally binding rules of conduct'. From the domestic legal viewpoint, the ground for the constitutional validity of Union law becomes clearer than it used to be; however, this paragraph still does not solve the problem of primacy, i.e. that a domestic legal act conflicting with an EU legal act is not applicable. The duty of the courts of law to ensure the consistency of domestic and Union law still stems from the EU Treaties (i.e. by way of requesting preliminary rulings) and not from the Constitution itself.[18]

The National Assembly inserted a new sentence into Article E) para. (2) in 2018, by the seventh amendment to the Constitution, creating a solid basis for the Constitutional Court to protect the so-called national constitutional identity:

> The exercise of powers under this Paragraph must be consistent with the fundamental rights and freedoms set out in the Fundamental Law, and it must not be allowed to restrict Hungary's inalienable right of disposition relating to its territorial integrity, population, political system and form of governance.

There are further provisions with regard to fair trial in the context of the EU's Area of Freedom, Security and Justice, which are cited in Sects. 2.3.1–2.3.2.

1.3.2–1.3.3 Contrary to expectations and the activism of the Constitutional Court in 1998, the Constitutional Court succinctly explained the meaning of Art. 2/A after EU accession. Article 2/A 'defines the conditions and the framework of the membership of the Republic of Hungary in the European Union, and the status of Community law in the system of the sources of Hungarian law'.[19] Only in 2008 was the authentic interpretation of the authorising provision further enriched. The Constitutional Court highlighted the function of Art. 2/A in Decision 61/B/2005 AB:

> The purpose of including this provision in the Constitution was to establish the conditions and the framework of the participation of the Republic of Hungary in the European Union. The cited provision of the Constitution authorises the Republic of Hungary to conclude an international treaty under which certain of its competences deriving from the Constitution may be exercised jointly with the other Member States of the European Union and the joint exercise of competences may be implemented through the institutions of the European Union.

The Court clarified the limitations on the exercise of competences within the Union as follows:

> Competences may be exercised jointly to the extent required for the exercise of rights and fulfilment of obligations stemming from the founding treaties of the European Union; only the joint exercise of certain concrete competences deriving from the Constitution is authorised, in other words, the scope of competences exercised jointly is limited.

In respect of the exercise of jurisdiction of the Constitutional Court, this decision for the first time expressly rejected the examination of a collision with EU law: 'The

---

[18] Chronowski 2012, p. 111.

[19] CC Decision 1053/E/2005 AB, judgment of 16 June 2006.

[Act on the Constitutional Court] contains no competence authorising the Constitutional Court to examine a collision with community law. Pursuant to the rules of community law, this questions falls within the competence of the organs of the European Community, ultimately the European Court of Justice.' It also follows that a collision with EU law does not in itself serve as a ground for alleging unconstitutionality. As regards the position of EU law within the Hungarian system of sources of law, the Constitutional Court widened the meaning of the authorising provision by identifying it as the ground for the constitutional validity of EU (Community) law: 'Under Article 2/A of the Constitution, community law applicable in Hungarian law is just as valid as is law adopted by Hungarian legislation.' This interpretation opens the way for the possible examination by the Court of collisions between EU law and Art. 2/A.[20]

In its decision of 143/2010. (VII. 14), the Constitutional Court ruled that the Act of Promulgation of the Lisbon Treaty is constitutional. According to the Court, Art. 2/A of the Constitution cannot be interpreted in a way that would deprive the constitutional provisions on sovereignty and the rule of law of their substance. It referred to its former decisions on the limitation of the exercise of sovereignty and came to the conclusion that although the reforms introduced by the Lisbon Treaty were of foremost importance, Hungary remained a sovereign and independent state with a prevailing rule of law.[21]

In Decision 22/2012 (V. 11.) AB on the interpretation of paras. (2) and (4) of Art. E) of the FL, the Court stated that Art. E(2) contains a provision identical to that of Art. 2/A. The Constitutional Court held that the interpretation of Art. 2/A of the previous Constitution, which was provided in the Decision 143/2010 (VII. 14.) AB, is also valid for the interpretation of Art. E) of the FL. In that decision of 2010, the Constitutional Court clarified the question whether the requirement of qualified majority was only applicable to the Accession Treaty or to other treaties as well. The Court found that the qualified majority 'is necessary for every treaty that leads to transferring further competences of Hungary, specified in the FL, through the joint exercise of competences by way of the institutions of the European Union'. The Court continued:

> Provided that it is based on an international treaty, the requirement of qualified majority is also applicable to the implementation of the founding treaties and their supervision: it means that the implementing measures based on the founding treaties (adoption of secondary legal acts) are not sufficient any more, and therefore the implementation tools need to be amended, or new tools are needed. It is not a condition, however, that the treaty specify itself as the European Union's law, and neither is it a requirement that it should belong to the founding treaties of the EU.

1.3.4 EU law has been regarded as a separate legal system by the Constitutional Court and the courts of law since accession. As such, the supremacy and direct applicability of EU legal acts are recognised; in most cases the courts ensure the

[20] CC Decision 61/B/2005. AB, judgment of 29 September 2008.

[21] See the press release on CC Decision 143/2010 (VII. 14.) AB, supra n. 17.

effectiveness of Community/Union law.[22] References to the principles of direct effect and supremacy are rather automatic;[23] See also Supreme Court Decision Kfv. I.35.052/2007/7, which referred to *Costa v. ENEL* and *Van Gend en Loos*. the courts follow the well-known textbooks on EU law or utilise the ministerial explanations attached to the bill of the applicable Hungarian law. The Curia (former Supreme Court) seems to be willing to establish the triangular relationship of EU law, the ECHR and domestic law, and interpret harmonised Hungarian legal acts in the light of the ECHR, if the implemented EC directive provides a minimum standard.[24]

So far, the Constitutional Court has established two principles marking the boundaries of future constitutional practice. First, it will not treat the founding and amending treaties of the European Union as international law for the purposes of constitutional review,[25] thereby setting up a three-tier system of legal rules applicable within Hungarian legal practice that distinguishes between national, international and EU law. Secondly, in the absence of jurisdiction to review substantive (un)constitutionality (as opposed to procedural constitutionality), the Constitutional Court does not regard a conflict between domestic law and EU law as a constitutionality issue,[26] and this mandates the ordinary courts to resolve such conflict of a sub-constitutional nature.[27]

1.4 Democratic Control

1.4.1 Article 19 of the FL provides:

> The National Assembly may request information from the Government on the government position to be represented in the decision-making procedures of the intergovernmental institutions of the European Union, and may take a position on the draft placed on the agenda in the procedure. In the course of the decision-making of the European Union, the Government shall act on the basis of the position taken by the National Assembly.

Through a scrutiny procedure regulated in Act XXXVI of 2012 on the National Assembly, the National Assembly takes part in the decision-making process

---

[22] See Dezső and Vincze 2012, pp. 208–209.

[23] See e.g. the Decision of Szabolcs-Szatmár-Bereg County Court 5.K.20. 631/2010/4.: '… the Community Treaty has the highest rank in the hierarchy of legal norms. … [T]he relationship of EU law and national law is determined by the principle of primacy, as the Supreme Court stated in principle: national law shall be interpreted in a way that is appropriate to fulfil (i.e. implement) Community law (EBH 2006/1568).'

[24] The Supreme Court established that only refugees are covered by the scope of Council Directive 2003/86/EC of 22 September 2003 on the right to family reunification [2003] OJ 251/12; however, in the light of Art. 8 of the ECHR, domestic law may recognise this right of other protected persons as well. The Supreme Court emphasised that Member States may maintain or introduce more favourable provisions than those laid down by the Directive. Supreme Court Kfv.III.37.925/2009/7.

[25] CC Decision 1053/E/2005. AB

[26] CC Decision 72/2006. (XII. 15.) AB.

[27] Blutman and Chronowski 2011, pp. 329–348.

indirectly, as the Government and the National Assembly cooperate according to special rules in formulating the national position regarding EU draft legislation. The National Assembly also monitors the activities of the Government in EU affairs. The instruments that already existed before accession have remained intact (such as interpellation, questions, committee hearings, parliamentary debates and committees of inquiry), and these instruments can also be used with regard to EU affairs. In addition, Art. 69 of the Act on the National Assembly defines further obligations for the Government in informing the Assembly.

Tasks stemming from subsidiarity checks are carried out by the Committee on European Affairs by virtue of Act XXXVI of 2012 on the National Assembly and Parliamentary Resolution 10/2014 (24 February 2014) on Certain Provisions of the Rules of Procedure. With regard to the *ex-ante* control of subsidiarity, if the Committee considers that a draft Union legislative act fails to comply with the principle of subsidiarity, it submits a report to the plenary on the adoption of a reasoned opinion. The adopted reasoned opinion is sent by the Speaker to the Presidents of the European Commission, the European Parliament and the European Council as well as to the Government of Hungary. With regard to the *ex-post* application of the subsidiarity principle, the Committee is entitled to propose to the Government that it bring an action before the CJEU on the grounds of infringement of the principle of subsidiarity in accordance with Art. 263 TFEU.

1.4.2 The referendum on accession to the EU was held on 12 April 2003, and 83.76% of the citizens who participated voted yes. This was 38% of all the electors. Of the 8 million citizens entitled to vote only 3.66 million voted, which means a participation rate of 45.6 %.

1.5 The Reasons for, and the Role of, EU Amendments

1.5.1–1.5.3 As mentioned earlier, a Constitutional Court finding was of considerable significance in respect of the 2002 amendment of the 1989 Constitution. This amendment was based on a wide consent of the parliamentary parties of that time, and a special parliamentary committee discussed the questions of constitutional authorisation and the accession referendum. The prime minister established a so-called 'council of wise men' composed of former ministers of justice and constitutional court judges. The bill on the amendment was also sent to universities and other academic institutions, which provided expert opinions upon the request of the Government.

However, before the 2007 amendment no such public debate took place.

In the course of the constitution-making in 2010/11, no specific attention was devoted to the Europe Clause or the experiences of the application of EU-related rules in the 1989 Constitution. The entire drafting of the constitution was a closed and almost secret process, and thus public debate or expert advice did not influence the content of the FL.

2 Constitutional Rights, the Rule of Law and EU Law

2.1 The Position of Constitutional Rights and the Rule of Law in the Constitution

2.1.1 Under the title 'Freedom and Responsibility' the FL lists the catalogue of fundamental rights (Articles II–XXIX) in 28 articles. These articles include constitutional rights (including new rights such as the right to good administration, some social rights of employees and the right to self-defence), prohibitions (including the new prohibitions *ne bis in idem*, non-refoulement and biomedical prohibitions) and principles (including the new principles of equality before the law and social responsibility for property). In the field of social solidarity, however, the FL is restricted to constitutional objectives instead of rights (protection of the elderly and persons with disabilities, striving to provide decent housing).

It is worthwhile to add that during the drafting of the Hungarian constitution in 2011 the question arose – and the Hungarian Government inquired from the Venice Commission – whether and to what extent it was necessary to incorporate the EU Charter of Fundamental Rights (Charter) into the national constitution. The adopted FL originally contained more or less the same rights as the Charter in its relevant Chapter ('Freedom and Responsibility'), and some sentences of the Charter were ultimately incorporated; however, compared to the Charter, the content of the rights enumerated in the FL is less detailed and the text leaves the possibility for a wider limitation of rights. It is also worth referring to the preamble of the FL, according to which 'individual freedom can only be complete in cooperation with others'. The Charter applies a completely different approach, with emphasises in its preamble that the Union 'places the individual at the heart of its activities'.

The Charter addresses individual responsibility only in connection with the enjoyment of rights.[28] Whereas the approach of the FL – considering also the numerous basic obligations – is communitarian and nationalist, the Charter focuses on the philos-ophy of individual freedom and supports pluralism.[29] The difference is not acci-dental. In the last decade, Hungarian society has become increasingly closed, exclusive and disunited, and discrimination, segregation, xenophobia and hate speech have become part of everyday life with the support of political populism. In the field of the most important human values, the FL has legalised and reaffirmed unprecedented solutions based on unacceptable societal practice.

---

[28] Charter Preamble: 'Enjoyment of these rights entails responsibilities and duties with regard to other persons, to the human community and to future generations.'

[29] This difference is also pointed out in European Commission For Democracy Through Law (Venice Commission) Opinion No. 621/2011, Strasbourg 20 June 2011, Opinion on the New Constitution of Hungary, point 57.

2.1.2 Article I(3) provides as follows:

> The rules for fundamental rights and obligations shall be laid down in an Act. A fundamental right may only be restricted to allow the effective use of another fundamental right or to protect a constitutional value, to the extent absolutely necessary, proportionate to the objective pursued and with full respect for the essential content of such fundamental right.

2.1.3 Article B) of the FL supports the most important principles of the 1989 Constitution – the rule of law and democracy. Art. C(1) of the FL explicitly provides the principle of division of powers. It is worth mentioning, however, that the division of powers should also be reflected in the rules on state organs in the FL and in constitutional practice.

An extremely alarming issue concerning the basic principles of the FL was that the Transitional Provisions supporting the entry into force of the FL (hereinafter TP-FL) undermined some rules of the FL itself.[30] The Constitutional Court declared that all provisions of the TP-FL that lack transitory character are invalid.[31] As a response, in 2013 the governing majority adopted the fourth amendment of the FL, which incorporated into the Constitution most of the abolished articles, and overrode several earlier Constitutional Court decisions. The Venice Commission expressed its serious concerns about the systematic shielding of ordinary law from constitutional review. The reduction (budgetary matters) and in some cases complete removal (constitutionalised matters) of the competence of the Court to review ordinary legislation on the one hand undermined the rule of law – as the constitutional protection of the standards of the FL became limited; and, on the other hand, infringed the democratic system of checks and balances – as the Constitutional Court lost its influence and is no longer able to provide effective control.[32]

Before the fourth amendment, some hope was given regarding 'constitutional continuity', in that the Constitutional Court seemed to be willing to refer to its jurisprudence and recall its previous argumentation where the formulation of text of the FL was the same as the wording of the Constitution. According to the Court's judgment in 2012:

> In the new cases the Constitutional Court may use the arguments included in its previous decision adopted before the Fundamental Law came into force in relation to the constitutional question ruled upon in the given decision, provided that this is possible on the basis of the concrete provisions and interpretation rules of the Fundamental Law, having the same or similar content as the provisions included in the previous Constitution. ... The

---

[30] On the TP-FL and other cardinal acts read more in Halmai and Scheppele 2012.

[31] The Constitutional Court annulled approximately half of the articles of the TP-FL in its decision of 28 December 2012 (CC Decision 45/2012. (XII. 29.) AB).

[32] Opinion No. 720/2013 of the Venice Commission, point 87.

> conclusions of the Constitutional Court pertaining to those basic values, human rights and freedoms, and constitutional institutions, which have not been altered in the Fundamental Law, remain valid.[33]

However, the fourth amendment of the FL repealed the decisions of the Constitutional Court delivered prior to the entry into force of the FL. This new regulation has reinforced the concern that the governing majority is ignoring the constitutional traditions of the last two decades.

2.2 *The Balancing of Fundamental Rights and Economic Freedoms in EU Law*

2.2.1 This issue has not been addressed in Hungarian judicial practice.[34] As indicated earlier, the Hungarian Constitutional Court has declined to recognise any formal competence to examine the compatibility of national legislation with EU law.[35] This excludes one of the main avenues in Hungarian law for contesting the order of priority of fundamental rights and fundamental economic freedoms.

The only, rather indirect indication of how Hungarian courts would approach the Court of Justice's balancing between fundamental rights and fundamental freedoms follows from an early judgment in the *Dog Breeders Association* case. In its ruling, the Budapest Metropolitan Court accepted that the fundamental rights jurisprudence of the Court of Justice is binding on Hungarian courts.[36] The judgment relied on Title I Article F(2) of the Maastricht Treaty and included citations from

[33] CC Decision 22/2012. (V. 11.) AB, paras. 40–41.

[34] There are examples of legislation establishing a balance favouring local, assumedly value-based considerations against fundamental freedoms, see the regulation of student contracts in Sect. 110 (1)23 of Act 2011: CCIV and Government Regulation 2/1012 requiring students in state higher education to enter into employment in Hungary. In the related judgment of the Constitutional Court in Decision 32/2012 of 4 July 2012, it was deemed necessary to take the rights provided by the free movement of persons in EU law into account in determining the appropriate level of legal protection available in Hungarian constitutional law. In contrast, the dissenting opinions, with a different degree of robustness, emphasised that the majority interpretation put the communitarian values of the new Fundamental Law in jeopardy and considered the individualistic fundamental economic rights in EU law to be in conflict with local social values.

[35] See, for instance, CC Decision 1053/E/2005 of 16 June 2006 where the claim that the 1997 Act on Gambling, which prohibited the sale and advertising of gambling activities organised abroad, breached Art. 56 TFEU, was refused, as the Constitutional Court had no jurisdiction to examine the compatibility of domestic legislation with the EU Treaties.

[36] Case No. 3.K-30698/2006/33. The issue was not addressed in the judgment of the Supreme Court, Case No. Kfv.IV.37.256/2008/14. In Case No. 5.K.20.155/2010/13, the reference to Case 44/79 *Hauer* [1979] ECR 03727, and its detailed discussion was *obiter* and, ultimately, EU law, despite the insistence of the first instance judge, was irrelevant in the case.

Internationale Handelsgesellschaft,[37] *Nold I*[38] and *Rutili*.[39] The impact of the judgment was considerably weakened by the fact that it failed to clarify whether EU jurisprudence was relevant in the case and whether the case fell within the scope of EU human rights law.

2.3 *Constitutional Rights, the European Arrest Warrant and EU criminal law*

2.3.1–2.3.2 The presumption of innocence; *nulla poena sine lege*

As was seen in Sect. 1.2.1, the 1989 Constitution was amended with regard to the EU AFSJ. Further provisions on this were included in the FL, where Art. XXVIII (4)–(6) provides as follows:

> (4) No one shall be held guilty of or be punished for an act which at the time when it was committed did not constitute a criminal offence under Hungarian law or, within the scope specified in an international treaty or a legal act of the European Union, under the law of another State.
> (5) Paragraph (4) shall not prejudice the prosecution or conviction of any person for an act which, at the time when it was committed, was a criminal offence according to the generally recognised rules of international law.
> (6) With the exception of extraordinary cases of legal remedy laid down in an Act, no one shall be prosecuted or convicted for a criminal offence for which he or she has already been finally acquitted or convicted in Hungary or, within the scope specified in an international treaty or a legal act of the European Union, in another State, as provided for by an Act.

The *principle of nullum crimen sine lege* is and was the focal element of the constitutional legality of criminal law in Hungary. According to the Constitutional Court, it is not just a state obligation but the right of the individual that a person be found guilty and sentenced only according to law. Reference to EU law first appeared on the constitutional level at the time of the ratification of the Lisbon Treaty. The former Constitution had already been amended (see Sect. 1.2.1) to enable judicial cooperation in criminal affairs. A new element in the FL is that the text – as an exception to the rule – explicitly refers to an 'act, which was, at the time when it was committed, an offence according to the generally recognised rules of international law'. However, this is not completely new, since the Constitutional Court in 1993 stated that war crimes and crimes against humanity are to be punished even in the absence of Hungarian criminalisation at the time of commitment.[40] The explicit formulation of the principle of *ne bis in idem* is also a new

[37] Case 11/70 *Internationale Handelsgesellschaft* [1970] ECR 01125.
[38] Case 4/73 *Nold* [1974] ECR 00491.
[39] Case 36/75 *Rutili* [1975] ECR 01219.
[40] CC Decision 53/1993. (X. 13.) AB.

element in the FL compared with the 1989 Constitution; however, this was previously guaranteed by the Constitutional Court under the principle of the rule of law. A definite novelty is that foreign judgments can be recognised not only on the basis of EU law but also on the basis of international treaties.[41]

Under the 1989 Constitution neither the Framework Decision on the European Arrest Warrant[42] nor the implementing law were subjected to a constitutional challenge.

The Framework Decision was transposed into Hungarian law by Act CXXX of 2003, which was later replaced by Act CLXXX of 2012.

Unlike in other Member States, the prohibition of the extradition or surrender of own nationals is not constitutionally entrenched. Although the prohibition of extradition of Hungarian nationals as a general rule is laid down in Act XXXVIII of 1996 on international legal assistance in criminal matters, the law of CLXXX of 2012 prevails on the basis of the principle *lex posterior derogat legi priori.*

A more difficult question arises in the case of a potential constitutional challenge against the 2012 Act. First, the former Art. 69 of the 1989 Constitution and Art. XIV of the FL currently in force on the prohibition of expelling Hungarian citizens from the territory of Hungary, or the statement that Hungarians always have the right to return to Hungary, may be interpreted as encompassing the prohibition of extradition or surrender of Hungarian nationals.

Secondly, the other ground-breaking novelty of the European Arrest Warrant, the departure from the principle of double criminality, may also be challenged on the basis of the Constitution or may be disputed in light of the FL. Since there are potential clashes between EU law and the Constitution/FL of Hungary, the matter is more delicate. However, these issues have not yet been raised in front of the Constitutional Court.

In Decision 32/2008. (III.12.) AB, the first case in relation to the European Arrest Warrant (EAW), it was not the implementing domestic law but a related piece of legislation, the Hungarian law promulgating the Convention on the surrender procedure between the European Union on the one hand and the Republic of Iceland and the Kingdom of Norway on the other (hereinafter EUIN), which became the subject of constitutional scrutiny in March 2008. Using his constitutional right of veto, the President of the Republic initiated the constitutional review of the law promulgating the EUIN, which had been approved by the Hungarian legislature on 11 June 2007. The EUIN Convention extended the jurisdiction of the Framework Decision to the above-mentioned two non-EU members, Iceland and Norway. Therefore, the Convention forms neither part of the primary nor of the secondary legal sources of the EU.

[41] Jakab 2011, p. 229.

[42] Council Framework Decision of 13 June 2002 on the European arrest warrant and the surrender procedures between Member States (2002/584/JHA), [2002] OJ L 190/1.

In Decision 32/2008. (III.12.), the Constitutional Court ruled that certain passages of the challenged law were unconstitutional. The Constitutional Court examined the correspondence of both Art. 2 of the Constitution, whereby 'Hungary is a sovereign, democratic state', and Art. 57(4), which enshrined the legal principles of *nulla poena sine lege* and *nullum crimen sine lege* in the 1989 Constitution. The Court was of the opinion that the turn of phrase 'according to Hungarian law' in Art. 57(4) was primarily meant to refer to the Criminal Code, but it also covers obligations that become part of the Hungarian sources of law through the ratification of an international convention, thus making allowance for possible exceptions to the principle of *nullum crimen sine lege*, and therefore also including the possibility of retrospective legislation.[43] Therefore, Art. 7 of the 1989 Constitution on international law complements Art. 57(4), and the two should be applied in parallel. According to the Constitutional Court's decision, however, the EU *acquis* does not qualify as international law. The Union can promulgate an article of international law only within the framework of the third pillar, but according to the Constitution these conventions do not become 'part of Hungarian law'. In light of the above, the Constitutional Court reviewed the various articles of the EUIN Convention and came to the conclusion that several sections of the Act ratifying the Convention were in fact in contradiction with the Constitution.

In Decision 3144/2013. (VII. 16) AB, the applicant challenged Act CXXX of 2003 (replaced by Act CLXXX of 2012 by the time the decision was delivered) implementing the EAW Framework Decision in the form of a constitutional complaint. According to the Act, execution of an EAW has to be refused if the criminal prosecution or punishment of the requested person is barred by statute under Hungarian law, provided that the act in question falls within the jurisdiction of Hungary.[44] Justice Miklós Lévay wrote the decision rejecting the complaint for the court unanimously. He emphasised that mutual trust and cooperation were the basis of surrender according to the EAW. This, however, does not mean an unconditional or unverified acceptance of the issuing authority's evaluation of the case. According to Art. 11(1) of the implementing Act, the Budapest-Capital Regional Court shall hold a hearing where the requested person has the opportunity to challenge the existence of circumstances which might affect the conditions of his or her surrender. Should the Budapest-Capital Regional Court not be able to decide on surrender based on the available data and facts provided by the issuing authority, it may request, by way of the responsible minister, that the issuing authority in an urgent procedure provide it with additional information, with special regard to data that might lead to a possible refusal to execute the EAW, including data on the statute of limitations. Should the Hungarian judicial authority ultimately come to the conclusion that the statute of limitations has expired, it will deny the execution of the EAW.

---

[43] CC Decision 2/1994. (I. 14.) AB.

[44] Article 4 of Act CXXX of 2003 and Art. 5 point c) of Act CLXXX of 2012.

In Constitutional Court Decision 3025/2014 (II. 17.), the judge of an ordinary court referred a constitutional issue in an on-going case to the Constitutional Court. The judge challenged Art. 15(3) of Act CXXX of 2003 implementing the EAW according to which, once located, the person requested has to be automatically arrested, i.e. the competent authority is not granted judicial discretion to opt for less rights-intrusive measures in lieu of arrest. The Constitutional Court's majority – in an opinion authored by Justice Mária Szívós – rejected the complaint.

The majority held that the regulation under review corresponds to the constitutional and international requirements on the limitation of fundamental rights. The limitation is prescribed by law. The limitation serves the aim of exercising state powers of criminal prosecution. In order to make the exercise of these powers efficient, the state organs need to have effective tools which by necessity severely limit certain rights. The necessity of employing these tools can be justified by the nature of criminal acts, which endanger or violate other persons' fundamental constitutional rights. The efficient enforcement of EAWs ensures the successful exercise of the state powers of punishment and necessarily involves rights infringing measures, such as arrest and detention.

Justice Miklós Lévay authored a dissenting opinion, joined by Justices Elemér Balogh, András Bragyova and László Kiss. In their view the Constitutional Court should have conducted a complex constitutional scrutiny (as opposed to examining surrender for the sake of execution of a sentence only) and it should have determined a violation of the FL. The dissenting opinion clarified that a Constitutional Court review conducted upon the initiative of a judge is an abstract review of the challenged provision. Often the Constitutional Court does not limit the scope of constitutional scrutiny to the subject or object of the case at hand, but reviews all elements of the attacked provision.[45] In the view of the dissenting judges, the only limitation is that the Constitutional Court must stick to the constitutional review of the provision to be invoked in the actual case at issue. Therefore, the majority Justices – in the opinion of the dissenting Justices – engaged in 'negative judicial activism' with regard to the scope of the constitutional scrutiny. In their view, a full constitutional analysis of the whole challenged provision should have been conducted. Neither the EAW Framework Decision nor the implementing domestic law differentiates between procedures conducted for the sake of a criminal proceeding and for the enforcement of a custodial sentence or detention order, which is a further reason to not limit the scope of constitutional review. In the view of the dissenting Justices, had the majority reviewed the whole provision, it would have come to the conclusion that the implementing legislation was, while necessary, disproportionate to the aim to be pursued and therefore unconstitutional.

In order to underpin his point, Justice Lévay also invoked EU law. He noted that the Constitutional Court must interpret domestic law – as far as possible – in line

[45] See e.g. CC Decision 37/2013. (XII. 5.) AB.

with the Framework Decision.[46] Although Art. 12 of the EAW Framework Decision leaves it primarily up to the Member States to decide whether a requested person should remain in detention after arrest, the main aim of this rights-infringing measure is the prevention of absconding. This provision thus does not oblige Member States to detain all requested persons. Quite to the contrary, in his view, severe doubts are raised regarding the compatibility of the Hungarian measures with EU law, with due regard to Art. 6 of the EU Charter of Fundamental Rights on the right to liberty and security of person.

2.3.2.1 Decision 32/2008. (III.12.) evoked harsh criticism among legal scholars who immediately reacted to the Constitutional Court's ruling.[47] It is quite telling that a Constitutional Court judge, Péter Kovács, authored one of the scholarly articles,[48] thereby departing from the well-established practice that constitutional court justices do not explain their decisions, and judgments shall speak for themselves. The majority of the experts in the field seem to agree with Justice Bragyova and have criticised the application of the *nullum crimen* principle to the law under scrutiny. As Krisztina Karsai and Katalin Ligeti have proved, whether and to what extent constitutional and other guarantees apply to procedures conducted in the framework of legal assistance depends on the branch of law. As the professors have rightly pointed out, the Constitutional Court entirely omitted such analysis and took it for granted that legal assistance in criminal matters belongs to the branch of criminal law,[49] although the various parts of an extradition procedure are characterised by their patchwork nature: on the one hand a certain duality between international and domestic law can be traced, and on the other the procedure has both criminal and administrative law elements. Compliance with a request for extradition or surrender is an administrative law decision, and cannot be regarded as an act where the criminal power of the requested state is being manifested, even if – like in the case of surrender – the principle of direct request applies, since the objective of the procedure is neither the establishment of criminal liability nor the imposition of sanctions.[50]

Although the rulings declaring the unconstitutionality of the domestic law giving effect to the international treaty which extended the ambit of the EAW to Iceland and Norway have created some difficulties, the overall situation is not as bad as it seems: in the day-to-day practice, this legal instrument more or less does the job. The overall experience indicates that in the face of all the constitutional worries, one-fifth of all arrest warrants end in effective surrender in the EU.[51]

---

[46] Cases C-105/03 *Pupino* [2005] ECR I-05285; C-397/01 *Pfeiffer and Others* [2004] ECR I-08835; C-282/10 *Dominguez* [2012] ECLI:EU:C:2012:33.

[47] Karsai and Ligeti 2008, pp. 399–408.

[48] Kovács 2008, pp. 409–413, commenting on the article by Karsai and Ligeti.

[49] Karsai and Ligeti 2008, pp. 399–408, 400.

[50] Ibid., pp. 401–402.

[51] See the aggregate number of EAWs issued and resulting in effective surrender between 2005–2013, http://www.europarl.europa.eu/EPRS/140803REV1-European-Arrest-Warrant-FINAL.pdf

2.3.3 Fair Trial and *In Absentia* Judgments

2.3.3.1 The expert has come across and is aware of a number of cases that raise doubts with regard to *in absentia* judgments rendered in other Member States decades ago, but these cases have not yet been heard by the courts.

2.3.4 The Right to a Fair Trial – Practical Challenges Regarding a Trial Abroad

2.3.4.1–2.3.4.2 Although constitutional issues did not directly arise in the following complex set of decisions, let us mention the perhaps best known EAW surrender case which has been extensively covered by the Hungarian and Irish media. The Tobin case illustrates the difficulties of the implementation of the EAW by the Member States.[52]

The case confirms that the European criminal justice that used to operate along the lines of intergovernmentalism was inefficient. A field of law that develops slowly on a case-by-case basis is not suitable for remedying the negative side-effects of an expanded freedom of movement.

Out of fear for loss of national sovereignty over criminal law, the Member States opted for mutual recognition-based instruments rather than harmonisation. However, mutual confidence has still not been fully achieved among the Member States. As long as certain states are worried about their citizens' basic rights and respect for their procedural guarantees due to different fundamental rights standards, they will leave shortcuts in their legislation to avoid the enforcement of EU law; they will interpret EU law in a restrictive way or even *contra legem*. Irish Justice Hardiman's opinion speaks volumes in this regard; he straightforwardly rejected the idea of mutual trust.[53] Had he adhered to the basics of EU criminal law, neither his devastating opinion about Hungarian criminal procedure nor his ignorance about the Hungarian legal system should have mattered. The fact that Hungary would not have extradited its own citizen but rather would have offered to execute the punishment itself should also have been irrelevant, since the EAW does not operate on the basis of reciprocity, but rather on the basis of confidence among the Member States.

Had the Member States not guarded their national sovereignty over criminal so jealously, a Luxembourg decision in the framework of a preliminary ruling procedure would have clarified how to interpret Irish law in conformation with EU law so as to correspond to the Framework Decision. Had the third pillar operated along the lines of supranationalism, the Commission or another Member State, including Hungary, could have initiated an infringement procedure for the wrongful

---

[52] Buda Surroundings District Court, case number: 2.B.1308/2000/20, 7 May 2002., Pest County Court as court of second instance, case number: 2. Bf. 740/2002/6, 10 October 2002, High Court, *Minister for Justice Equality & Law Reform v. Tobin*, [2007] IEHC 15, 12 January 2007, Supreme Court of Ireland, *Minister for Justice, Equality & Law Reform v. Tobin*, [2008] IESC 3, 3 July 2007., High Court, *MJELR v. Tobin*, [2011] IEHC 72, 11 February 2011, Supreme Court of Ireland, *Minister for Justice Equality and Law Reform v. Tobin*, [2012] IESC 37, 19 June 2012.

[53] Supreme Court of Ireland, *Minister for Justice Equality and Law Reform v. Tobin*, [2012] IESC 37, 19 June 2012.

implementation of the Framework Decision. Had the Court of Justice had more powers, it could have condemned Ireland for disrespecting the maximum 90-day deadline applicable for the determination of a request for surrender, and the length of proceeding argument would not have arisen.

2.3.5 The Right to Effective Judicial Protection: The Principle of Mutual Recognition in EU Criminal Law and Abolition of the Exequatur in Civil and Commercial Matters

2.3.5.1 The dissenting opinion of Justice Lévay to the EUIN decision, which clarified what procedural and substantive safeguards need to be available for the constitutional operation of the EUIN, seems to have embraced the necessity of mutual recognition and trust under the European framework for criminal cooperation. The separate opinion of Justice Bragyova, however, suggested that even though the *nullum crimen sine lege* principle may not constitute a constitutional limit to the EUIN, other constitutional principles, such as the right to asylum, the prohibition on the extradition of own nationals, the equal treatment principle, the right to a fair trial or the prohibition of the death penalty may offer sufficient constitutional grounds for the potential refusal of EU criminal cooperation measures.

The *EAW Transfer Detention* decision of the Constitutional Court[54] – reported above at Sects. 2.3.1–2.3.2 – was also not particularly critical of the mutual recognition principle. It merely took notice that criminal cooperation under the EU framework represented a closer system of cooperation among the Member States, and that the obligations of national criminal justice systems under the mutual recognition principle can be scrutinised domestically when the grounds for the execution of an EAW are examined by national courts. A more critical position was formulated in the dissenting opinion of Justice Lévay and others, arguing that the domestic implementation of the Framework Decision, which prescribed the mandatory detention of the person being transferred under an EAW and which did not regulate the possibility of using other alternative instruments, represented a disproportionate interference with the right to personal freedom. The EAW Framework Decision interpreted together with Art. 6 EU Charter contributed to the conclusion by the dissenting judges that the domestic regulation of mandatory detention following a mandatory arrest under an EAW was unconstitutional, as it represented a violation of the right to personal freedom by making the decision automatic and not subjecting it to a test of justification in the light of the circumstances of the individual case.

2.3.5.2 The Expert is not aware of any debates regarding the transplantation of mutual recognition from internal market to criminal law in Hungary.

Technically, the mutual recognition principle is an effective principle for the governance of large and diverse areas. It ensures that without engaging in politically treacherous and legally risky harmonisation, private and public activity across

[54] CC Decision 3025/2014 (II. 11.) AB.

borders between the participating states can be secured, and conflicts between the different participating regulatory systems are settled. It places emphasis on horizontal cooperation and communication, and conflicts are settled in a bilateral framework. It creates an essentially decentralised framework for governance which, in harmony with the principle of subsidiarity, favours local discretion. Its safe operation, however, requires that exemptions from the obligation of mutual recognition be available. Mutual recognition, because of increased horizontal cooperation and communication between the participating states, may lead to voluntary harmonisation through the conduct of the individual participants.

2.3.5.3 The Expert is not aware of any such concerns raised with regard to the role of courts.

In the Expert's view, the mutual recognition principle assumes the approaches of both trust and cooperation and of protection. While there is pressure to cooperate horizontally and to safeguard the effectiveness of the overall governance framework, it is possible to protect locally formulated considerations in what is an essentially decentralised system. The sensitive issue is how these functions may be reconciled, and to what extent the protection function is allowed to be exercised in light of the inherent pressure to secure the effective operation of the governance framework. Again, this is a question of gradation.

In the Expert's view, a conflict between the different functions exercised by national courts is likely to arise in the area of cooperation in family matters. National courts are likely to be conflicted by their obligations to protect the rights of the child and to secure the effective execution of court orders issued in a foreign jurisdiction, in particular when the parents have initiated parallel proceedings concerning child custody in different jurisdictions.

2.3.5.4 In the Expert's view, it first needs to be considered whether the current safeguards available in the EU measures concerned enable effective protection in all circumstances and whether through the extension of the relevant safeguards at the EU level any hiatuses can be remedied. When the introduction of further nationally driven safeguards beyond these possibilities is considered, how they would affect the regulatory objectives of the relevant EU measures and whether they are liable to reproduce the procedural and other problems the relevant EU measures were intended to resolve in the first place needs to be taken into account. The Expert considers that while a reintroduction of judicial review could increase the level of protection of individuals, it is difficult to foresee the cross-border implications of such a solution. It must not be ignored that the effective resolution of cross-border matters is also in the interest of the individuals concerned.

Locally engineered responses could also raise the issue of different standards of protection being available to individuals in different Member States. It is not only questionable that the same institutions of judicial protection could be introduced in the different Member States in the different areas where the mutual recognition principle applies, but it is also unclear whether the relevant judicial remedies would have the same scope and intensity. These differences could reflect deeper divergences between the different legal systems and therefore, introducing a uniformly applicable solution at the national level may be problematic not only as a matter of competences, but also substantively. Revisiting the rules of the existing EU measures in light of the experiences of the past year may offer a more easily achieved solution.

2.4 *The EU Data Retention Directive*

2.4.1 The implementation of the Data Retention Directive[55] did not raise constitutional issues in Hungary. The Hungarian Civil Liberties Union filed a petition with the Constitutional Court in 2008 against several articles of Act C of 2003 on electronic communications,[56] alleging that beyond the violation of several fundamental rights (e.g. right to privacy, right to protection of personal data, right to property) the domestic legislation also infringed Art. 2/A of the 1989 Constitution by implementing an ultra vires EU act. However, the Constitutional Court did not address the petition, and when the 1989 Constitution was repealed by the FL, the petitioner was unable to re-initiate the procedure as a constitutional complaint under the new legal conditions.

2.5 *Unpublished or Secret Legislation*

2.5.1 The principle of loyalty does not require the Member States to overlook the principles governing the legality of domestic administrative action completely, and it does not prevent the Member States from observing domestic legal requirements in the execution of EU measures, provided that the effectiveness of EU law is not placed in jeopardy. The Hungarian approach was placed under the scrutiny of the Court of Justice in its 22 May 2014 judgment in the *Érsekcsanádi Mezőgazdasági Zrt.* case.[57] The Court of Justice, as a matter of the formal requirements of EU law, confirmed the Hungarian practice by accepting that the adoption of national administrative decisions and administrative opinions for the execution of Commission Decisions are not excluded by those decisions.[58] This, however, does

[55] Directive 2006/24/EC of the European Parliament and of the Council of 15 March 2006 on the retention of data generated or processed in connection with the provision of publicly available electronic communications services or of public communications networks and amending Directive 2002/58/EC, [2006] OJ L 105/54.

[56] Petition of the Hungarian Civil Liberties Union: http://tasz.hu/files/tasz/imce/Eht_AB_vegleges.pdf

[57] Case C-56/13 *Érsekcsanádi Mezőgazdasági Zrt* [2014] ECLI:EU:C:2014:352.

[58] The Court of Justice paid no attention to matters arising in domestic law relating to the adoption of national measures for the execution of Commission Decisions – specifically, the use of an administrative opinion as opposed to an administrative decision to decide on the rights and

not mean that as a matter of national law, and provided that EU law requirements are not violated, national courts cannot demand that the domestic requirements of administrative law be met.[59] This is particularly important in circumstances where the legality of administrative action, for example the choice of administrative instrument (here administrative decisions and a formally non-binding administrative opinion) restricting the rights of and imposing obligations on individuals, is questionable under domestic law. Arguably, the Court of Justice implied, whilst denying that it had competence to rule on the issue, that the lawfulness of the executing national measures may also depend on their meeting domestic legal requirements.[60] This follows from the fact that the questions referred to the Court of Justice were aimed at clarifying whether not providing compensation for damage caused by national executing measures is an acceptable practice in general considering, especially, the requirements following from EU law.

See also the *György Balázs* case in Sect. 2.8.1.

2.6 Rights and General Principles of Law in the Context of Market Regulation: Property Rights, Legal Certainty, Non-retroactivity and Proportionality

2.6.1 It has been suggested that the declaration by the Constitutional Court that a domestic executing/implementing measure is unconstitutional could be considered as an indirect constitutional criticism towards EU market regulation, although formally it would have no effect on the legality of any EU instruments, and the Constitutional Court has always been cautious to indicate that its decisions do not involve an assessment of EU legislation.[61]

The *Agricultural Surplus Stock* decision[62] offers a clear image of the hesitant approach of the Constitutional Court, which placed more emphasis on domestic conundrums of constitutional adjudication than on investigating the potential for

obligations of individuals, and it was only interested in the effective execution of the Commission decisions, which did not specify the rules of their domestic implementation (paras. 40–43).

[59] This question was not put to the Court of Justice, and it is likely that the Court may not have jurisdiction to answer the question in its entirety.

[60] See paras. 47–49, 51–56, and 62–65 of the judgment. The Court of Justice held that in the absence of explicit requirements in EU law, it is exclusively for the national legislature to decide whether a system of compensation for any damage caused by the executing national protection measures should be established. In the relevant questions referred to the Court of Justice, the referring court wanted to clarify whether the principles of EU law would require the Hungarian state to set up a system of compensation, or liberate it from any such (European and domestic) obligation.

[61] Fazekas 2014, p. 53.

[62] CC Decision 17/2004 (V. 24.) AB. Annotated in Albi 2009, pp. 46–69; Sajó 2004, pp. 351–371 and Uitz 2006, pp. 41–63.

diverging constitutional standards of economic regulation at the European and the national level. The main limitation of the decision is that, unlike the Estonian Supreme Court and the Czech Constitutional Court,[63] the Constitutional Court refused to acknowledge that it is necessary to examine matters under EU law. Therefore, only the domestic implications of the relevant EU regimes were examined on the basis of domestic constitutional law. This enabled the Hungarian court to avoid the constitutional controversies of addressing the constitutional deficits of EU regulation and of giving precedence to EU law over the Hungarian Constitution.

The Court claimed that that 'the question about the provisions challenged in the petition concerns the constitutionality of the Hungarian legislation applied for the implementation of the EU regulations, rather than the validity or the interpretation of the EU regulations themselves. This meant that the act was reviewed on the basis of the standing jurisprudence of the Constitutional Court on the principle of legal certainty, which resulted in a declaration that several provisions of the act were unconstitutional. The Constitutional Court confirmed, in particular, that the payment obligations were introduced retroactively, and that the temporal complications of implementing the EU regulations in the first half of 2004 compromised the constitutional principle of legal certainty. The Commission regulations were subjected – albeit indirectly – to the control offered by Hungarian constitutional requirements.[64] Although the intention to uphold core domestic constitutional requirements, such as the rule of law, was evident,[65] it is far from certain that this was inspired by the suspected more relaxed demand for legal certainty in EU law. Similarly, the Constitutional Court did not specify whether the decision might be regarded as a challenge to the supremacy of EU law (of the Commission regulations) over the Hungarian Constitution.[66]

There is perhaps a clearer indication of what the Constitutional Court thinks of the standard of fundamental rights protection at the EU level in the jurisprudence in which the protection of rights as offered by EU legislation is contrasted indirectly with national requirements.[67] As noted in the Hungarian commentary, these cases reveal a more receptive attitude towards the EU dimensions of constitutional

---

[63] EU legislation on transitional agricultural measures also caused constitutional problems immediately after EU accession in Estonia and the Czech Republic. See Albi 2009.

[64] Fazekas 2014, p. 53.

[65] As Fazekas noted, it is unclear 'whether legal certainty was given precedence because it was one of the most significant constitutional principles of the democratic Hungarian state based on the rule of law, or other provisions of the constitution would also be treated in this way'. Ibid., p. 53.

[66] Fazekas argued that the Constitutional Court, first among the constitutional courts of the new Member States, was under considerable pressure to avoid a solution which would have represented a limitation of state sovereignty and independence, and of the constitutional values of Hungarian democracy. Fazekas 2014, p. 55.

[67] The *Lisbon Decision* made it clear that the Charter of Fundamental Rights binds the Member States and they are subjected to the jurisdiction of the Court of Justice under the Charter. It also accepted that the Lisbon Treaty reinforced fundamental rights protection in the EU.

disputes than the cases – discussed above – that deal with more visible conflicts between national and EU constitutional law.[68]

There are several cases where EU law has enhanced the protection of employees and equal treatment on the grounds of gender.

Finally, it needs to be considered that recent jurisprudence from the Constitutional Court concerning the constitutional benchmarks of economic regulation by the Hungarian state under the FL seems to be pursuing a rather reduced constitutional agenda. The rulings, which aimed to lay down the foundations of economic constitutionalism under the FL, recognise a particularly broad discretion for the legislature to interfere with the economy, and they, therefore, seem to contradict any expectation that EU economic regulation may fall below Hungarian constitutional benchmarks, as now regulated under the FL. Nevertheless, the relevant decisions may serve as a source of conflict between EU economic regulation and Hungarian constitutionalism. While they do not represent an outright denial that the economic constitution under the FL follows the idea of a market economy,[69] their conclusions are based on explicit – if rather misunderstood – criticisms of global and regional market integration, and on concerns for the devastating consequences of unregulated markets. They also recognise the global fiscal and economic crisis as a ground for curbing back the market and expanding the influence of the state. This, in the interpretation of the recent jurisprudence, entails that normal rule of law requirements may be accorded lesser relevance and that the right to property and the freedom of enterprise may need to tolerate more robust interventions by the state. At this point, it must be noted that there is no evidence that the examination of the individual grounds by the Constitutional Court has actually been affected by these considerations. Beyond general declarations, the decisions in question have all failed to establish a link between the crisis/regulatory failure/globalisation and the legal provisions in question.

The June 2014 decision in the *Cooperative Banking Restructuring* case[70] indicated that in matters of economic policy and regulation, the Constitutional Court is prepared to trust the judgement of the Government. It also made it clear that the right to property and the freedom to pursue an economic activity represent a rather undemanding constitutional limitation on government discretion, and it seems to have set the benchmarks for justifiability, rationality and necessity applicable to economic regulation comparably lower than in the jurisprudence under the 1989

---

[68] Fazekas 2014, pp. 65–68.

[69] In Art. M), the Fundamental Law holds that the Hungarian economy is based on value-producing work and on the freedom of enterprise, and that Hungary ensures the conditions of fair and undistorted competition in the market. Contrast this with Art. 9(1) and (2) of the 1989 Constitution, which holds that the Hungarian economy is a market economy in which the equality of private and public ownership are guaranteed, and that Hungary recognises and supports the freedom of enterprise and the freedom of competition in the market.

[70] CC Decision 20/2014 (VI. 30.) AB.

Constitution.[71] The decision was allegedly influenced by the exigencies of post-crisis economic and fiscal recovery. The Court was anxious to make the general point that global and regional market integration and the governance of global and regional markets have proved to constitute a risk for the Hungarian social and economic order, but without any elaboration on how this might actually affect constitutional standards.

The socially and politically highly controversial November 2014 *Foreign Currency Consumer Loan* decision[72] ruled that Act XXXVIII of 2014 implementing the 'uniformity decision' by the Curia (uniformity decision in civil law 2/2014) concerning the fairness of foreign currency consumer loan contracts delivered on the basis of the *Kásler* judgment of the EU Court of Justice,[73] did not constitute a violation of legal certainty, the prohibition of retrospective legislation or the right to a fair trial. The Act had sought to alleviate the exposure to currency fluctuations of individuals affected by foreign currency mortgages. In setting the premises, the Constitutional Court claimed that the contested legislation needed to be interpreted in the light of the commitment of the FL to protect vulnerable individuals, in particular poor and vulnerable consumers. While this in principle is unproblematic, there is no evidence that the assessment of the Constitutional Court of the individual grounds was influenced by such commitment.

Concerning the requirement of legal certainty, the Constitutional Court held that the extremely limited amount of time available between the adoption and the entry into force of the act in question – although it was recognised as unusually short – cannot be regarded as unconstitutional, as in the circumstances of the case the financial institutions affected by the legislation were in fact able to make the necessary preparations. Fundamentally, it argued that the Act contained nothing new which the financial institutions affected would not have known from judicial practice or from other pieces of legislation, and that the Act, although it introduced considerable negative consequences for the financial institutions affected, did not contain provisions which would have required lengthy preparations.

Regarding the claim relating to retrospective legislation (and in this connection to legal certainty), the Constitutional Court stated that the conditions of contractual fairness as regulated by the Act – although not as explicitly as made out in the Act – had in fact been part of the Hungarian legal system before the introduction of foreign currency consumer loans in the Hungarian market. It argued that the fairness of consumer contracts have always been regulated clearly and unambiguously in Hungarian law and that the explicit conditions of the Act on contractual fairness,

[71] See, also CC Decision 3194/2014 (VII. 7.) AB on the regulation of the sale of tobacco products, which by examining only the manifest unreasonableness of the regulatory instrument in light of its general objectives has created an extremely low constitutional benchmark for economic regulation, aiming to re-regulate and re-partition entire sectors of the economy. The generally applicable benchmarks, such as transparent and non-discriminatory regulation, and the adequate regulation of the discretion made available to the public body concerned, were ignored.

[72] CC Decision 34/2014 (XI. 14.) AB.

[73] Case C-26/13 *Kásler and Káslerné Rábai* [2014] ECLI:EU:C:2014:282.

which followed directly from the judgment of the EU Court of Justice in *Kásler* interpreting Directive 93/13/EC, have been part of Hungarian law since the implementation of the directive into Hungarian law. In reaching this conclusion, the Constitutional Court was not disturbed by the fact that until the judgment in *Kásler*, the uniformity decision 2/2014 and the adoption of the Act, the particular meaning of contractual fairness as specified in length by the Act had not been defined at all in Hungarian law or in Hungarian judicial or other practice. It seemed satisfied that the vulnerable position of consumers and the information deficit favouring financial institutions should have been sufficient to allow for an interpretation of fairness in consumer contracts as determined in legislation in 2014.

2.7 The ESM Treaty, Austerity Programmes and the Democratic, Rule-of-Law-Based State

2.7.1 There is no evidence that any constitutional discussions on the Treaty Establishing the European Stability Mechanism (ESM Treaty) have taken place in Hungary, which is not a eurozone country and has not ratified the ESM Treaty.

The Constitutional Court decision dealing with the constitutionality of the Treaty on Stability, Coordination and Governance (TSCG) dealt with the interpretation of the 'Europe clause' (Art. E(2) and (4) of the FL).[74] It focused, in particular, on the issue of whether the binding nature of the TSCG, which regulates policy and institutional matters relating to the EU framework, should be considered under Article E of the FL, which requires a two-thirds majority in the Hungarian Parliament in the ratification process. The technical reasoning of the decision, which did not address the substantive legal and policy consequences of the TSCG, examined under these premises whether the TSCG should be classified as a treaty constituting the European Union, or as a treaty modifying or supplementing the rights and obligations laid down in the treaties constituting the European Union. Ultimately, it found that if the TSCG does not affect the transfer of constitutional competences under the EU framework, the provisions of Art. E(2) and (4) need not be applied. The reasoning is far from clear, and the use of the conditional in the conclusion ('if')[75] was not particularly helpful for the legislator in determining whether the TSCG in fact required a two-thirds majority for ratification by Parliament. The refusal of the Constitutional Court to look into the substance of the TSCG was based on the fact that its review powers were limited by the application

[74] CC Decision 22/2012 (V. 11.) AB.

[75] On the basis of EU constitutional law and as indicated in Art. 3(1) of the TSCG, the TSCG cannot be regarded as constituting a transfer of competences for their exercise under the EU framework, and the TSCG (therefore) was not adopted as a modification of the Founding Treaties. There are, nevertheless, TSCG provisions which affect – beyond explicit EU legal obligations – the fiscal sovereignty of its signatories (Arts. 3(1)a, 3(1)e, 3(2), and 11), which should justify its recognition as a treaty falling under Art. E) of the FL.

in the given case, which did not touch upon substantive issues. The Court nevertheless indicated that it was prepared to examine the substance of the Hungarian legislation incorporating the TSCG in light of the FL, provided that it receives an admissible application in that matter.

2.7.2 There have been no constitutional discussions regarding Eurobonds in Hungary.

2.7.3 As seen earlier, the constitutional order established after 2010 in Hungary went particularly far in guaranteeing unrestrained discretion for the Government to tackle the economic and social impact of the financial and economic crisis. The partial suspension of the jurisdiction of the Constitutional Court in reviewing economic regulation enabled the Government to make the necessary reforms through legislation. This is reflected in the constitutional case law dealing with the admissibility of petitions against fiscal and economic legislation aimed – supposedly – at managing the crisis, which despite inventing the potentially useful instrument of interpreting the right to human dignity together with the non-discrimination principle have left Governmental discretion untamed. However, the fact that these constitutional provisions were left in force in 2015 and that they are potentially of unlimited temporal applicability begs the question of whether their aim was ever to guarantee effective crisis management by the Government, and it is extremely controversial that these immunities apply to the non-crisis related re-regulation and re-partitioning of different markets in Hungary.

More importantly, the essence of these constitutional changes has never been the rein-forcement of democratic controls, rule of law requirements, transparency or the adequate balancing of rights with regard to Government austerity/bail out/emergency and other nationalisation measures. Conversely, their intention was to exclude any form of potential control over Government policy-making.

This, necessarily, can be explained by some form of new government philosophy regarding the post-crisis role of the state in the market and by a newly found emphasis on solidarity and social rights in fiscal and economic regulation, as attempted in the previously commented recent case law of the Constitutional Court. The FL is also available to provide a potential communitarian interpretation of these changes, with the argument that the interest of the community of Hungarian people should enjoy priority over the rights and interests of individuals, economic operators or particular social groups. Nevertheless, there is no convincing evidence available that these interpretations of the Hungarian social order comprehensively influence government policy-making and regulation, and that austerity and other crisis management measures have been introduced to satisfy citizens' demand for control, transparency and accountability. It is a more likely interpretation that liberal constitutionalism has been suspended while the Government is 'at work'.

2.8 *Judicial Review of EU Measures: Access to Justice and the Standard of Review*

2.8.1 The Expert is aware only of one instance in which the invalidity of the relevant EU measure was raised and the respondent petitioned for a reference for a preliminary ruling to this end.[76] It was claimed that Art. 5(3)j of Directive 2001/29/EC[77] – governing one of the exceptions and limitations to EU copyright law – violated Arts. 50 and 95 EC, without clarifying the grounds of that claim. The regional appeal court refused to refer the case to the CJEU. It indicated that the directive was irrelevant for the facts of the case and that the Treaty provisions cited were wrongly raised in the case.
There were two other cases in which this matter was addressed, although very indirectly. The question in *GSV* was whether the Common Customs Tariff was enforceable against individuals when its Hungarian version, containing an obvious mistake, supported the legal position of the individual in question.[78] In a preliminary ruling, the Court of Justice held that the linguistic discrepancy 'is not liable to entail the annulment (of the tariff classification under EU law) made by the customs authorities on the basis of all the other language versions (of the Common Customs Tariff and the related regulations).[79] In *György Balázs*, a question was put to the CJEU in a preliminary reference on whether the unavailability of legal measures in the national language had an impact on the lawfulness of their application under the relevant EU legislation (Directive 98/34/EC[80]) by domestic public authorities.[81]

2.8.2 The Expert has found no evidence of discussion on the standard of review by the EU courts in Hungary. The focus of all actors – the ordinary courts, the Constitutional Court and the administration – has been on ensuring that EU law is given effect in a manner required by the relevant principles of EU law and as it follows from the FL and the accession documents. The main indication that the scope and effectiveness of judicial review may actually matter for the political and constitutional order under the FL is the notorious delimitation in the constitutional text of the competences of the Constitutional Court in questions of fiscal policy and of the related economic policies. In the instances where in the Expert's view the effective application of EU law has not been adequately ensured, the cause of non-enforcement must be sought in individual professional incompetence rather

[76] Budapest Regional Appeal Court 8. Pf. 21.417/2011/6.

[77] Directive 2001/29/EC of the European Parliament and of the Council of 22 May 2001 on the harmonisation of certain aspects of copyright and related rights in the information society, [2001] OJ L 167/10.

[78] Case C-74/13 *GSV* [2014] ECLI:EU:C:2014:243.

[79] Ibid., para. 53.

[80] Directive 98/34/EC of the European Parliament and of the Council of 22 June 1998 laying down a procedure for the provision of information in the field of technical standards and regulations, [1998] OJ L 204/37.

[81] Case C-251/14 *György Balázs* [2015] ECLI:EU:C:2015:687.

than in conscious resistance against expanding, strictly enforced but judicially inadequately controlled EU law. Nonetheless, considering the increasingly critical approach of the Constitutional Court to global and regional economic integration, it is not excluded that it will strike a more critical tone with regards to the legality and the impact of EU economic regulation. Although it is bound to obey EU law under domestic constitutional law and it would be extremely reluctant to contradict a formal obligation laid down in law, it is not completely excluded that the Constitutional Court – in circumstances where Hungarian interests are gravely affected, relying on the social and communitarian values of the FL as a rather thin veil hiding its true intentions – would question the applicability of EU law based on this or other gaps in EU constitutional law.

Considering that with the introduction of the FL and the recent jurisprudence on the economic constitution in Hungary the availability of judicial review against domestic economic and social legislation has been considerably reduced, arguments comparing the standard of judicial review before EU Courts and before the Constitutional Court do not appear particularly convincing. Both avenues of judicial review seem to acknowledge and defer to the discretion of the legislator, and both are prepared to annul legislative provisions in the case of a manifest breach of the requirements of legality. Since the examination by the EU Courts – in terms of the justification, regulatory design, balancing of competing objectives and the availability of sufficient regulatory and other safeguards – seems better executed than that of the Constitutional Court, compared to the current state of Hungarian jurisprudence, the judicial review carried out by the EU Courts appears to have a more solid legal footing.

2.8.3 As a necessary disclaimer to the assessment of Hungarian jurisprudence, a clear dividing line must be drawn between the approach of the 'old' and the 'new' Constitutional Court. Because of the new approach taken in recent years – predominantly following considerations of political nature – towards the constitutional limits and controls of legislative action, the jurisprudence cannot be conceived as having developed in a linear fashion under more or less constant institutional supervision.[82]

2.8.4 See also the answer in Sect. 1.3.4.

In Decision 61/2011 (VII. 13.) AB, as a direct continuation of the thoughts first quoted, the Court adjusted the domestic level of constitutional protection of fundamental rights to the international level, not on a hierarchical basis, but as a consequence of the *pacta sunt servanda* principle:

> In case of certain fundamental rights, the Constitution defines the substance of the fundamental right in the same way as it is in some international treaty (for example the Covenant on Civil and Political Rights and the European Convention on Human Rights). In these cases, the level of protection of fundamental rights provided by the Constitutional Court may in no instance be lower than the level of international protection of rights

[82] Szente 2015, p. 186.

> (typically elaborated by the Strasbourg Court of Human Rights). As a result of the *pacta sunt servanda* principle [Section 7(1) of the Constitution, Article Q(2)-(3) of the FL], the Constitutional Court is required to follow the Strasbourg jurisprudence and the level of protection of fundamental rights defined therein, even if they did not necessarily arise from its own previous case law.[83]

Later, the Court broadened the international determination of the level of protection of fundamental rights to include the stipulations of EU law; moreover, it considered the above quoted conclusion to be 'even more true' for the law of the European Union, having regard to Art. E(2)–(3) of the FL (compared to the rules of the Constitution, however, it did not elaborate in detail the meaning of the new Article E(3)).[84]

2.8.5 The Expert is not aware of concerns about the standard of review by the CJEU having been raised in Hungary. As indicated earlier, the discussions have focused on the adequate and effective implementation and application of EU law as it follows from the formal legal provisions which bind the relevant national actors in EU matters.

In the Hungarian context, there is a more directly damaging gap in judicial protection under EU law, which follows from the above-mentioned refusal of the Constitutional Court to assume jurisdiction to examine the compatibility of national legislation with EU law, which forces individuals to seek redress in litigation before ordinary courts.

The Expert understands the practical rationale for presuming equivalent standards of review in an environment characterised by the overlap of multiple constitutional jurisdictions. The Expert also understands that the threshold for the rebuttal of the presumption of equivalent standards was determined at such a high level in order to avoid disagreement between the affected courts on minor issues concerning the balance established between the policy aims pursued and the fundamental rights protected, or concerning the right combination of safeguards available for the protection of rights, and to confine inter-systemic constitutional conflicts to matters where there is a manifest breach of requirements or a fundamental backsliding in the standard of protection offered.

Considering that the presumption of equivalence is rebuttable as established in *Bosphorus* (and in the jurisprudence of national courts), the resulting gap in judicial protection does not seem as threatening and damaging as perhaps suggested by the question. Although the different assessment of EU legislation on fundamental rights grounds by different courts is not excluded, it does not seem likely that genuine fundamental rights concerns would be overlooked by one court and declared as vital by another. The state of the Strasbourg jurisprudence itself indicates that the protection of human rights by courts is not a task that could not be fulfilled by other courts within their jurisdiction, and that adequately prepared legislative measures, which duly incorporate the legal signposts indicated by human rights law, would

---

[83] CC Decision 61/2011. (VII. 13.) AB.

[84] CC Decision 32/2012. (VII. 4.) AB.

not have much to fear in Strasbourg or Luxembourg. With intensive cross-fertilisation between the Strasbourg and the Luxembourg jurisprudence, the potential for divergent judicial treatment of EU legislation and a gap in judicial protection does not seem particularly high. It is also unclear whether the Strasbourg court because of its institutional position as a transnational court would not guarantee the same, or even greater, deference to the intention of the EU legislator in matters of policy as expressed in an otherwise adequately drafted and designed piece of EU legislation. It must not be overlooked that the Strasbourg jurisprudence regards international cooperation and effective transnational governance as a significant common objective of European states which, as expressed in *Bosphorus*, must be given some form of recognition in the judicial control of EU or other transnational legislation.

2.8.6 The Expert is not aware of concerns regarding the equal treatment of citizens falling under the scope of EU law and falling under the scope of domestic law having been raised in Hungary. The Expert notes that similar concerns have been raised in the academic literature regarding the legal treatment of individuals in the Member States that qualify and do not qualify as EU citizens. In the Expert's view, this has less to do with the constitutional credentials of EU legislation and more with the political willingness and unwillingness of the Member States to address the situation at the European and at the national level.

2.9 *Other Constitutional Rights and Principles*

2.9.1 The Hungarian case regarding surplus sugar stocks noted in the Questionnaire has partly been explored above in Sect. 2.6.1.

2.10 *Common Constitutional Traditions*

2.10.1 In the Expert's view, the common constitutional traditions of the Member States as sources of EU constitutional law have indeed failed to fulfil the role(s) assumedly intended for them in previous jurisprudence. The concept – with a few exceptions – has proved to be unworkable and impractical in judicial practice, and a substitute was found in the more practical and workable law of the ECHR. In other instances (e.g. the fundamental rights guarantees in EU competition enforcement procedures), a genuinely European solution needed to be found, as the common constitutional traditions of the Member States appeared to be unable to provide workable legal principles, and they would not have been able to offer legal solutions suiting the particular context. The doctrinal, conceptual and other differences in that particular area in the then developing national legal orders were irreducible, and there was no common approach which would have satisfied both the constitutional demands and the interests of the effective administration of EU policies. Furthermore, judicial practice showed that principles of EU law could be developed and then applied on a whim, without taking into account their origins and workability as common constitutional traditions. Nevertheless, this does not mean that they have not influenced EU legislation and EU Treaty reform. The Treaties do in fact recognise – mainly, at the level of declarations – a number of shared constitutional norms and values, and the EU now seems unable to legislate without having regard to requirements recognised in national constitutions and also in European treaties governing the human rights dimension of human activity (e.g. the autonomy and informed consent of patients, the value of human life and human biological material).

In other words, the listing of common constitutional traditions depends on what normative content is expected to be expressed and how that normative content is expressed. In the case of *nulla poena sine lege*, finding common ground among the Member States as to its normative content – also considering that its guarantees have been subject to dilution – does not seem particularly problematic. However, establishing consensus regarding how that normative content may be regulated, especially in the European setting, may be more difficult, as the potential technical rules/arrangements and safeguards provided, as in the EAW, may not satisfy all expectations. Regarding the German expectation of citizens' private lives not being recorded, the fundamental question is how its assumed normative content can be expressed in EU legislation. If it can find expression in a limitation or exceptions clause agreed by the Member States, then within that framework it can be recognised as a common constitutional tradition of the Member States. In a similar manner, the requirement under legal certainty in Central and Eastern European Member States that adequate time must be afforded to enable preparations for the application of tax measures, as it emerged in the sugar quotas affairs, can be expressed in the shared, neutral requirement that the EU legislative process must have regard to the exigencies of the domestic implementation of EU instruments.

2.10.2 As noted earlier, the exploration of common constitutional traditions could be impractical and unworkable, it could lead to a downscaling of the protection offered or it could entail technical difficulties in expressing the qualifications, reservations, exceptions, etc., that could be attached to common requirements. These problems apply mainly with regard to the judicial recognition of common constitutional traditions. Their expression in EU legislative or other processes may be less problematic, although examples show that finding common constitutional ground can delay the adoption of EU legislation considerably (e.g. Directive 98/44/EC on biotechnological inventions). The democratic and other credentials of a judicial exploration of common constitutional traditions may also be problematic, as it may contradict the different conceptions in the different Member States of the extent and of the role of judicial power, and also because the method and the execution of a comparative exercise leading to the establishment of common constitutional traditions – as discussed in the academic literature on the difficulties and distortions of such comparative exercises – are not foolproof.

Furthermore, unless it is carried out with the purpose of highlighting that in a particular Member State a particularly high standard of protection is applicable, urging EU Courts to develop their judgment on the basis of a genuine exploration of common constitutional traditions may not be particularly relevant. Arguably, it may be more important to direct EU Courts towards the right assessment and the right balancing of considerations relevant in the legal appreciation of the case than to develop a legal test or legal formula genuinely shared among the Member States, which could be deduced from EU or ECHR law. For example, in the classic judgment in *Hauer*,[85] a thorough comparative analysis regarding the constitutional protection of property rights would not have added much to the legal formula that was available through less complicated sources or to the final assessment of the interference with focus on its justifiability and on the availability of safeguards/compensation.

2.11 *Article 53 of the Charter and the Issue of stricter Constitutional Standards*

2.11.1 There is very little evidence that the issue of the ECHR setting a minimum floor influences deliberations and decisions in the Hungarian courts. Borrowing from foreign jurisdictions and from ECHR law has always been standard practice in Hungarian constitutional law; therefore, the ECHR predominantly represents a standard to adhere to, and not a standard adherence that should be criticised.

In the Expert's view, Art. 53 of the Charter needs to be interpreted together with the actual provisions of EU law in relation to which the application of a right or freedom included in the Charter is raised. As demonstrated by *Omega* and *Schmidberger*,[86] the structure made available for the application of the fundamental freedoms of the Single Market enables – as reinforced by judicial deference to the national level by the EU Court – the application of higher national standards in a scenario in which the Charter is clearly applicable. Also, EU legislative instruments, such as Directive 98/44/EC on biotechnological inventions, through their clauses that allow for derogations from the main obligations in the protection of national constitutional values (e.g. human dignity), can ensure the enforcement of higher national standards under the scope of the Charter. Finally, there are EU measures in the case of which the standard of rights protection will depend on the conduct of national authorities in the implementation and enforcement of the measure in question.[87] In such instances, it is the responsibility of the national public authorities to provide at least the minimum protection demanded by EU law.

---

[85] Case 44/79 *Hauer* [1979] ECR 03727.

[86] Case C-36/02 *Omega* [2004] ECR I-09609 and Case C-112/00 *Schmidberger* [2003] ECR I-05659.

[87] See, for example, Joined cases C-411/10 and C-493/10 *N.S.* [2011] ECR I-00865.

Therefore, the scenario envisaged by the question could only arise in circumstances where the structure developed for the application of EU law does not allow for the vindication – in one way or another – of domestic constitutional concerns. Arguably, *Melloni* represented such an occasion, as the preliminary reference by the Spanish Constitutional Court was returned with the EU Court refusing to give effect to higher national standards. That judgment, however, must be interpreted in light of the fact, also indicated by the EU Court, that the regulation of the EAW reflects a 'consensus reached by all the Member States regarding the scope to be given under EU law to the procedural rights enjoyed by persons'.[88] This implies that in the EU Court's interpretation, the Member States, in the interest of the effective operation of a system for administering cross-border justice based on mutual trust and recognition, have waived their entitlement to enforce their higher national constitutional standards.

2.12 Democratic Debate on Constitutional Rights and Values

2.12.1–2.12.3 These points are not relevant in the context of Hungary's recent constitutional developments.

In the Expert's view, when important constitutional issues have arisen and have been referred to the Constitutional Court at the stage of implementing EU law, the present system and the preliminary ruling procedure allow sufficient space for democratic deliberation at the EU level. In the Hungarian context, the problem is that the Constitutional Court has not clarified its position on the relationship between EU law and the constitutional protection that had been controversially developed in the previous jurisprudence. It also does not seek formal contact, in the form of requests for a preliminary ruling, with the CJEU; this would have been possible not only in the case of the retirement of judges but also in the review of the Hungarian regulation on the implementation of the EAW. In the latter case, it could have inquired about the harmony of the rules with the Charter, thus contributing to development of the protection of fundamental rights at EU level. The Constitutional Court also did not invoke the procedural bond between the ordinary courts and the CJEU, i.e. the procedure of a preliminary ruling with constitutional emphasis on the interpretation of the right to a legitimate judge to establish if EU legal conditions have been met.[89] According to the permanent jurisprudence of the German Federal Constitutional Court, the CJEU may also be a 'legitimate judge' by virtue of Sentence 2 of Art. 101(1) of the German Basic Law. Namely, if a German judge

---

[88] Case C-399/11 *Melloni* [2013] ECLI:EU:C:2013:107, para. 62.

[89] CC Order 3110/2014. (VI. 17.) AB; reinforced by CC Order 3165/2014. (VI. 23.) AB. The petitioners argued in both cases that the court had not fulfilled the request to initiate a preliminary ruling in the base case and Art. XXVIII(1) of the FL had therefore been infringed.

fails to request a preliminary ruling even though the relevant EU conditions are met, then reference may be made to the infringement of the right to a legitimate judge within a constitutional appeal procedure.[90] According to the Hungarian Constitutional Court, this is not a constitutional issue but a technical legal issue falling within the scope of the judge of the proceedings. Although the Constitutional Court does not refuse or endeavour to actively participate in the network of cooperative constitutionalism, it might nevertheless emphasise the importance of a Europe-friendly interpretation of the Fundamental Law in a political environment in which rejection of an otherwise constructive European criticism, questioning of the decisions of Strasbourg and Luxembourg and a generally anti-EU rhetoric are typical. It appears that the political circumstances do not favour an extensive and activist constitutional judicature.

2.13 *Experts' Analysis on the Protection of Constitutional Rights in EU Law*

2.13.1 The Expert has not found evidence of EU law – unquestionably, systematically or fundamentally – having affected the protection of constitutional rights or the rule of law in a negative manner.

When addressing the standard of the EU's performance, it must not be ignored that EU constitutional requirements have been developed for a collective of different states in an environment characterised by a high degree of diversity. Finding common ground in such circumstances entails finding what could be expressed as optimum requirements which go beyond the minimum but which may not reach the maximum expectations. A certain degree of levelling out is necessary to be able to provide workable constitutional rules for a polity such as the EU. As a result, it is arguable that the development of common requirements cannot exclude the lowering of standards as recognised in individual Member States. This circumstance is particularly important when claims concerning the negative impact of EU law on the protection of constitutional rights and rule of law requirements are considered.

2.13.2 As stated earlier, the levelling out of standards could be necessary for the legal order of a collective polity such as the EU to develop common standards of protection of constitutional rights. The Expert also believes that while the protection offered in individual instances could be open to criticism, it would be controversial to formulate general conclusions concerning the performance of EU law in this domain on this basis. The Expert is willing to accept the argument that any levelling out of standards in EU law has been necessary to establish a collective polity and a collective system for the enforcement of common rights and obligations.

[90] *BVerfGE 73, 339, 366 ff.; 75, 223, 233 ff.; 82, 159, 192 ff.; 126, 286, 315 ff.*, latest in 2010: *1 BvR 1631/08* http://www.bundesverfassungsgericht.de/entscheidungen/rk20100830_1bvr163108.html.

Nevertheless, in frameworks establishing essentially horizontal systems of governance among the Member States, which aim to negotiate between the benefits of mutual trust/recognition and the fundamental rights implications of the regulated activity, because of the weaknesses of these governance structures, the guarantees offered by EU law may not be satisfying in all circumstances.

2.13.3 In the Expert's view, the responsiveness of the EU Court and also of national courts to national constitutional concerns depends primarily on the ethos of the different institutions, and also on individual factors, such as the preparedness, sensitivity, etc., of individual judges. Courts of law – national and international – seem quite satisfied to present themselves as special adjudicatory agencies with the task of resolving legal disputes and matters of legal interpretation in a continuously growing number of cases. They are keen to explore avenues to increase administrative efficiencies, and are likely to have an interest in getting involved in the cases before them only to the extent necessary. The prevailing institutional culture – e.g. decision by consensus, lack of dissenting or other opinions, etc. – may also dictate a reserved approach to matters of broader relevance. In their everyday operation as agencies, the understanding of matters of context, of local priorities, of the anticipation of individuals of their decisions, or of the potential and often controversial domestic implementation of their rulings could be limited. Unless the national constitutional concerns are adequately presented – by the referring national court which is assumed to be aware of them, or by the intervening governments – their relevance can be lost in such an institutional environment.

A strict reading of the jurisdiction of the EU Court – certainly before the Treaty changes commencing in the 1990s – could exclude any responsiveness from the EU Court towards national constitutional concerns. Its mandate covers interpreting and upholding the law developed in the collective enterprise among European states that is the EU polity. On the other hand, its institutional position and legitimacy as a transnational court, and its role in governing the participation of national administrative and judicial systems in the enforcement of EU law make it absolutely necessary to pay attention to concerns raised at the domestic level on constitutional grounds. The overall image of its jurisprudence indicates that national constitutional concerns – directly or indirectly – have been taken on board. This, however, does not mean that in individual, often very significant cases, the EU Court does not follow a strict reading of its mandate under the Treaties and sidelines the constitutional dilemmas raised by particular Member States. The attitude of the EU Court might, however, be changed by Art. 4(2) TEU on the protection of national (constitutional) identities, which has made the commitment of the Member States to conserve their positions in EU integration explicit. Nevertheless, it is still unclear how Art. 4(2) might influence the adjudication of Member State compliance before the EU Court, and whether the principle might represent a categorical departure from the EU as a collective enterprise and legitimate Member State particularism beyond the traditional constitutional remits.

The references for a preliminary ruling from the Hungarian courts have not raised national constitutional concerns in a manner that would have affected the EU Court's judgments.[91]

2.13.4 In the Expert's view, the possible institutional, procedural and substantive instruments are already available at the national level. Constitutions are rather explicit about the mandate of national constitutional organs, and also about the constitutional values and principles which should be safeguarded by them. National courts, although they are bound to apply EU law on the terms of the EU Court as it follows from national law, are not prevented from raising constitutional concerns regarding the application and interpretation of EU law in a particular case. National parliaments have been granted the right under national law to control their government's action in EU decision-making, in the course of which they are not prevented from raising their own constitutional concerns. Provided that national actors approach these matters with appropriate individual and institutional attitudes, it seems rather difficult, and perhaps unnecessary, to develop further instruments for safeguarding national constitutionalism at the national level. This may even be true for Member States which have experienced a recent regression in constitutionalism and constitutional protection. The Expert holds the view that if adjustments are indeed necessary at the national level, they must focus on attitudes, knowledge and understanding instead of rules and institutions.

3 Constitutional Issues in Global Governance

3.1 Constitutional Rules on International Organisations and the Ratification of Treaties

3.1.1 The conduct of international co-operation is governed by Art. Q(1) of the FL: 'In order to establish and maintain peace and security and to achieve the sustainable development of mankind, Hungary shall endeavour to co-operate with all peoples and countries of the world.' The provision is modelled on the text of Art. 6(2) of the 1989 Constitution,[92] but unlike its immediate predecessor, it explicitly mentions two objectives of international co-operation: the establishment and maintenance of peace and security, and the achievement of the sustainable development of humanity. These objectives were most likely incorporated into the text for exemplificative purposes. This constitutional clause is supplemented by a declaration in the National Avowal of the FL, which expresses the intention of members of the

[91] The reference in Case C-328/04 *Vajnai* [2005] ECR I-08577 would have raised significant issues of national constitutional law; however, the EU Court ruled – correctly – to decline its jurisdiction since the case fell outside the scope of EU law.

[92] 'The Republic of Hungary shall endeavour to co-operate with all peoples and countries of the world.'

Hungarian nation to strive to co-operate with every nation of the world. Although the wording of the provisions concerned is extremely broad, a comprehensive interpretation reveals all the essential details of international co-operation, including the potential partners, the scope of discretion, the primary objectives and the relevant limitations.[93]

The Rome Statute of the International Criminal Court, although it was ratified as early as 30 November 2001, has yet to be promulgated in Hungary. There was an unsuccessful attempt to promulgate the Rome Statute at the time of ratification, but the relevant bills were subsequently withdrawn. It has been assumed by members of the scholarly community that the long-awaited promulgation of the instrument would probably necessitate the amendment of the FL. The previously planned promulgation of the Rome Statute would also have required the amendment of the Constitution to permit the criminal prosecution of the President of the Republic by an international judicial organ. A new bill on the promulgation of the Rome Statute was submitted to the National Assembly in 2016, but at the time of writing, it has yet to be adopted.

The expression of consent by Hungary to be bound by an international treaty is governed by the FL and Act L of 2005 on the Procedure Relating to International Treaties (hereinafter APRIT). The authorisation to express consent to be bound is granted either by the National Assembly for treaties falling within its functions and powers,[94] or by the Government for all other treaties (Art. 1(2)(d) FL; Art. 7(1) APRIT). The authorisation itself is contained in the law promulgating the treaty (Art. 7 (2) and Art. 10(1)(a) APRIT). Following the adoption of the promulgating law, the minister of foreign affairs must immediately initiate the expression of consent to be bound by the President of the Republic, if the authorisation has been granted by the National Assembly, or if the treaty provides that the consent to be bound must be expressed by the head of state. The consent to be bound by the treaty is then expressed by the President of the Republic, and the related instrument is exchanged or deposited, or the required notification to the other party or parties is provided by the minister of foreign affairs (Art. 9(4)(a) FL; Art. 8(1)–(2) APRIT). The consent to be bound by all other international treaties is expressed, as appropriate, by the minister of foreign affairs, or if the treaty provides that the consent to be bound must be expressed by the head of government, by the Prime Minister. The exchange or deposit of the related instrument is likewise performed by the minister of foreign affairs (Art. 8(4) APRIT).

3.1.2 The constitutional provisions on treaty ratification and international co-operation were, without exception, introduced by the adoption of the FL, and were designed to replace the corresponding provisions of the 1989 Constitution. Nevertheless, there is a close textual resemblance between the old and new provisions, and the former apparently served as a model in the formulation of the latter.

---

[93] Sulyok 2013a, pp. 464–489.

[94] Treaties in the field of EU cooperation (pursuant to Art. E(2) of the FL); the subject matter of the treaty is already regulated by an Act of Parliament or pursuant to the FL, it shall be regulated in a cardinal or other Act of Parliament; the treaty influences other matter belonging to the competence of the Parliament on the basis of Art. 1(2) (a)–(c) and (e)–(k) of the FL.

In the preliminary stages of the making of the FL, selected state organs, representative bodies, social organisations and the scholarly community were requested to submit proposals regarding the future constitution. The few submissions that touched upon the provisions concerned include the detailed proposals presented by the Institute for Legal Studies of the Hungarian Academy of Sciences.[95] The actual impact of these proposals is largely unknown: some were manifestly disregarded; others may have been accepted.

3.1.3 In spite of occasional criticism by members of the scholarly community, amendment of the provisions concerned, to our knowledge, has not been seriously raised since the adoption of the FL. Previously, in the period between the political transition and the entry into force of the FL, the 1989 Constitution was amended, *inter alia*, upon Hungary's accession to the North Atlantic Treaty Organization[96] and to the European Union.[97] The unsuccessful attempt to promulgate the Rome Statute of the International Criminal Court, as has been mentioned, would also have required the amendment of the Constitution.

3.2 The Position of International Law in National Law

3.2.1 The application and position of international treaties in the domestic legal system are governed by the FL and APRIT. The second sentence of Art. Q(3) of the FL provides that '[o]ther sources of international law shall become part of the Hungarian legal system by promulgation by law'. This provision can only be interpreted in the light of the first sentence of the same paragraph, which concerns the generally recognised rules of international law, including customary international law, the general principles of law and the peremptory norms of international law.[98] Hence the scope of the second sentence covers the other sources of international law: international treaties, binding decisions of international organisations, judicial decisions and unilateral acts of states.

International treaties become part of domestic law by promulgation by law. The detailed reasoning of Bill T/2627 on the FL of Hungary placed special emphasis on the requirement of promulgation: 'Accordingly, the Bill expresses that other rules of international law binding on Hungary, including above all international treaties, only become part of the Hungarian legal system and applicable in the procedure of

[95] Magyar Tudományos Akadémia Jogtudományi Intézete (2010), *Javaslatok a Magyar Köztársaság Alkotmányának szabályozási koncepciójához* [Proposals for the Regulatory Concept of the Constitution of the Republic of Hungary], pp. 16–21.

[96] Act XCI of 2000 on the Amendment of Act XX of 1949 on the Constitution of the Republic of Hungary. See also CC Decision 5/2001. (II. 28.) AB.

[97] See supra n. 11. See also CC Decision 30/1998. (VI. 25.) AB.

[98] 'Hungary accepts the generally recognised rules of international law.'

Hungarian law enforcement agencies by promulgation by law'.[99] Earlier, the Constitutional Court had also pronounced that ensuring harmony between international law and domestic law demands the promulgation of international treaties, including self-executing treaties, and the inadequate or incomplete promulgation of treaties does not meet the constitutional requirements.[100]

The detailed rules of promulgation are laid down by APRIT. The Act, as amended in 2011 in the wake of the adoption of the FL, provides that treaties falling within the functions and powers of the National Assembly must be promulgated by a Parliamentary Act; other treaties must be promulgated by Government decree.

Similarly to the 1989 Constitution,[101] Art. Q(2)–(3) of the FL do not determine the position of promulgated international treaties in the domestic hierarchy of sources of law. Their position may nevertheless be explored by recourse to a range of related provisions. The provisions of the FL on the competences of the Constitutional Court and the provisions of Act CLI of 2011 on the Constitutional Court relating to procedures that may promote harmony between international law and domestic law, contain particularly useful guidelines.[102] The same holds true for the case law of the Constitutional Court. These guidelines indicate that the position of international treaties in the domestic hierarchy formally corresponds to the level of the promulgating law. However, promulgated international treaties function differently than, and have precedence over, ordinary sources of domestic law. This precedence is largely based on procedural factors.

The requirement of faithful observance of international treaties, in addition to the relevant rules in international law, may be derived from several interrelated constitutional provisions. These provisions include Art. B(1) and Art. Q(2)-(3) of the FL on the constitutional principle of the rule of law,[103] on ensuring harmony between international law and domestic law,[104] and the domestic incorporation of norms of international law, respectively. The Constitutional Court has also pronounced that

[99] Bill T/2627 on the Fundamental Law of Hungary, Detailed reasoning to Art. P, 38.

[100] CC Decisions 30/1998. (VI. 25.) AB; 54/2004. (XII. 13.) AB; 7/2005. (III. 31.) AB; 30/2005. (VII. 14.) AB.

[101] 'The legal system of the Republic of Hungary accepts the generally recognized rules of international law, and shall ensure harmony between obligations assumed under international law and domestic law.' 1989 Constitution, Art. 7(1).

[102] FL Art. 24(2)–(3); Act CLI of 2011 on the Constitutional Court (hereinafter ACC), Art. 23–25, 32, 37–38, 40–42, and 46. The provisions of the FL prohibiting conflicts between various sources of law also offer guidance. FL Art. T(3), Art. 15(4), 18(3) 23(4) 32(3), 41(5).

[103] 'Hungary is an independent, democratic rule-of-law State.' FL Art. B(1).

[104] 'In order to fulfil its obligations under international law, Hungary shall ensure harmony between international law and Hungarian law.' FL Art. Q(2). The Venice Commission welcomed the incorporation of the provision into the Fundamental Law. European Commission for Democracy through Law, *Opinion on the New Constitution of Hungary*, CDL-AD(2011)016, 10, para. 42.

> [t]he implementation of an international commitment ... is a duty originating from [the constitutional provision] containing the rule of law, including the fulfilment in good faith of obligations under international law, as well as from [the constitutional provision] demanding the harmony of international law and domestic law that exists from the moment from which the international treaty binds (in the sense of international law) Hungary. ... Those obliged by international treaties are, as a general rule, the states parties to the treaty. It is the duty of these states to ensure the implementation of the treaty.[105]

3.2.2 The relationship of international law and domestic law traditionally ranks among the most problematic issues of Hungarian constitutionalism. The first constitutional clause to explicitly regulate the matter, Art. 7(1) of the 1989 Constitution, received a tremendous amount of criticism for its infamously imprecise and vague wording which left room for conflicting interpretations. The Constitutional Court ultimately pronounced that the provision established a dualist system,[106] but even this authoritative interpretation could not put an end to the debate. Following several failed initiatives, the drafting of the FL offered an opportunity to remedy the theoretical and practical shortcomings by introducing a progressive new provision. However, Art. Q(2)-(3) of the FL were formulated on the model of their predecessor, the text of which seems to have been simply rearranged, partly rephrased and modestly supplemented. Due to the close resemblance of the two provisions, the early commentators of the new regulation mostly observed that essentially nothing had changed.[107] The FL is authoritatively interpreted so as to maintain the dualist tradition, wherein the generally recognised rules of international law and other sources of international law become part of domestic law by general transformation and by special transformation, respectively. The possibility of conflicting interpretations nevertheless remains.

3.3 *Democratic Control*

3.3.1 Parliamentary involvement in the initial negotiation of international treaties is rather limited in Hungary. The FL at present does not contain detailed provisions on the early phases of treaty-making, leaving the regulation of the process to Act L of 2005 on the Procedure Relating to International Treaties (APRIT). This Act assigns the relevant functions and powers to the Government in order to reduce the workload of the National Assembly.[108] Hence the conclusion of international treaties is initiated and arranged by the competent minister, with the consent of the minister of foreign affairs, and in observance of the foreign policy principles laid

---

[105] CC Decision 7/2005. (III. 31.) AB. (Inserts added).

[106] CC Decision 53/1993. (X. 13.) AB.

[107] E.g. Blutman 2014a, p. 30; Kovács 2011, pp. 75–76; Molnár 2013, p. 60; Sulyok 2013b, pp. 48–49.

[108] Molnár 2013, p. 117.

down by the National Assembly and by the Government (Art. 4(1) APRIT). The authorisation to adopt the text of the treaty and to designate the person representing the state in the process is granted by the Government, or in exceptional cases, between two sessions of the Government, by the Prime Minister. The granting of authorisation is initiated by the minister who has proposed the conclusion of the treaty, with the consent of the ministers of foreign affairs and justice (Art. 5(2) APRIT). If the treaty falls within the functions and powers of the National Assembly, the resolution authorising the adoption of the text of the treaty and the available text of the treaty must be forwarded to the competent parliamentary committee (Art. 5(3) and 7(1) APRIT). The National Assembly is certainly not precluded from expressing its political opinion on a treaty, and may even request or endorse the Government in a resolution to adopt the text of a treaty.[109] The National Assembly, therefore, may discuss various issues related to international treaties. Parliamentary discussion is most likely to take place upon the granting of authorisation to express consent to be bound by/promulgation of a treaty, or at any later stage following the promulgation.

3.3.2 Similarly to Art. 28C(5)(b) of the 1989 Constitution, Art. 8(3)d) of the FL explicitly prohibits the holding of a national referendum on 'an obligation arising from an international treaty'.[110] This provision only applies to existing international treaty obligations and does not prohibit the holding of referendums before the assumption of such obligations. These referendums may pursue several interrelated objectives, such as to consult the public in the preliminary stages of decision-making or to enhance the legitimacy of outstandingly important foreign-policy decisions. National referendums were indeed held prior to Hungary's accession to NATO on 16 November 1997 and to the European Union on 12 April 2003. Both referendums were valid and conclusive. The Constitutional Court later pronounced that the holding of a referendum on the accession to NATO did not entail that a similar referendum could also be held on the question of withdrawal.[111] More recently, two politicians of the opposition initiated a national referendum on the planned expansion of the Paks Nuclear Power Plant, the only nuclear power station in Hungary, but the initiative was rejected by the National Election Commission on 17 February 2014.[112] The Commission pointed out that the initiative was incompatible with the constitutional prohibition concerned, as it would have affected existing international obligations arising from the Convention between the Government of Hungary and the Government of the Russian Federation on the Conduct of Co-operation in the Field of Peaceful Use of Nuclear Energy.

---

[109] Ibid., pp. 117–118.

[110] See also Act CCXXXVIII of 2013 on the Initiation of a Referendum, the European Citizens' Initiative, and the Referendum Procedure. For more details, see Csatlós 2014, pp. 337–346.

[111] CC Decision 35/2007. (VI. 6.) AB.

[112] National Election Commission Decision 91/2014. The decision was upheld by Curia Order Knk.IV.37.178/2014/3, and the subsequent constitutional complaint was rejected by Constitutional Court Order IV/938/2014.

3.4 *Judicial Review*

3.4.1 National courts are not in a position to perform a review of promulgated international treaties or binding decisions of international organisations; they are only expected to apply them appropriately.[113] Recent investigations have nevertheless exposed considerable reluctance on the part of the judiciary to invoke international law, particularly when ordinary domestic provisions are equally sufficient to decide a given case.[114] Domestic judges are further expected to turn to the Constitutional Court upon encountering conflicts between international law and domestic law. The Constitutional Court has several procedures in its inventory in which international treaties may be subjected to scrutiny. (The provisions of Act CLI of 2011 on the Constitutional Court do not explicitly mention the binding decisions of international organisations.) These procedures include the *ex ante* review of conformity with the FL (preliminary norm control),[115] the *ex post* review of conformity with the FL (posterior norm control but of the domestic promulgating law rather than of the treaty),[116] the judicial initiative for norm control in concrete cases[117] and the examination of conflicts with international treaties.[118]

3.5 *The Social Welfare Dimension of the Constitution*

3.5.1 As noted earlier, over the summer of 2014 the Hungarian Constitutional Court made an attempt to develop the bases of a new economic constitution under the FL, which would reinstate the roles and the power of the Hungarian state as stabiliser, regulator and provider. The relevant decisions either build on a fervent criticism of economic regionalisation and globalisation, or they rely on the social provisions of the FL and the resulting social obligations of state actors.[119] As criticised earlier, these observations are often rushed and wrong, and they never surpass the crude level of detail of simple declarations. More importantly, they do not seem to have affected the actual scrutiny of the Constitutional Court beyond accepting the discretion of the Government and rolling back the usual standards of constitutional

[113] E.g. Blutman 2014b, pp. 167–179; Chronowski and Csatlós 2013, pp. 7–28.

[114] E.g. Chronowski et al. 2011, p. 278.

[115] ACC Art. 40(3).

[116] FL Art. 24(2)e); ACC Art. 24(1).

[117] FL Art. 24(2)b); ACC Art. 25(1).

[118] FL Art. 24(2)f); ACC Art. 32.

[119] See also CC Decision 3062/2012 (VII. 26.) AB on price regulation in the district heat market, where the Constitutional Court accepted that, inter alia, the impact of the global financial and economic crisis necessitated the local reregulation of the public and private law framework available for determining prices in the sector, despite legitimate expectations for the previous framework to remain in place.

control of Governmental economic governance. The Constitutional Court seems to be prepared to support the Government's efforts by failing to question the legitimacy and validity of the purpose of Government action, and by refusing to investigate the suitability and the necessity of the relevant measures. The Constitutional Court is satisfied with a rather relaxed circumregulation of the discretion made available to the responsible bodies under the measures in question, it raises no issue with the rather low standards of legal safeguards and remedies, and it is rather untroubled by the actual impact on individuals of the measures in question and by the potential for the application of the measures in question to lead to further violation of constitutional guarantees. Overall, the new economic constitutionalism in Hungary emerging in the wake of the crisis is less concerned with transparency, classical state roles in capitalist markets, and with issues of solidarity and social protection than with assisting the restructuring of the market in Hungary following undisclosed (or rather well-known but not openly advertised) economic policy priorities. Having regard to the apparent exclusionist, protectionist and possibly chauvinist economic policies of the Government, the anti-globalisation and anti-regionalisation agenda of the Constitutional Court seems to support a very particular transformation of the economy and society in the final years of the decade after the crisis.

Hungarian economic and social policies[120] and the erosion of the constitutional environment available to keep Government policies under control in light of social protection or other policies indicates that the states are equally responsible for the demise of the social dimension of constitutions. Following Bartolini, it may not seem controversial to suggest that the threat of globalisation and regionalisation on local social regulation and on local systems of social protection has resulted from conscious decisions by local political elites to transfer sensitive decisions of economic and social policy to the transnational level in order to avoid the confines of national constitutions and the control of national parliaments and courts.[121] Furthermore, while pressures for deregulation, privatisation and liberalisation may come top-down from the global and/or regional level, states – the economies of which seem to benefit from these changes – are not prevented from compensating for any negative impacts of these transformations. Often, in structures of social governance favouring subsidiarity, they are even urged to make autonomous choices as to the compensatory measures or regarding the suitable extent and intensity of these changes in the particular domestic environment. The responsibility for failing to exploit these opportunities to level out the negative social effects of economic policies must be borne by states and their governments.

The Expert, therefore, would be very reluctant to argue that the social welfare dimension of constitutions is threatened only by global and regional governance,

[120] E.g. a flat income tax rate, tax benefits to high earners, the increase of VAT, the deregulation of employment law, the reduction of social benefits, an export driven exchange rate for the domestic currency, financing public debt through high premium sovereign bonds, etc.

[121] Bartolini 2005, p. 405.

and that attempts by states to safeguard their social constitutions are thwarted by the binding rules of global and regional economic regulation. States can pursue economic, social, fiscal, etc., policies which are known to compromise social protection and social regulation.

3.5.2 Hungary participated in a post-crisis bailout programme administered jointly by the World Bank, the IMF and the EU[122] including an IMF Stand-by Arrangement,[123] but with the change of Government in 2010, this participation was reconsidered. It is suspected that the Government insisted on excluding these international partners because it aimed to regain control over matters of domestic economic policy in order to bring about the restructuring of markets and the rechannelling of market based income without being confined by demands of transparency, accountability, sustainability and balanced rationality. It is likely that the fairly obvious plans of the Government for the Hungarian public and private economy would have been thwarted if they had been carried out under the close supervision of an international agency.

References

Albi A. (2009) Ironies in Human Rights Protection in the EU: Pre-Accession Conditionality and Post-Accession Conundrums. ELJ 15:46–69.

Arato A., Halmai G., Kis J. (eds.) (2011) Opinion on the Fundamental Law of Hungary. http://lapa.princeton.edu/hosteddocs/amicus-to-vc-english-final.pdf.

Bárd, P. (2013) The Hungarian Fundamental Law and Related Constitutional Changes 2010–2013. Revue des Affaires Européennes: Law and European Affairs 20:457–472.

Bartolini S. (2005) Restructuring Europe. Centre Formation, System Building, and Political Structuring between the Nation State and the European Union. Oxford University Press, Oxford.

Blutman L. (2014a) A nemzetközi jogi klauzula az Alaptörvényben (The clause on international law in the Fundamental Law). In: Blutman L., Csatlós E., Schiffner I. (eds.) A nemzetközi jog hatása a magyar joggyakorlatra (The effect of international law on Hungarian legal practice). HVG-ORAC, Budapest, pp. 29–36.

Blutman L. (2014b) A nemzetközi jog érvényesülése a magyar belső jogban: joghatások (The enforcement of international law in Hungarian domestic law: legal effects). In: Blutman L., Csatlós E., Schiffner I. (eds.) A nemzetközi jog hatása a magyar joggyakorlatra (The effect of international law on Hungarian legal practice). HVG-ORAC, Budapest, pp. 119–180.

Blutman L., Chronowski N. (2011) Hungarian Constitutional Court: Keeping Aloof from European Union Law. ICL Journal 5:329–348.

Bragyova A. (2012) No New(s), Good News? The Fundamental Law and the European law. In: Tóth G.A. (ed.) Constitution for a disunited nation. CEU Press, Budapest-New York, pp. 335–358.

Chronowski N. (2005) Integrálódó alkotmányjog (Constitutional law under integration). Dialóg-Campus, Budapest-Pécs.

Chronowski N. (2012) The New Hungarian Fundamental Law in the Light of the European Union's Normative Values. Revue Est Europa 2:111–142.

[122] http://www.imf.org/external/pubs/ft/survey/so/2008/car102808b.htm.

[123] http://www.imf.org/external/np/sec/pr/2008/pr08275.htm.

Chronowski N., Csatlós E. (2013) Judicial Dialogue or National Monologue? The International Law and Hungarian Courts. ELTE Law Journal 1:7–28.

Chronowski N., Drinóczi T., Ernszt I. (2011) Hungary. In Shelton D. (ed.) International Law and Domestic Legal Systems: Incorporation, Transformation, and Persuasion. Oxford University Press, Oxford, pp. 259–287.

Csatlós E. (2014) Alkotmánybírósági határozatok: ahol a nemzetközi jog mérce vagy felülvizsgált norma (Constitutional court decisions: where international law is a standard or a reviewed norm). In: Blutman L., Csatlós E., Schiffner I. (eds.) A nemzetközi jog hatása a magyar joggyakorlatra (The effect of international law on Hungarian legal practice). HVG-ORAC, Budapest, pp. 337–386.

Dezső M., Vincze A. (2012) Magyar alkotmányosság az európai integrációban (Hungarian constitutionality in the European integration), 2nd edn. HVG-ORAC, Budapest.

Fazekas F. (2014) EU Law and the Hungarian Constitutional Court. In: Varju M., Várnay E. (eds.) The Law of the European Union in Hungary. HVG-ORAC, Budapest, pp. 32–76.

Halmai G., Scheppele K.L. (eds.) (2012) Amicus Brief for the Venice Commission on the Transitional Provisions of the Fundamental Law and the Key Cardinal Laws. http://halmaigabor.hu/dok/426_Amicus_Cardinal_Laws_final.pdf.

Jakab A. (2011) Az új Alaptörvény keletkezése és gyakorlati következményei (Formation of the new basic law and its practical implications). HVG-ORAC, Budapest.

Karsai K., Ligeti K. (2008) Magyar alkotmányosság a bűnügyi jogsegélyjog útvesztőiben (Hungarian constitutionalism in the labyrinth of legal assistance in criminal matters). Magyar Jog 55:399–408.

Kovács P. (2008) Az EUIN-megállapodás és az alkotmányosság (The EUIN convention and constitutionality). Magyar Jog 55:409–413.

Kovács P. (2011) Nemzetközi közjog (Public international law), 2nd edn. Osiris, Budapest.

Molnár T. (2013) A nemzetközi jogi eredetű normák beépülése a magyar jogrendszerbe (The incorporation of norms originating from international law into the Hungarian legal system). Dialóg Campus-Dóm, Budapest-Pécs.

Sajó A. (2004) Learning Co-operative Constitutionalism the Hard Way: the Hungarian Constitutional Court Shying Away from EU Supremacy. Zeitschrift für Staats- und Europawissenschaften 3:351–371.

Sonnevend P., Jakab A., Csink L. (2015) The Constitution as an Instrument of Everyday Party Politics: The Basic Law of Hungary. In: Bogdandy A. von, Sonnevend P. (eds.) Constitutional Crisis in the European Constitutional Area. C.H.BECK-Hart-Nomos, Oxford and Portland, pp. 33–109.

Sulyok G. (2013a) A nemzetközi együttműködés alaptörvényi szabályozása (The regulation of international co-operation under the fundamental law). In: Szoboszlai-Kiss K., Deli G. (eds.) Tanulmányok a 70 éves Bihari Mihály tiszteletére (Studies in honour of Mihály Bihari at 70). Universitas-Győr, Győr, pp. 464–489.

Sulyok G. (2013b) Incorporation of International Law into Domestic Law under the Fundamental Law of Hungary. In: Smuk P. (ed.) The Transformation of the Hungarian Legal System 2010–2013. CompLex Wolters Kluwer, Budapest, pp. 31–50.

Szente Z. (2015) The Decline of Constitutional Review in Hungary – Towards a Partisan Constitutional Court? In: Szente Z., Mandák F., Fejes Z. (eds.) Challenges and Pitfalls in the Recent Hungarian Constitutional Development. L'Harmattan, Paris, pp. 185–210.

Uitz R. (2006) EU Law and the Hungarian Constitutional Court: Lessons of the First Post-accession Encounter. In: Sadurski W. et al. (eds.) Après Enlargement. Legal and Political Responses in Central and Eastern Europe. European University Institute, Florence, pp. 41–63.

Vincze A. (2013) Wrestling with Constitutionalism: the supermajority and the Hungarian Constitutional Court. ICL Journal 7:86–97.

Vörös I. (2014) The constitutional landscape after the fourth and fifth amendments of Hungarian Fundamental Law. Acta Juridica Hungarica 55:1–20.

Zeller J. (2013) Nichts ist so beständig… Die jüngsten Novellen des Grundgesetzes Ungarns im Kontext der Entscheidungen des Verfassungsgerichts. Osteuropa-Recht 59:307–325.

3

The Constitution of Greece: EU Membership Perspectives

Xenophon Contiades, Charalambos Papacharalambous and Christos Papastylianos

Abstract The Constitution of Greece, adopted in 1975 after the collapse of the military dictatorship, was drafted with provisions providing the constitutional grounds for European integration. Subsequently, two EU related amendments were introduced and, additionally, constitutional interpretation is used to overcome further conflicts. The Constitution is described in the report as detailed and comprehensive, with a legal character and strong normative force. It includes a detailed list of rights, including social rights. The Constitution refers to the concept of 'welfare state rule of law'. By way of an exception to constitutional systems of this type, Greece does not have a constitutional court, but instead a decentralised system of review of constitutionality. Adhering to the French '*État de droit*' and the German '*Rechtsstaat*' traditions, the rule of law works in conjunction with specific constitutional provisions. In particular, *nulla poena sine lege* is a cornerstone

Xenophon Contiades is Professor of Public Law at the Panteion University, Athens, and Managing Director, Centre for European Constitutional Law, Athens. e-mail: xcontiades@hotmail.com.

Charalambos Papacharalambous is Associate Professor in Criminal Law and Law Philosophy, Law Department, University of Cyprus. e-mail: papacharalambous.charalambos@ucy.ac.cy.

Christos Papastylianos is Assistant Professor for Public Law, University of Nicosia School of Law. e-mail: papastylianos.c@unic.ac.cy.

Xenophon Contiades wrote Sects. 1, 2.1 and 3.1. Charalambos Papacharalambous wrote Sects. 2.3–2.6. Christos Papastylianos wrote Sects. 2.2, 2.7, 2.8, 2.9, 2.10, 2.11, 2.12, 2.13, 3.3–3.6.

X. Contiades (✉)
Panteion University, Athens, Greece
e-mail: xcontiades@hotmail.com

C. Papacharalambous
Law Department, University of Cyprus, Nicosia, Cyprus
e-mail: papacharalambous.charalambos@ucy.ac.cy

C. Papastylianos
School of Law, University of Nicosia, Nicosia, Cyprus
e-mail: papastylianos.c@unic.ac.cy

principle of constitutionality and the rule of law, and has prompted extensive scholarly concerns in relation to the European Arrest Warrant system. More widely known are the constitutional and fundamental rights issues raised in the context of the EU and IMF austerity and conditionality programmes, marking, according to the report, a darker side of sovereignty loss. The report summarises a broader concern in Greek academic commentary that constitutional rights and values have been given marginal protection, as the national constitution is no longer the guarantor of popular sovereignty rooted in a political decision made by the people, but rather has become a guarantor of the state's compliance with EMU obligations.

Keywords The Constitution of Greece · Constitutional amendments regarding European and international co-operation · Decentralised constitutional review 'Welfare state rule of law' · The French '*État de droit*' and German '*Rechtsstaat*' traditions · European Arrest Warrant · *nulla poena sine lege* and defence rights in extradition cases · Fundamental rights · EU and IMF austerity and conditionality programmes · Social rights · Trade union rights and the economic emergency regime · Data Retention Directive · Limitation of rights and public interest Change away from popular sovereignty based on the Constitution

1 Constitutional Amendments Regarding EU Membership

1.1 Constitutional Culture

1.1.1 The current constitution of Greece was promulgated in 1975 after the collapse of a seven-year military dictatorship. The constituent power exercised by the Parliament elected in 1974 was described as delegated power to convey the image of constitutional continuity. Indeed, the 1975 Constitution, which has been revised three times (1986, 2001, 2008) has its roots in the Constitution of 1864, the most long-lived Constitution in Greek constitutional history, which contributed greatly to the establishment of the rule of law and parliamentarism. The 1864 Constitution had been enacted after a revolution against the monarch and was influenced by the 1831 Constitution of Belgium and the 1849 Constitution of Denmark. The election of a new king by the Constituent Assembly and the enactment of a liberal constitution marked the passage from constitutional monarchy to parliamentary democracy.

The Constitution of Greece is written and difficult to amend.[1] Detailed, analytical and comprehensive, the Constitution has legal character and strong normative force. Due to the existence of a system of diffused constitutional review, all courts have competence to review the constitutionality of laws. In other words, Greece does not have a constitutional court, but instead a tradition of diffused review. The current Constitution thus enshrines a decentralised system of judicial

[1] Spyropoulos and Fortsakis 2009.

review of the constitutionality of laws (Art. 93(4)). However, constitutional review is to a great extent concentrated through jurisdictional mechanisms of appellate review by the three supreme courts, i.e. *Areios Pagos* (Supreme Civil and Criminal Court), the Council of State (Supreme Administrative Court), and the Court of Audit. Article 100(5) of the Constitution regulates constitutional review as follows:

> When a section of the Supreme Administrative Court or chamber of the Supreme Civil and Criminal Court or of the Court of Audit judges a provision of a statute to be contrary to the Constitution, it is bound to refer the question to the respective plenum, unless this has been judged by a previous decision of the plenum or of the Special Highest Court of this article. The plenum shall be assembled into judicial formation and shall decide definitively, as specified by law. This regulation shall also apply accordingly to the elaboration of regulatory decrees by the Supreme Administrative Court.

Thus, the Greek Constitution belongs to the type of constitutions that have legal character, contain detailed norms and are enforceable in courts.

1.1.2 The Constitution sets out the form of government, establishes the separation of powers and provides for checks and balances. Furthermore, it includes a detailed list of fundamental rights enshrining civil, political and socio-economic rights. It is noteworthy that all former Greek constitutions have also included catalogues of rights, gradually incorporating the three generations of rights. Since the adoption of the Constitution of 1864, the principle of popular sovereignty has been enshrined in constitutional texts. According to Art. 1 of the current Constitution, '[s]overeignty lies with the people; all powers derive from the people and exist for the people and the Nation'.

The Constitution of Greece sets out the basic rules of the game, organising and allocating powers and providing for the detailed protection of fundamental rights. It has therefore been central to the legal and political life of Greece, generating a strong culture of constitutionalism; constitutional narratives are dominant in the Greek political discourse.

1.2 Amendment of the Constitution in Relation to the European Union

1.2.1, 1.2.3 The application for accession to the EU was submitted on the day the Constitution of 1975 was enacted. Specific provisions were included in the constitutional text in order to provide the constitutional grounds for the accession. Thus, accession to the EU did not take place under an aged constitution, rather the Constitution itself was drafted in such way as to include provisions facilitating this goal. The advice of legal scholars in favour of this choice proved invaluable for a smooth accession procedure.

Articles 28(2) and (3) of the Constitution[2] set out the substantive and procedural requirements allowing the accession as follows:

> Article 28(2) Authorities provided by the Constitution may by treaty or agreement be vested in agencies of international organizations, when this serves an important national interest and promotes cooperation with other States. A majority of three-fifths of the total number of Members of Parliament shall be necessary to vote the law ratifying the treaty or agreement.
>
> Article 28(3) Greece shall freely proceed by law passed by an absolute majority of the total number of Members of Parliament to limit the exercise of national sovereignty, insofar as this is dictated by an important national interest, does not infringe upon the rights of man and the foundations of democratic government and is effected on the basis of the principles of equality and under the condition of reciprocity.

In 2001 an interpretative clause was added, according to which: 'Article 28 constitutes the foundation for the participation of the Country in the European integration process'. Still, the wording of the above provisions was rather ambiguous and left room for different interpretations. Thus, Greek scholars disagreed on whether the accession of Greece to the EU should be understood as vesting powers in agencies of international organisations, which would require the three-fifths majority of the total number of Members of Parliament (MPs), or it constituted a limitation on the exercise of state sovereignty, which could be made through the enactment of legislation voted by the absolute majority of the total number of MPs. The dominant view was that both paras. (2) and (3) of Art. 28 in combination provided the constitutional grounds for the accession. Thus, a combination of the stricter substantive conditions provided for by para. (3) and the stringent procedural requirements set by para. 2 was applicable. What the Parliament actually did was to vote the law ratifying the accession of Greece to the EU with a three-fifths majority, leaving open the relevant interpretative issues. The same procedure was followed for the ratification of the treaties of Maastricht, Amsterdam, Nice and Lisbon, leaving the interpretational ambiguity unresolved. However, all ratifications took place smoothly since the two major political parties of the pre-financial crisis period were pro-European.[3]

1.2.2, 1.2.4 So far, constitutional amendment procedures have not been used to address the application of EU law. Although the relationship between EU law and the Greek Constitution from the aspect of the hierarchy of legal rules has been the subject of debate, with the doctrine of primacy of EU law having gained ground during recent years, in practice the issue has not yet created serious problems. So far, the incompatibility of constitutional norms with EU law has emerged as a problem with regard to two provisions. The first is Art. 14(9) of the Constitution, which provides that the capacity of owner, partner, major shareholder or managing

---

[2] The official translation, which is used here and subsequently in the report, is available at http://www.hellenicparliament.gr/UserFiles/f3c70a23-7696-49db-9148-f24dce6a27c8/001-156%20aggliko.pdf.

[3] For details and references to further literature, see Contiades and Fotiadou 2014.

director of a media enterprise is incompatible with the capacity of owner, partner, major shareholder or managing director of an enterprise that undertakes to perform works or to supply goods or services to the public sector, with the prohibition extended to all types of intermediary persons. The Greek Council of State[4] referred questions to the European Court of Justice (CJEU) regarding the compatibility of the 'major shareholder' provision with EU law. The CJEU in its judgment of 16 December 2008[5] concluded that an incompatibility existed. The contested provision has not been enforced since, and its revision is pending because, due to procedural hurdles set by the amending formula, no constitutional revision to allow such amendment has as yet taken place.

The second provision of the Constitution that creates tension with EU law is Art. 16(5), according to which 'education at university level shall be provided exclusively by institutions which are fully self-governed public law legal persons'. Incompatibility with EU rules on the recognition of professional rights with regard to graduates of private colleges, as well as with EU rules on freedom to offer and receive services, has often triggered discussion about amending this constitutional provision. Nonetheless, agreement among the political parties to do so has been hard to achieve.

As mentioned, such tensions with EU law are difficult to promptly address through formal amendment, since the amending formula is very stringent, rendering the Greek Constitution difficult to change. In particular, formal amendment rules consist of a combination of procedural and material limits. Procedural limits set out in Arts. 110(2)–(6) are very strict, providing for a two-phase process, with intervening general elections. In the first phase, the need for a constitutional revision is ascertained by a resolution of Parliament, adopted on the proposal of at least fifty Members of Parliament either by a three-fifths majority or by an absolute majority of the total number of its members in two ballots, held at least one month apart. This resolution specifically determines the provisions that are to be revised. In the second phase, the next Parliament proceeds with the amendment of the provisions that are to be revised. It is noteworthy that the timing of the intervening elections is not influenced by the initiation of the amending process. If a proposal for amendment of the Constitution receives an absolute majority of the votes of the total number of members but not the three-fifths majority, the next Parliament shall proceed with the revision of the proposed provisions by a three-fifths majority of the total number of its members, and vice versa. Constitutional revision is concluded with the publication of the revised provisions in the government gazette within ten days after their adoption by order of the Speaker of Parliament. Rigidity is enhanced by a mandatory time lapse between revisions: revision of the Constitution is not permitted before a lapse of five years from the completion of a previous revision.[6] Material limits are provided for by Art. 110(1), which

[4] Decision 3760/2006 of the Greek Council of State.

[5] Case C-213/07 *Michaniki* [2008] ECR I-09999.

[6] Contiades and Fotiadou 2014, p. 712.

entrenches the provisions defining the form of government and also Art. 2(1) (respect of human dignity), Arts. 4(1), (4) and (7) (equality before the law, eligibility of Greek citizens for public service, and prohibition of titles of nobility or distinction), Arts. 5(1) (right to free development of personality) and (3) (personal liberty), Art. 13(1) (freedom of religious conscience) and Art. 26 (separation of powers).

The stringency of the amending formula works within a predominant culture of political distrust between the political parties. Thus, the constitutional culture enhances the rigidity level.[7] Within this context, the sort of constitutional maintenance culture required to 'fix' incompatibilities of specific constitutional provisions with EU law does not exist. Consequently, in the course of the three revisions of the 1975 Constitution, EU law exerted implicit influence in shaping the content of specific provisions. For example, EU law influenced the design of constitutional provisions such as Art. 116(2), according to which the adoption of positive measures for promoting equality between men and women does not constitute discrimination on grounds of sex. According to this provision, the state shall take measures for the elimination of actual inequality, in particular to the detriment of women. Another provision shaped in light of EU law is Art. 4(4), providing that only Greek citizens shall be eligible for public service. This provision was subject to interpretation imposed by EU law, opening the Greek public service to EU citizens, while Art. 102(2), according to which the authorities of local government agencies which enjoy administrative and financial independence are elected by universal and secret ballot, was influenced by EU law introducing interpretations that allow EU citizens to vote in municipal elections.[8] Thus, these examples show that informal amendment was the route chosen and that formal amendment is neither a necessary nor suitable tool to address incompatibilities between the Constitution and EU law.

Consequently, the strictly and directly EU-related formal amendments are two interrelated interpretative clauses. The first is the above-mentioned clause added to address the debate regarding the foundation for participation in the European integration process. The clause adopts the view, which prevailed during the discussions in Parliament as part of the revision process, that different possibilities exist, which may accordingly trigger the application of different paragraphs of Art. 28. This interpretative clause was complemented in 2001 by the interpretative clause of Art. 80 of the Constitution, providing in para. 2 that the minting or issuing of currency shall be regulated by law. According to this interpretative clause, '[p]aragraph 2 does not impede the participation of Greece in the process of the Economic and Monetary Union, in the wider framework of European integration, according to the provisions of article 2'.

---

[7] Contiades and Fotiadou 2012, p. 450.

[8] Contiades and Tassopoulos 2012, p. 166.

1.3 Conceptualizing Sovereignty and the Limits to the Transfer of Powers

1.3.1, 1.3.4 For many years the supremacy of EU law appeared to puzzle constitutional scholars and judges alike.[9] Reluctant to clearly recognise the supremacy of legal norms over the Constitution, theory and jurisprudence found refuge in the concept that such rules have a different scope and cannot be in conflict. In extreme cases of tension, interpretative choices that harmonise the crucial constitutional provision with EU law should prevail.[10] This hesitation to address the issue gradually gave way. In Decision 161/2010, the Grand Chamber of the Council of State stated that when reviewing a law, the courts must first consider whether the law is contrary to the Constitution. Only if the answer to that question is negative should the courts consider whether the law is contrary to EU law. If the contested provision is found to be in violation of the Constitution, it is rendered inapplicable, and thus there is no reason to review it further. The Court stressed that this way of reviewing national laws is not contrary to the principle of the primacy and direct effect of EU law, but appropriate, since in order to assess the compatibility of a national law with EU law (and perhaps ask the European Court of Justice for a preliminary ruling), the exclusively competent national judge should firstly adjudicate on all the issues of interpretation and applicability of national law. It is noteworthy that 13 members of the Court dissented, stating that the Court in the specific case should first have adjudicated on the compatibility of the specific law with EU legislation, since the specific piece of legislation was enacted in order to comply with rulings of the European Court of Justice. The dissenting opinion also stressed that in accordance with the principles of primacy and direct effect of EU law, the Court should interpret the relevant constitutional provisions in line with EU law, so as to minimise the possibility of conflict between the Constitution and EU legislation.[11]

As a whole, although sovereignty narratives have not changed, in practice the Constitution operates in harmony with EU law, the supreme courts refer questions to the Court of Justice of the EU, and EU-friendly interpretation of legislation is common practice.

It is noteworthy that the crisis-related EU treaties were ratified via the normal law-making procedure provided for in Arts. 70–77 of the Constitution. In other words, Art. 28(1) of the Constitution, which dictates that international conventions are ratified by law, was applied instead of the special procedures set up by Art. 28(2) for vesting constitutional powers in agencies or international organisations. Statute 4063/2012 contained, among other rules, the ratification of the Treaty

---

[9] Chryssogonos 2003, pp. 210–213.

[10] See Decision 247/1997 of the Council of State recognising the supremacy of EU law, and contrarily Decision 2809/1997 not recognising supremacy of EU law over the national Constitution.

[11] See Association of European Administrative Judges, Greek Report, 2013.

Establishing the European Stability Mechanism (ESM Treaty), the amendment of Art. 136 TFEU and the ratification of the Fiscal Compact. The balance of political powers in Parliament allowed for this to happen quite smoothly, although concerns about the informal amendment of the Constitution effected by these treaties were expressed by parties of the opposition. So far, the dilemma about the constitutionalisation of the balanced budget rule implementing the Fiscal Compact has not been addressed due to the stringency of the amending formula. Nonetheless, when a constitutional revision process is initiated, the issue will inevitably emerge.

For more recent discussion on sovereignty in the context of the judicial adjudication of the financial crisis, see Sect. 1.5.

1.4 Democratic Control

1.4.1 The Standing Orders of Parliament[12] (Standing Orders) provide for the rules governing the relation of the Greek Parliament with the EU decision-making process. According to Art. 70(8) of the Constitution, 'the Standing Orders of Parliament shall specify the manner in which the Parliament is informed by the Government on issues being the object of regulation in the framework of the European Union, and debates on these'. This amendment, explicitly mentioning the EU, was added in the 2001 constitutional revision.

Article 32 of the Standing Orders sets out the rules on the Committee of European Affairs, providing that the Speaker of the Parliament shall, at the onset of every parliamentary term, establish by his/her decision a special standing Committee of European Affairs. The Committee is composed by 30 MPs and one of the Parliament's Deputy Speakers, acting as the Committee's president. In the sittings of the Committee, Greek members of the European Parliament can participate with a right to speak. The Speaker of the Parliament may refer to the Committee any issue that he/she deems as relevant or any issue submitted to him/her by the standing or special committees of the Parliament or by MPs and Members of the European Parliament. The competences of the Committee mainly include the following: (a) institutional issues of the EU, (b) issues of co-operation between the Hellenic Parliament and other national Parliaments of the EU, of the European Parliament and of the Conference of Community and European Affairs Committees of Parliaments of the EU (COSAC), (c) issues of European policy and (d) acts of EU bodies with a regulative content. The Committee can express its consultative opinion on the aforementioned issues through the submission of a respective report to the Parliament and the Government.

With regard to opinions on the regulatory acts of the European Parliament, Art. 41B of the Standing Orders provides that the Government shall forward the draft legislative acts of the EU to the Speaker of the Parliament immediately after they

[12] http://www.hellenicparliament.gr/en/Vouli-ton-Ellinon/Kanonismos-tis-Voulis/.

are communicated to the Council of Ministers. The Speaker of Parliament refers the documents to the competent standing committee or/and to the Committee on European Affairs. The Speaker of Parliament or the Committee by its own decision may invite the competent Minister to provide information to the Committee if it is so requested by one third of its members. The competent committee delivers its opinion, which is forwarded to the competent Minister and, if this is provided by EU legislation, to the Union's competent bodies. By a decision of the Speaker of Parliament or if this is requested by the competent Committee, the issue on which an opinion is delivered is entered in the Plenum's parliamentary control order of the day. In recent years, the Hellenic Parliament Committee on European Affairs has adopted several opinions on EU legislative acts, which it has then submitted to the European Commission, and has taken part in consultation procedures with regard to green papers.

1.4.2 Since constitutional referendums are not provided for and referendums have not been employed in practice during the last 40 years, democratic control is exercised by the Parliament.

However, it is noteworthy that in the midst of the financial crisis that struck Greece in 2010, the idea of holding a referendum was brought forth by the then Prime Minister George Papandreou. His Government was constantly under stress caused by general strikes and violent clashes between police and protestors, and narrowly won a vote of confidence in June 2011 while Parliament approved a five-year austerity package. On 26–27 October, a second bailout loan, which reduced Greece's debt by 50%, was agreed by EU leaders, the IMF and banks. As the adoption of new harsh measures was due, Papandreou decided to hold a referendum to request the opinion of the people on the conditions of the new agreement. Under immense pressure exerted by both the French and German leaders, by his own party, and by the opposition parties as well, Papandreou called off the referendum on 3 November. As a vote of confidence was pending in Parliament and Papandreou was faced with the imminent danger of losing it, a constitutional absurdum occurred: the Prime Minister won the vote of confidence under the unprecedented condition that he would subsequently resign so that a coalition Government would be formed. One week later, on 11 November, an interim coalition Government was indeed formed with the participation of PASOK, New Democracy and a far right wing party, the Popular Orthodox Rally (LAOS). The new Prime Minister, Loukas Papademos, was a highly regarded technocrat, a former Vice-President of the European Central Bank, while the Government's main task was to lead the country up to new elections. Thus, the referendum proposal actually led to the collapse of the Papandreou Government.

1.5 The Reasons for, and the Role of, EU Amendments

1.5.1–1.5.2 The limited scope of EU-related formal amendments is explicable by a combination of factors. The Constitution of Greece is recent and modern, its very drafting was done with the aim of EU membership and thus it included the appropriate accession mechanisms. The detailed and extensive protection of fundamental rights is in line with the EU culture of rights protection, which is also reflected in the addition of modern aspects of rights protection, such as the protection of genetic identity and the protection against biomedical interventions (Art. 5(5)), the right to information (Art. 5A(1)), the right to participate in the information society (Art. 5A(2)) and the protection of the person against the electronic processing of personal data (Art. 9A). Although the amending formula and the constitutional culture create a context of augmented constitutional rigidity, alternative routes for relieving possible tensions exist. Issues such as the ban of non-state university-level education, even if the political context fails to produce the level of consent required for a formal revision, can be resolved by way of judicial interpretation.

Furthermore, there has always been strong support for EU membership among the public in Greece, with Euroscepticism being expressed mostly by smaller political parties.

1.5.3 Sovereignty issues with regard to the EU integration process had been merely the subject of discussion among scholars, at least until the financial crisis broke out. The bailout agreements, however, marked a darker side of sovereignty loss. Delayed dismay at this loss apparent in the political discourse and in constitutional challenges against the bailout agreements suggest that an abrupt realisation of waning sovereignty in the age of globalisation occurred as a result of the financial crisis.[13] Its concrete expression was the challenge against Law 3845/2010 incorporating the Memorandum of Understanding (MoU) between Greece and its international lenders brought before the Greek Council of State, in which it was argued that this law, despite the fact that it made concessions of sovereignty and transferred state competences to international organisations (i.e. the Troika), was not adopted with the necessary enhanced majority of three-fifths of votes, as provided by Art. 28 of the Constitution. It is clear that despite the participation of the International Monetary Fund (IMF), which did however complicate matters legally, the bailout scheme was important if Greece was to remain in the eurozone. The Court resolved the issue by rejecting the very applicability of Art. 28 of the Constitution, characterising the Memorandum not as an international treaty but a political programme.[14] Although the Court thus did not invoke sovereignty issues to resolve the case, narratives of lost sovereignty are part of the influence of the financial crisis on the Constitution. Constitutional normativity has often been challenged because of the impact of austerity measures on the application of fundamental rights and because of deviations from normal law-making processes and the enhanced role of the executive in law-making.

Nonetheless, the Constitution is far from becoming obsolete. As regards the EU, it creates no problems with regard to the integration process, while it has an

[13] Contiades and Fotiadou 2013, pp. 9–59.

[14] Contiades and Tassopoulos 2013, pp. 195–218.

immense role in adjudication and politics. Still, the financial crisis has put a severe strain on the Constitution and exerted a continuous influence on it, as it has on most constitutions in the legal orders that have been struck by the financial crisis. It is arguable that the amending formula itself could be considered as an area in demand of reconsideration. Over-stringency has proved to be an obstacle to constitutional updating as well as to allowing the people to be more involved in the amending process.

2 Constitutional Rights, the Rule of Law and EU Law

2.1 The Position of Constitutional Rights and the Rule of Law in the Constitution

The Greek Constitution protects individual and social rights, while political rights are also enshrined in other constitutional provisions. Ever since the creation of the Greek state, fundamental rights have been constitutionally protected. All Greek Constitutions have included catalogues of rights that have gradually acquired their present status. This gradual evolution has been marked by the continuous enhancement of rights protection. The current Constitution of 1975 has a comprehensive and very detailed list of rights, which was further enhanced in the 2001 constitutional revision that was also marked by the constitutionalisation of interpretative principles.

As part of the 2001 revision, the proportionality doctrine and the horizontal application of rights were explicitly included in the Constitution (Art. 25(1)), which also guarantees the rule of law and the welfare state. The provision also provides that restrictions to rights may be imposed by the Constitution or by statute. In accordance with the wording of Art. 25(1):

> [t]he rights of the human being as an individual and as a member of the society and the principle of the welfare state rule of law are guaranteed by the State. All agents of the State shall be obliged to ensure the unhindered and effective exercise thereof. These rights also apply to the relations between individuals to which they are appropriate. Restrictions of any kind which, according to the Constitution, may be imposed upon these rights, should be provided either directly by the Constitution or by statute, should a reservation exist in the latter's favour, and should respect the principle of proportionality.

It is noteworthy that proportionality had already been extensively elaborated in the case law as a normative principle delineating the permissibility of restrictions imposed on constitutional rights. Interpretatively derived from the rule of law principle in a landmark case of the Council of State in 1984,[15] the proportionality doctrine is constantly employed by the Greek courts. The constitutionalisation of the principle encourages the judge to employ all tiers of the test rigorously. Under

[15] Decision 2112/1984 of the Council of State.

the rule of law umbrella, the principles of legal certainty and legitimate expectation have been judicially elaborated.

Greek courts in exercising judicial review of the constitutionality of laws often address constitutional rights protection issues. The absence of a constitutional court often works against a unified, coherent jurisprudence. Nonetheless, a large part of Greek constitutional jurisprudence deals with the delineation of the protective scope of rights and the permissibility of restrictions.

2.1.3 The rule of law principle was explicitly enshrined in 2001, although it had been part of the Greek constitutional culture ever since the birth of the Greek state, with a landmark point in its evolution being the Constitution of 1864. The above-mentioned concept of the 'welfare state rule of law'[16] is considered to be one of the fundamental principles of the state, along with the principle of democracy and the separation of powers doctrine. The Greek constitutional literature had interpretatively derived the principle from a combination of a long list of constitutional provisions. Jurisprudential references to the doctrine had also found multiple constitutional grounds for its elaboration. The welfare state dimension operates under the rule of law rationale, while welfare state redistribution complements the constitutional protection of social rights. Adhering to the French '*État de droit*' and the German '*Rechtsstaat*' traditions, the Greek conceptualisation of the rule of law works in conjunction with other specific constitutional provisions.

Article 42 of the Constitution dictates that statutes passed by the Parliament shall be promulgated and published by the President of the Republic. Statutes obtain formal legal effect with their publication in the government gazette, and substantive legal effect ten days after publication; i.e. legal validity begins with publication and legal enforceability ten days later. Statutes may also contain provisions that set a different starting point for legal bindingness. Retroactivity is possible if explicitly provided for under the condition that this is not prohibited by the Constitution. Retroactive force is not constitutionally permissible in the following provisions: Art. 7(1), according to which no crime exists and no punishment can be inflicted unless specified by law in force prior to the perpetration of the act, while criminal liability also cannot be retroactively increased; Art. 77(2), according to which pseudo-interpretative statutes may not be used to produce retroactivity;[17] and Art. 78(2), according to which taxes or other financial charges may not be imposed by a retroactive statute effective prior to the fiscal year preceding their imposition.[18] In other words, the rule of law is substantiated through specific constitutional provisions that pre-existed the explicit enshrinement of this principle, providing the grounds for its interpretative conceptualisation, while these provisions are currently read in conjunction with the doctrine.

[16] The terminology used in the official translation of the Constitution, see supra n. 2.

[17] 'A statute which is not truly interpretative shall enter into force only as of its publication.'

[18] Contiades and Fotiadou 2014, p. 714.

2.2 The Balancing of Fundamental Rights and Economic Freedoms in EU Law

2.2.1 According to the CJEU's jurisprudence, conflicts that may arise between fundamental rights and fundamental freedoms enshrined in the Treaties are resolved when the Court, following a balancing procedure, rules whether or not a fundamental right can prevail over fundamental freedoms. In the light of the CJEU's jurisprudence, fundamental freedoms can justify a restriction of rights, which are not considered as absolute.[19] The evaluation of whether a right is considered absolute or not is based, among other criteria, on the European Convention on Human Rights (ECHR). Consequently, in relation to all the rights which, according to the ECHR, can be subject to limitations justified by objectives of public interest, fundamental freedoms are considered by the jurisprudence of the CJEU as a 'form' of public interest, the protection of which potentially requires the restriction of rights.[20] The CJEU's jurisprudence is not clear about whether rights generally prevail over freedoms. In every case the balancing procedure is based on the principle of proportionality. Consequently, the limitation of a freedom is considered legitimate if it takes place within the framework of the exercise of a fundamental right, and is considered to be appropriate, necessary and proportional *stricto sensu* for the achievement of the objectives of the right at issue. On the other hand, the limitation of a right is appropriate, necessary and proportional *stricto sensu*, if it serves the achievement of a given end which is protected by the freedom at issue. Nevertheless, the most crucial issue is that according to the CJEU's jurisprudence, fundamental freedoms must be balanced against fundamental rights even in those circumstances in which the exercise of rights concerns activities that fall outside the scope of the EU's competence, given that the CJEU has ruled that the exercise of rights cannot jeopardise the achievement of goals protected by fundamental freedoms.[21] Within the balancing context, fundamental rights do not prevail over economic freedoms. As a commentator on case C-112/00[22] has observed, 'the language of *prima facie* breach of economic rights, suggests that it remains something, which is at the heart wrong, but tolerated'.[23]

With regard to the question of constitutional issues in Greece due to the jurisprudence of the CJEU on the balancing of fundamental rights with economic freedoms, we can observe that the jurisprudence of the Council of State has been influenced by the CJEU's approach concerning the primacy of fundamental

---

[19] See Case C-112/00 *Schmidberger* (2003) ECR I-05659.

[20] Ibid., para. 79. The CJEU makes a direct reference to the text of Arts. 10 and 11 of the ECHR and their limitations due to objectives in the public interest.

[21] Case C-438/05 *International Transport Workers Federation (Viking)* [2008] ECR I-10779, para. 40 and Case C-341/05 *Laval un Partneri* [2007] ECR I-11767, para. 87. On this issue see Amtenbrink 2012, pp. 35–64, especially pp. 60–62.

[22] Case C-112/00 *Schmidberger* [2003] ECR I-05659.

[23] Brown 2003, p. 1508.

freedoms of EU law over national constitutions, which may act as trumps over the enforcement of certain constitutional provisions. However, the Council of State has not developed a sound constitutional policy regarding the relation between the Greek Constitution and EU law (see below Sects. 2.7–2.8).

2.3 *Constitutional Rights, the European Arrest Warrant and EU Criminal Law*

2.3.1 The Presumption of Innocence

2.3.1.1–2.3.1.2 This presumption applies in Greece; Greece has incorporated the ECHR as well the International Covenant on Civil and Political Rights (ICCPR), among other conventions, into its legal order. Both academic commentary and the courts hold that the presumption is not violated through the execution of a European Arrest Warrant (EAW).

According to the national provisions concerning arrest, an arrest warrant is in conformity with the law if there is probable cause indicating guilt, and the proceedings are controlled by the judiciary (Arts. 5(3) and 6(1) of the Constitution; Art. 276 et seq. of the Code of Criminal Procedure (CCP)). Although these are provisions of domestic law, they apply to the EAW along the same lines, since it is considered as a procedural means in the common EU space, where mutual trust and especially the principle of mutual recognition have to prevail. Therefore, the Supreme Court (*Areios Pagos*, hereinafter AP) has no competence to control the substance of the case; it can only control the legality of the EAW.[24] However, part of the academic commentary holds that control must always be carried out in cases where procedural requirements for the execution of the EAW are not met. This is the case especially when the issuing state has no jurisdiction over the alleged deed.[25]

One aspect of the presumption of innocence that could be regarded as having been violated is the '*pro mitiore*' principle, which means that if several reasoned scientific views exist, the one that best safeguards the rights of the accused ought to be preferred. Such a violation occurs when national 'indictment' (i.e. charging the person sought, which in Greece is a ground not to execute an EAW according to the law (Arts. 12(1a') and (b') of Law No. 3251/2004), is interpreted narrowly by the courts and thus its scope is not exhausted to allow the person to be treated in more favourable terms. This narrow interpretation runs contrary to the very meaning of the legislative ground for non-execution, as long as the latter aims at avoiding

---

[24] Kedikoglou 2014, pp. 29–30, 71; Mouzakis 2009, pp. 572 et seq.; Mouzakis 2012, p. 67. From the case law see e.g. AP 1836/2007, Poiniki Dikaiosini 2008, p. 535 (summary); 1811/2009, Poiniki Dikaiosini 2010, pp. 37 et seq.

[25] Kedikoglou 2014, pp. 71–72.

double jeopardy and thus should be interpreted generously to benefit the person sought. Since, according to the commentary, a preliminary investigation, possible henceforth in Greece for almost all crimes and obligatory now for felonies (Laws Nos. 3904/2010 and 4055/2012, accordingly amending Art. 43 CCP,) blocks the execution of an EAW as an indictment does, the execution of an EAW should be denied also in the case of such an investigation. Contrary, however, to the viewpoint in the above commentary, the Supreme Court considers preliminary investigation as separate from indictment (which as such may or may not follow, according to the evidence obtained after the investigation has ended). Here one could consider the Court's approach to identifying indictment in the wider sense of the EAW Framework Decision[26] (EAWFD) with the formal and narrow meaning that this term has in domestic law to be erroneous. The case seems ripe for a request for a preliminary ruling from the CJEU.[27] However, the Supreme Court has recently held that indictment, even if thus narrowly conceived, may exclude the execution of an EAW even when it temporally follows the issuing of the latter; the only condition is that indictment take place during the hearings on the EAW at the Appeals Judicial Council or the Supreme Court and not later.[28] However, pending indictments may adversely impact the proper application of the EAWFD, given that the optional refusal of execution has been reshaped as obligatory with regard to nationals under Arts. 11(h') and 12(a') of Law No. 3251/2004, which provides for a possibility of abuse since consciously unfounded complaints may be submitted with the aim of paralysing the execution of an EAW through a subsequent indictment. This reshaping into an obligatory ground deprives the judge of the discretionary power that he/she otherwise had to declare such submissions abusive and allow execution. The Greek legislator has thus distorted the EAWFD in a 'nationalist' manner.[29]

2.3.2 *Nullum crimen, nulla poena sine lege*

2.3.2.1 The principle *of nullum crimen, nulla poena sine lege* is recognised in Greece as a cornerstone of criminal law and, as discussed in Sect. 2.1.3 above, as part of the rule of law (Arts. 2(1), 6(1) and especially Art. 7(1) of the Constitution

---

[26] Council Framework Decision of 13 June 2002 on the European arrest warrant and the surrender procedures between Member States (2002/584/JHA), [2002] OJ L 190/1.

[27] Kedikoglou 2014, pp. 129–134. As to commentary, see also Anagnostopoulos 2005, pp. 855–856; Fytrakis 2006, pp. 219; Kalfelis 2006, pp. 203; Mouzakis 2012, pp. 59-60. Cf. the opposite stance of the judiciary in AP 591/2005, Poinika Chronika 2005, pp. 840 et seq.; AP 2149/2005, Poiniki Dikaiosini 2006, pp. 169 et seq.; AP 1773/2007, Poinika Chronika 2008, pp. 556 et seq., as well as of Karaflos 2013, p. 98.

[28] Kedikoglou 2014, pp. 136–137. Cf. AP 678/2012, Poinika Chronika 2013, pp. 440–441; AP 558/2007, Poinika Chronika 2007, pp. 597 et seq.; AP 2135/2005, Poinika Chronika 2006, pp. 597 et seq.

[29] Togias 2013, pp. 1156–1157.

and Arts. 1 and 2 of the Criminal Code (CC)). Article 2(1) of the Constitution provides that '[t]he primary obligation of the State is to respect and protect human dignity'. Art. 6(1) provides that '[w]ith the exemption of *in flagranti* crimes, nobody shall be arrested or imprisoned without a reasoned warrant, which must be presented at the time of arrest or detention'. Article 7(1) provides:

> No crime is constituted and no criminal sanction shall be imposed without a law valid before the commission of the deed and defining its component elements. A criminal sanction that is harsher than the one provided for at the time of commission of the deed, shall never be imposed.

Therefore, the legal commentary has strongly contested the EAW from the point of view of respect of the principle of *nulla poena sine lege*, especially as regards the erosion of the dual criminality principle. The points stressed in the theory are the following: it is absurd for the executing state to extradite a person for an act which the state itself does not consider as punishable; the very fundamentals of extradition are thus dismantled; the guarantees of the person sought and laid down in the above-mentioned constitutional provisions are undermined; sovereignty is negated; without dual criminality, criminalisation overwhelms the EU legal space.[30] It seems clear that despite the symbolic maintenance of the principle of dual criminality, it has in fact been totally eroded, especially if the 32 'crime types' in Art. 2(2) of the EAWFD (Art. 10(2) of Law No. 3251/2004) are taken into consideration, whereby dual criminality is already *ex lege* excluded. The principle functions only marginally, e.g. when an execution is refused due to defects in the legality principle traced *in concreto* when, for instance, the crime for which a person is sought is not provided for as such in Greece and simultaneously is not included in the 32 'crime types'.[31] The removal of double criminality has been considered problematic in Greece in particular with regard to the following crimes and offences in the list, which are not considered as crimes or offences in Greece. First, Greece may face problems as to the forms of certain crimes: e.g. in Greece, 'homicide' does not include participation in suicide or acts of euthanasia, both specifically provided for

[30] Kedikoglou 2014, pp. 56–57, 68; Kaiafa-Gbandi 2004, pp. 1297–1301, noting '… for the person sought the offering of procedural guarantees for the materialization of extradition cannot counter the eventual dismantlement of basic obstacles blocking it, since, as it is obvious, there is no comparison between the possibility of non-extradition and the extradition under procedural safeguards' (at p. 1297); Fytrakis 2006, pp. 214–215, noting: '… narrowing the requirement of dual criminality constitutes a dangerous diversion from the fundamental principles of criminal law, as they are laid down in our Constitution' (at 215)'; Kalfelis 2006, p. 201; Vasilakakis 2006, p. 207, noting: '… the deletion of dual criminality produces an over-incrimination at a European level, since the probability of being confronted with a EAW grows … under conditions of intense international mobility like nowadays the possibility grows that somebody may behave legally according to the law of his/her nationality or usual residence, in conformity with which he/she coordinates his/her behavior, but illegally according to another country's law, which he/she may ignore'.

[31] See in this regard Togias 2013, pp. 1154–1156, referring in this regard e.g. to AP 116/2011, as well as Decision 8/2011 of the Piraeus Appeals Judicial Council and Decisions 38/2012 and 89/2012 of the Athens Appeals Judicial Council.

in Greece separately from the former; however these may be part of 'homicide' in some other Member States. Problems may also arise with regard to the question whether crimes procedurally related to those in the EAW are to be considered as included in the list. Secondly, issues around dual criminality may arise with regard to crimes concerning tax evasion, customs fees or currency (Art. 10(1a'), last sentence of Law No. 3251/2004, incorporating Art. 4 of the EAWFD), whereby Greece is obliged to extradite persons even to countries that do not accept this EAWFD clause, like some Scandinavian and Baltic countries or the Netherlands. Furthermore, Greece in its domestic law has also widened the list of offences provided for in the EAWFD by providing also for 'violations of sexual freedom' in general, 'corruption' and preparatory acts of currency-related crimes.[32] Finally, the case law of the Supreme Court does not consider it to be a violation of the *nulla poena* principle if the EAW provisions also apply to alleged deeds committed before the entry into force of Law No. 3251/2004, provided that the EAW request has been received after this temporal point; the reasoning is that in procedural law matters, unlike in substantive law, the *nulla poena* principle is not binding, allowing thus for retroactivity.[33]

Counterarguments to the above critical points could be that the above-mentioned constitutional provisions concern only indictments made by the Greek state, whereas in the case of the EAW, Greece is only assisting another EU Member State legally and, moreover, the crimes included in the 32 'crime types' will mainly be committed abroad (however, in this case the problem remains with regard to crimes that are not punishable in Greece and have been allegedly committed by nationals).[34] There is thus a clear setback for the constitutional guarantees for arrested persons, which has been considered as a necessary 'sacrifice' for the good functioning of co-operation inside the EU legal space.

2.3.3 Fair Trial and *In Absentia* Judgments

2.3.3.1 According to Greek law (Art. 13(1) of Law No. 3251/2004, incorporating Art. 5 EAWFD), the execution of an EAW for the execution of a penal sanction based on a court judgment issued *in absentia* is not automatic; it may be made dependent on a declaration from the part of the issuing state, satisfying the executing state, that procedural possibilities exist for a new trial in the issuing state in the presence of the person sought. This declaration should originate only from a court, not from any other, administrative authority. A practical difficulty as to the handling of such cases is the multiplicity of the Member States' legislation on

32 Kedikoglou 2014, pp. 59–67, and pp. 72–75.

33 See Art. 39 of Law No 3251/2004 and Mouzakis 2012, p. 65, respectively. In favour of the judiciary's stance also Karaflos 2013, p. 99. For a comprehensive critique of the viewpoint that favours retroactivity in criminal procedure, see passim Fytrakis 1998.

34 Kedikoglou 2014, p. 69.

summonses and subpoenas, which makes the respective control of whether the foreign law has been respected rather complicated for the executing state.[35] When the person sought for extradition is a national, Art. 11(f') of Law No. 3251/2004 also applies: the Greek state may insist on execution in Greece as a condition for execution of the EAW. It may then also refuse execution due to the fact that the *in absentia* judgment, if issued without compliance with the proper procedure on summonses and subpoenas, violates the principle of fair trial (scil. Art. 6(1) ECHR) and therefore execution of the sanction cannot be allowed by the Greek state (this rule applies both to nationals as well as non-nationals).[36] The 'collateral damage' of such potential refusals is of course the loss of a new trial of the person sought, i.e. the loss of the chance of an acquittal or a diminution of the sanction, and the risk of the judgment becoming final, if Greece, instead of taking refuge in Art. 6(1) ECHR, chooses to execute the sanction.[37] A solution in such cases could be that the Greek courts would adjudicate in conformity with the *I.B.* judgment of the CJEU. In that case, the CJEU would approach EAW requests for extradition for the execution of sanctions as requests for initiating criminal proceedings, provided that there exists in the issuing state an exceptional appeal for a new trial (in the form of a *'revisio propter nova'* or something analogous to it); meanwhile the execution of the existing judgment would be left pending.[38]

2.3.4 The Right to a Fair Trial – Practical Challenges Regarding a Trial Abroad

2.3.4.1 The absence of the protection guaranteed by domestic legislation is a real challenge for the person sought, as well as for the family. In Greek legislation there are no special measures provided for assisting these persons in such cases. The Ombudsman cannot be involved, since this institution mediates between public administration services and citizens; cases having to do with the judiciary, like EAW cases, are excluded. As to legal aid, Law No. 3226/2004 provides that every EU resident of low income may become a beneficiary. Low income means an income less than two-thirds of the annual family income as stipulated by the conditions of the General National Collective Labour Agreement. Such aid must be applied for. The aid also covers appeals, provided that they are not blatantly unfounded (Arts. 1, 2 and 7(4) of Law No. 3226/2004).

One can consider perhaps the provisions of the Law incorporating the EAWFD in Greece concerning residents and inhabitants (Arts. 12(1e'), 13(3) of Law No. 3251/2004) as a kind of pre-emption and thus 'circumvention' of the challenges mentioned above. According to these provisions, Greece may refuse to execute an

[35] Kedikoglou 2014, p. 162.

[36] Kedikoglou 2014, pp. 162–163.

[37] Mouzakis 2012, p. 60.

[38] See Case C-306/09 *I.B.* [2010] I-10341, paras. 56–57; cf. on this also Mouzakis 2012, pp. 60–61.

EAW if execution of the sanction in Greece (provided that such execution is possible according to domestic law) is guaranteed, if the person sought is resident in Greece, which is judged depending on the ad hoc personal, economic and social relations the person has to the country, indicating a link or connection of a more or less stable character. A certain period of stay is not a prerequisite, nor is it required that the person originate from an EU country, nor that he/she have no criminal record. Provided that the same conditions are fulfilled, custody of the arrested person may be replaced by non-custodial restrictive terms (Arts. 16(1)–(3) of Law No. 3251/2004). Exceptionally, when the person sought is a citizen of the issuing state, the link to the latter will probably prevail as to the execution of the EAW, but there is still a margin of appreciation for the Greek courts when the rights and freedoms of the person sought might be put at risk.[39]

The aim of the provisions is the successful rehabilitation of the person sought into the social circumstances with which he/she is familiar. This aim is also in harmony with Art. 8 ECHR, a provision the EAWFD also aims at enhancing.[40] Despite the conformity of the statute and the case law with the ruling in the *Szymon Kozłowski* case,[41] the differentiation of the treatment of nationals where refusal is obligatory (cf. Art. 11(f') of Law No. 3251/200[42]), is not in full compliance with the EU scope of protection for aliens, in so far as e.g. the court judgment may depend on administrative prerequisites like the possession of a valid residence permit. The CJEU preliminary ruling which was expected after the French request submitted in *Joao Pedro Lopes Da Silva Jorge* concluded that a Member State's legislation restricting the power not to execute an EAW to cases where the requested persons are its nationals runs contrary to the principle of non-discrimination.[43] A final complication that negatively impacts the situation of the sought person is the incorrect stance of the prevailing opinion in the Supreme Court's jurisprudence concerning the costs of the proceedings. Such costs, according to the Supreme Court's opinion, shall be borne by the person sought according to the respective domestic legislation, when he/she is extradited after his/her appeal has been rejected; however, Art. 37 of Law No. 3251/2004 provides otherwise, putting such charges at the expense of the executing state. This provision, especially as regards dealing with the costs of EAW proceedings on the basis of the territory on which they have arisen, has to apply in lieu of the general

[39] Kedikoglou 2014, pp. 91–94. See from the respective case law AP 854/2012, Poinika Chronika 2013, p. 116; AP 437/2012, Poinika Chronika 2013, pp. 113–115.

[40] See e.g. AP 1676/2010, Poinika Chronika 2011: 670–672.

[41] Case C-66/08 *Kozłowski* [2008] ECR I-06041.

[42] Whereby it remains contentious whether the court judgment of the issuing state should be 'irrevocable' (and not merely 'final' without suspension of the sanction's execution); fair trial considerations promote the affirmative answer, whereas the letter of the law allows for a negative one: cf. Karaflos 2013, p. 95.

[43] See Case C-66/08 *Kozłowski* [2008] ECR I-06041and Case C-42/11 *Joao Pedro Lopes Da Silva Jorge* [2012] ECLI:EU:C:2012:517. See also: Mouzakis 2012, pp. 57–59.

provisions of the Greek CCP.[44] It would seem recommendable to establish institutions and procedures aimed at appropriate assistance for persons extradited and for their relatives, and it is obvious that Greece is far behind in doing so. One possible solution could be an NGO-based model of assistance.

2.3.4.2 As to statistics regarding extraditions, throughout the years 2005 to 2009, Greece executed 82 EAWs. Between 38–49% of persons sought did not consent to their extradition; the average time needed for the extradition of persons not having consented to extradition was 48 days.[45] To date, 10 Greek citizens have been extradited to be indicted abroad and serve the sentence in Greece; in four cases concerning alien residents, no return has been decided due to the fact that they were citizens of the issuing state; in one case return was impossible because the Greek authorities did not apply for it; in five cases the aliens were deemed non-residents and the EAW was executed unconditionally.[46]

2.3.5 The Right to Effective Judicial Protection: The Principle of Mutual Recognition in EU Criminal Law and Abolition of the Exequatur in Civil and Commercial Matters

2.3.5.1–2.3.5.4 Given the strong adherence in the EAW system to the institution of mutual recognition, judicial review tends admittedly to become rather weak (and more so if the issuing state's authority is a non-judicial one). Since, however, fundamental liberties and rights are at stake in criminal law matters, the standpoint that seeks legitimacy for such weakness through the argument that criminal court decisions have to be assimilated to freely circulating consumer goods, cannot be regarded as acceptable. This is so because orders pertaining to deprivation of freedom, as inherently resistant to any kind of commodification, cannot be normatively equated with rules applicable to consumer goods. In this regard even the exequatur in civil and commercial matters is of dubious legitimacy, especially when the sanctions are so severe that they must be equated to quasi criminal sanctions; the same holds even more true when genuine criminal sanctions are to be imposed. Therefore, we will subsequently highlight six points which provide some additional safeguards in the Greek legal order.

First, one substitute for the lacking judicial review may be found in refusal of execution when the alleged deed does not fall under the jurisdiction of the issuing state, and Greece has no such jurisdiction either. However, this would run contrary to the interpretation of the EAWFD by the Greek courts; according to the judicial interpretation, the courts may not control the substance of the case underlying an EAW which Greece has been requested to execute.[47]

---

[44] Mouzakis 2012, p. 64.

[45] Togias 2013, p. 1154.

[46] Kedikoglou 2014, pp. 101–102.

[47] Kedikoglou 2014, pp. 71–72 and 150–152. See also under Sects. 2.3.1.1–2.3.1.2 above.

Secondly, by way of an analogous substitute, one may consider refusal of execution when a national is sought for execution of a sanction where either the act is not punishable in Greece or simply the sanction is not provided for as such in Greece (e.g. a certain type of internment in a workhouse conceived of as a form of security in the issuing state, but not existing in Greece as such).[48]

Thirdly, along the same lines, one could request a more generous use of the human rights clause and thus the refusal to execute an EAW on the grounds of a potential violation of Art. 6 of the EU Treaty (Art. 1(3) of the EAW FD; Art. 1(2a') of the implementing Law No. 3251/2004). The standpoint of the Greek Supreme Court, which holds that these rights or the fairness of the procedure are not at stake when deciding on the execution of an EAW and that these become relevant only after execution,[49] is very narrow. In opposition to this, commentary is strongly in favour of taking principles laid down in instruments like the ECHR or the case law of the European Court of Human Rights (ECtHR) like the judgment in the *Soering*[50] case into consideration. In such a framework, detention conditions that violate Art. 3 ECHR could provide grounds to refuse execution.[51]

Fourthly, it was noted that an appeal against a decision to execute an EAW taken by the President of the Appeal Court is not permitted when the person sought has consented to the extradition. Whilst this is in accordance with the speedy nature of the procedure and the freedom of choice of the consenting person and thus complies with Art. 20(1) of the Constitution ('right to be heard'), Art. 6 of the ECHR, Art. 2 (1) of Protocol No. 7 to the ECHR and the ICCPR, the non-permissibility of a refusal to execute such decision, at least in exceptional cases, seems less justified. It is obvious that a decision is not to be executed in the case of invalid consent (e.g. the person sought consents without having a lawyer and without being e.g. informed about the real consequences of consent to waiving the specificity rule (Art. 34 (2) e'-f') of Law No. 3251/2004), despite the fact that this case is not expressly regulated in the law.[52]

Fifthly, when an appeal is submitted (when the person sought has not consented to the extradition) but the appellant is absent when the court convenes, the Supreme Court will reject the appeal on the formal ground that it is 'unsupported' through the appellant's presence; such presence is indeed required according to Art. 501(1) CCP. This standpoint has, however, been strongly and persuasively contradicted by the minority opinion in Supreme Court Judgment No. 651/2011,[53] rejecting the

---

[48] Kedikoglou 2014, pp. 87–90. If an alien is sought who is resident in Greece and who is a citizen of the issuing state, the link to the issuing state may lead Greece not to refuse to execute the EAW; see also above Sect. 2.3.4.1.

[49] See for instance AP 1303/2011, Poinika Chronika 2012: 494. See also Mouzakis 2012, p. 67.

[50] *Soering v. the United Kingdom*, 7 July 1989, Series A no. 161.

[51] Togias 2013, p. 1161 and footnote 52. As to the impact of international human rights and protective legal means on the EAW, see also Vasilakakis 2006, p. 208. Critically to the conception of the notion of the EAW as an overreacting 'combat norm', see also Papacharalambous 2002.

[52] Mouzakis 2012, pp. 63–64.

[53] AP 651/2011, Poinika Chronika 2012, p. 347.

application of this article. The argument is that the article in question has to do with genuine decisions taken after real trials and not with rulings issued by judicial units acting as mere councils (as in EAW cases), whereby publicity and orality are not followed as in trials. It is further pointed out in the minority opinion that rejection of the appeal significantly deteriorates the procedural status of the person sought also for another reason: it is not permissible to claim that the procedure is invalid, as normally possible for an appellant according to domestic law when the non-appearance of the appellant was due to 'force majeure' (Art. 341 CCP), because of the specific and accelerated procedure of the EAW.[54] Moreover, and according to the same minority opinion, even the appellant's declaration that he/she 'will not appear' before the Supreme Court cannot always be interpreted as a waiver of the initially launched appeal. Such waivers must be made explicitly; tacit waivers are not recognised by the respective provisions of Art. 474(1) and 475(1) CCP. Finally, the presence of the appellant in and of itself adds nothing to the judicial procedure regarding the EAW: it is not matters of evidence but only complex juridical issues that are at stake at this stage. For all these reasons, the rejection of the appeal on formal grounds falls short of the requisite level of due protection of procedural rights.[55]

Finally, a clear case of disproportionate deterioration of the procedural status of the person sought is the formalistic reference in Art. 22(1) of Law No. 3251/2004 to Art. 451(1) CCP as regards the procedure of appealing against the initial decision to execute an EAW. The latter provision requires the person sought to submit an appeal exclusively with the Appeal Court's secretary within 24 hours after the issuing of the initial decision. Thus, the appeal becomes nearly impossible for a person in custody, since he/she is not permitted to address the director of the penal institution for that purpose, as it is provided for in principle according to Art. 474(1) CCP.[56] Additionally, this option is misleading: Art. 451 CCP presupposes that the appellant is not in custody. Finally, the disproportionate outcome of this option is evident from the fact that addressing the prison's director is, according to the jurisprudence of the Supreme Court, allowed if the detainee intends to waive the right to appeal.[57]

[54] Mouzakis 2012, pp. 62–63; Togias 2013, pp. 1162–1163.

[55] Mouzakis 2012, p. 63; Baltas 2014, p. 287. Contra AP 241/2013, Poinika Chronika 2014, pp. 286–287.

[56] Togias 2013, p. 1162, where, as to the rejection of the appeal as inadmissible, the author refers e.g. to AP 478/2011, Nomiko Vima 2011, p. 1005; see also AP 117/2013, Poinika Chronika 2014, p. 285. Regarding the narrow time limit of 24 hours for the appeal, see also the critique in Vasilakakis 2006, p. 208.

[57] Voulgaris 2014, p. 286. See also against the AP jurisprudence on this, Fytrakis 2006, pp. 219–220.

2.3.6 Constitutional Rights Regarding Other Aspects of EU Criminal Law

Amongst other challenges to constitutional rights in the context of EU criminal law, six issues will be briefly mentioned here.

First, the territoriality and the notion of the identity of the 'same act' ('*idem*') present significant problems as to a stable and foreseeable application of the EAW. According to Art. 11(g)i)' of Law No. 3251/2004, Greece shall refuse execution if the act has been committed, even partly, on Greek soil; the optional ground of refusal has also here been recast as an obligatory one. This has been relevant to crimes committed through the Internet, trans-border crimes like cigarette smuggling and other forms of smuggling or drug trafficking, and they have been dealt with in a contradictory manner by the Greek courts. In some cases these have been considered as having been committed (partly) on Greek soil (which leads to a refusal of execution), whilst in others as not influencing the jurisdiction of the issuing state (which leads to execution of the EAW). Whereas the former interpretive option is in concordance with the spirit of the CJEU ruling in *Gaetano Mantello*, which also refers to Art. 54 of the Schengen Treaty and promotes the *idem factum* in lieu of the *idem crimen* approach,[58] the academic commentary has seen in the latter option a risk of enhancing what is already an overly extensive tendency to affirm execution of an EAW.[59] In the case of concurrence of more than one crime (and the same holds true for so-called 'continuous crimes', i.e. repetitious conduct of more or less the same kind, like more acts of theft, robbery or embezzlement), the point of departure remains their autonomy. Therefore, the Greek judicial authority shall require the urgent delivery of information from the issuing state as to whether the person sought had, even partly, committed separate act(s) of the 'crime chain' on Greek soil (according to Arts. 5 and 16 CC and Art. 19(2) of Law No. 3251/2004), in which case execution must be denied.[60] Inherent in all the above constellations is the risk that the 'wholeness' of the criminal event is not taken under proper consideration as long as it is 'chopped' into pieces, whereby the complexity of the facts, the involvement of more persons and the differences in the procedural laws among the Member States may cause delays and undeserved harm for the accused. A reform at EU level seems unavoidable.[61]

---

[58] Cf. Case C-261/09 *Mantello* [2010] ECR I-11477, paras. 38–41.

[59] See also Togias 2013, pp. 1157–1161; Mouzakis 2012, pp. 65–67; AP 108/2013, Poinika Chronika 2013, pp. 468–469. These authors refer, respectively, to AP 1557/2012, AP 200/2011, AP 2006/2010 and the opposite (refusing the commission on Greek soil) AP 1074/2012, AP 678/2012, AP 994/2010, AP 810/2010. See also on territoriality AP 200/2011, Poiniki Dikaiosini 2011, pp. 579–581 and the respective remarks of Vrioni 2011, p. 582. In favour of the '*idem factum*' conception as to the identity of the act, see AP 1/2011, Poinika Chronika 2011, pp. 501–504, with approving remarks of Anagnostopoulos 2011, pp. 504–505; see also Karaflos 2013, pp. 91–92.

[60] Vrioni 2011, p. 583.

[61] This is correctly pointed out by Karaflos 2013, p. 97.

A second area of concern is whether an initial refusal of execution results in blocking the affirmation of a repeated EAW for the same person and deed. Since a clear provision is lacking in the Law, Art. 454 CCP applies *per analogiam*: in contrast to the final (i.e. irrevocable) judgment as to the substance of the case on which the EAW is based,[62] there is no *res judicata* in extradition cases, because the substance is never examined at this stage. Thus, the affirmation of a repeated EAW remains possible, provided that it contains new facts.[63]

The third point to note is that the requirement of specificity, i.e. the prohibition of being prosecuted or sentenced for an offence other than that for which surrender occurs, is dangerously undermined in Greece. Article 34 paras. (2)–(4) of Law No. 3251/2004 provide for exemptions from this principle, among which is the consent of the executing state after an application from the Appeals Court Prosecutor in this regard.[64]

The fourth point concerns the finding in Supreme Court Judgment No. 1/2011 that where a sentence has in fact been served, this is no longer a prerequisite for denying the execution of the EAW; the Supreme Court interprets Art. 50 of the EU Charter of Fundamental Rights (with regard to the *ne bis in idem* principle) as so indicating. However the issue cannot be considered as definitely settled.[65]

Another point that has arisen is that minors under 13 are not criminally responsible in Greece. EAWs regarding such persons cannot be executed in Greece.[66]

Last but not least, it is very important that EAWs are not unconditionally executed when human rights and discrimination issues arise in cases where the person sought may be further extradited via the issuing state to a third state of ambiguous democratic legitimacy. In Decision No. 1303/2011, the Supreme Court approved Germany's EAW request concerning a suspect for supporting DHKP-C (the acronym for '*Devrimci Halk Kurtuluş Partisi-Cephesi*', meaning 'Revolutionary People's Liberation Party/Front') in Turkey under the condition of no further extradition to third countries (according to Art. 36(2) of Law. No 3251/2004). The minority of the judges in this decision proceeded to an interpretation that was more generous and distinctly protective of human rights; the minority judges called for a rejection of the request on the grounds of a lack of clarity of the accusations and because of the fact that they saw the acts ascribed to the suspect as intrinsically legitimate.[67]

---

[62] Whether the judgment is final on the substance is determined according to the legislation of the Member State in which the case has been tried and not according to the legislation of the executing state: Karaflos 2013, p. 92.

[63] Togias 2013, pp. 1163–1164.

[64] Karaflos 2013, p. 99.

[65] Cf. respectively Karaflos 2013, p. 100.

[66] Karaflos 2013, p. 93.

[67] See the majority and the courageous minority in this decision in AP 1303/2011, Poinika Chronika 2012, pp. 494–495 and 495–496, accordingly.

2.4 The EU Data Retention Directive

2.4.1 According to the Greek Constitution, home, private and family life are inviolable; home searches are subject to law and carried out in the presence of representatives of the judiciary (Art. 9(1)). Violations of this right are punishable as crimes of breaches of peace of home and abuse of power, and the perpetrator shall also pay damages to the victim (Art. 9(2)). Further, every person is protected from the collection, elaboration and use, especially through electronic means, of his/her personal data; an Independent Authority is established for this purpose (Art. 9(a)). Finally, correspondence is inviolable except in cases where national security and the fight against especially serious crime so warrant, and an Independent Authority is also established for this purpose (Arts. 19(1) and (2)). Evidence obtained through violations of all of these three articles is not admissible in court.

EU Directive 2006/24[68] has been incorporated into the Greek legal order through Law No. 3917/2011. The Law provides for some guarantees for the preservation of the rule of law: a) access to data is dependent upon the rules and restrictions laid down in Law No. 2225/1994 concerning the interception of communications (Art. 4); (b) the procedure is supervised by independent authorities like the one protecting personal data (Art. 9); (c) illegal access, elaboration and dissemination of retained data is punishable as a felony with long-term imprisonment (especially when the constitutional order is endangered) or with imprisonment of 2 to 5 years as a misdemeanour when the crime is committed through negligence (Art. 11); (d) data produced in public places may be retained only when serious crimes (treason; public order offences; violent crimes; drug trafficking, crimes against property) or vehicular circulation are concerned (Art. 14).

There have been no judicial challenges with regard to the implementation of the Directive in Greece. However, even with the above safeguards, the Law cannot stand up against the critique already exerted against the Directive itself. The proportionality principle is in particular blatantly violated, in a framework of a general inconsistency of the Directive with Art. 8(2) ECHR: principles like fair warning, foreseeability and the necessity of the measures in a democratic society are not satisfied. The Directive proves unclear, allows retention for disproportionately long periods of time, contains no sufficient procedural safeguards and infringes upon the very meaning of the right to privacy, establishing an Orwellian EU 'Super-Panopticon' undermining freedoms and pluralism as fundamental EU values. Thus, the Directive seems totally unconstitutional, empirically unverified as to its necessity and counter-productive. This is evidenced by the annulment or bypassing of the implementing laws of the Directive in Bulgaria, the Czech

[68] Directive 2006/24/EC of the European Parliament and of the Council of 15 March 2006 on the retention of data generated or processed in connection with the provision of publicly available electronic communications services or of public communications networks and amending Directive 2002/58/EC, [2006] OJ L 105/54.

Republic, Cyprus, Germany and Romania[69] and of course by the respective decision of the CJEU in the jointly judged cases *Digital Rights Ireland* and *Seitlinger and Others*.[70] Nevertheless, Law No. 3917/2011 still remains in force.

2.5 Unpublished or Secret Legislation

2.5.1 This issue has not arisen in Greece. As was noted in Sect. 2.1.3, the requirement of publication of laws is regarded as part of the concept of a rule-of-law-based state. Article 42 of the Constitution provides that statutes passed by the Parliament are promulgated and published by the President of the Republic. Statutes obtain formal legal effect with their publication in the government gazette, and substantive legal effect ten days after publication; i.e. legal validity begins with publication and legal enforceability ten days later.

2.6 Rights and General Principles of Law in the Context of Market Regulation: Property Rights, Legal Certainty, Non-retroactivity and Proportionality

2.6.1 The constitutional rules on legal certainty and non-retroactivity are addressed in Sect. 2.1; see also Sect. 2.8 on judicial review.

2.7 The ESM Treaty, Austerity Programmes and the Democratic, Rule of Law Based State

2.7.1–2.7.3 As noted in academic commentary, especially in a recent Policy Paper of the Robert Schuman Centre of the European University Institute, the establishment of the European Stability Mechanism (ESM) transforms the nature of the EU. The EU is no longer considered a community whose members enjoy only benefits; it is also a community that shares risks.[71] Although the ESM is not formally an institution of the EU, scholars have underlined that we cannot overlook that its function concerns managing financial risks relating to EU members; therefore the

---

[69] Lachana 2013, pp. 1143–1153 and generally. With regards to Bulgaria, cf. the Decision of the Supreme Administrative Court of 11.12.2008, http://secile.eu/wp-content/uploads/2013/11/Data-Retention-Directive-in-Europe-A-Case-Study.pdf, under Sect. 5.2.

[70] Joined cases C–293/12 and C–594/12 *Digital Rights Ireland and Seitlinger and Others* [2014] ECLI:EU:C:2014:238.

[71] Poiares Maduro et al. 2012, p. 8.

ESM must not function in a way that is incompatible with the principles of transparency and accountability, which are fundamental for the operation of the EU.[72] However, in the decision-making process within the context of the ESM, the dominant role belongs to a body composed by the Ministers of Finance of the countries participating in the ESM. The choice of means for a country's rescue belongs exclusively to this body, and their decisions do not require any justification in the form of presenting the ground on which they are based, a requirement that exists for all EU institutions, in accordance with Art. 296 TFEU. This absence of justification is even more significant if we consider that the operation of the ESM is not accompanied by the usual accountability mechanisms for EU bodies, i.e. access to documents and the obligation to report to the European Parliament.[73]

Scholars have additionally identified two other changes brought by the ESM to the institutional architecture of the EU: (a) it alters the balance in favour of transnational over supranational elements of governance and (b) it breaks the unity of the EU legal order, as the legal regime of the ESM is in the form of an international treaty ratified by some members of the eurozone.[74] The first change is particularly important, if we consider that within the ESM, some countries play the role of the lender and others the role of the debtor, and therefore the power relations between them are unbalanced. This development weakens the economic sovereignty of some members, since the loss of their ability to make decisions on specific issues is not accompanied by the creation of decision-making mechanisms at the EU level that would enjoy democratic legitimacy.[75] Regarding the second change, it should be mentioned that this undermines the institutional unity of the EU, as the ESM introduces mechanisms that are not governed exclusively by EU law, allowing deviations in the decision-making process from the guarantees given by the institutional architecture of the EU.[76]

As Chiti and Teixeira have observed, whereas the establishment of the ESM and the amendment of certain provisions of the TFEU lead to constraints of national sovereignty over budgetary matters, this does not involve the reinforcement of all EU institutions, especially those which contribute to the transparency and accountability of the decision making process.[77] Thus, the current structure of the decision-making process of the ESM may contribute to the widening of the EU's democratic deficit and, consequently, also to the democratic deficit in the Members States. Furthermore, scholars have identified that the Memoranda of Understanding

---

[72] Ibid., pp. 8–10.

[73] Ibid., p. 10.

[74] Chiti and Teixeira 2013, pp. 673–708, especially p. 685.

[75] Ibid., pp. 705–706.

[76] A side effect of the non-inclusion of these mechanisms in the EU legal order is that national courts invoking such specificity may refuse to refer cases to the CJEU for a preliminary ruling, as did the Council of State in Decision 1117/2014 (para. 29), arguing that measures taken in the implementation of these mechanisms are not taken under EU law and therefore there is no need to refer a case for a preliminary ruling.

[77] Chiti and Teixeira 2013, p. 689.

(MoUs) signed by Greece and other countries make it clear that such instruments constitute a binding framework that Member States which receive financial assistance must respect in order to continue obtaining financial assistance.[78] As Kenneth Armstrong has observed:

> The degree and manner of the constraint on the policy autonomy of the states is significant. The regular mechanisms of accountability and governance are formally not suspended, yet they are in reality restricted for the states which are subject to the discipline imposed via MoU and controls exercised in the context of the adjustment programmes.[79]

Moreover, no legal evaluation of the international bailout agreements can escape considerations about state sovereignty. However, the Greek Council of State evaded the question as to whether the MoU implied a transfer of sovereignty by characterising the MoU as a political programme and not a legally binding document, since the MoU, unlike in other countries, had the support of the Parliament. In all of the relevant cases,[80] the Council of State has held that the measures taken by the Greek Government (salary cuts and cuts to bonds issued by the State of Greece) in order to comply with the loan agreements are compatible with the Geek Constitution (see below Sect. 2.8).

It is evident from the above-mentioned analysis that only issues within the field of Question 2.7.3 have arisen in Greece, since the Questions in Sects. 2.7.1 and 2.7.2 concern creditors and not debtors, such as Greece.

2.8 *Judicial Review of EU Measures: Access to Justice and the Standard of Review*

It should be noted that Greek courts, from 1984 onwards, recognise the principle of proportionality as a general principle of law, which should rule limitations of rights. Since the 2001 constitutional revision, this principle is enshrined in the Greek Constitution (Art. 25(1)d)). However, as has been pointed out, during the financial crisis, the Council of State has significantly eased or relaxed its control as to the second stage of this principle, in which the necessity of the measure is examined, and has tended to accept the legislature's choices as to the necessity of the measures. At the same time, invoking the principle allows the judge to place some limits on the legislator as to the interference with rights that will be deemed to be compatible with the Constitution.[81]

As regards the principle of legal certainty, it should be noted that recognition of this principle in the jurisprudence of the Greek courts has not led the Greek courts,

---

[78] See Fabrini 2014, p. 73.

[79] Armstrong 2013, as cited by Fabrini 2014, p. 15.

[80] Judgment 668/2012 considering the implementation of the First MoU and Judgments 1117/2014 and 2307/2014 considering the implementation of the Second MoU.

[81] See Contiades and Fotiadou 2013, p. 33.

in the past, to recognise a form of social acquis as regards the level of benefits associated with social rights.[82] The settled case law of the Greek courts is that the legislature has wide discretion in determining the amount of benefits of this type, and thus the level of benefits cannot be taken for granted. Therefore, the recent case law on the cuts in social benefits does not constitute a change of paradigm within the context of Greek jurisprudence. According to the principle of legal certainty as conceived in the Greek legal order, this principle does not guarantee a specific amount of benefits. Moreover, in accordance with the case law of the Greek courts, this principle does not apply to the expectations of bondholders. According to a recent decision of the Council of State, the application of the principle of legal certainty in relations between bondholders and the issuer of the bonds presupposes that the solvency of the state remains unchanged over time, which, according to the Court, is contrary to reality. Therefore, a 'haircut' of bonds is not contrary to the principle *pacta sunt servanda*, since in cases of changed circumstances, the guiding principle is *rebus sic stantibus.*[83]

As for the rule of law, it should be noted that even if we consider that the review of constitutionality of laws is one of the key aspects of this concept, the Greek courts have traditionally been very discreet in relation to the economic choices of the legislature, recognising the primacy of the latter on these issues over time.[84] We should note that the underlying reasoning of the jurisprudence of the ECtHR concerning the review of financial measures is similar, since it recognises a wide margin of appreciation in favour of the legislator.[85] Thus, the recent case law of the Greek courts in relation to the countermeasures of the economic crisis is not a deviation from the established case law.[86] The maximum that the judge can review is whether the legislature has provided sufficient evidence to support its choices.

The judicial review of the measures undertaken by Greece in the implementation of the MoUs does not exceed the limits of the judicial review exercised by the Greek courts in cases in which the crucial legal issue is the compatibility of a rule of EU law with the Greek Constitution. The Greek courts systematically avoid examining the cases at issue from the viewpoint of the protection of the constitutional identity of a Member State or a breach of competence by an EU institution, unlike is the case with the jurisprudence of other supreme courts. In the cases concerning the MoUs, the Council of State has followed this strategy and limited its judicial review of the measures only from the viewpoint of their compatibility with the Greek Constitution and the ECHR, ruling that they are compatible. Furthermore, the Council of State has avoided making a preliminary reference to the CJEU on the issue of whether EU law applied at that time (before the reform of the Treaties), conferred competence on the EU to adopt Council Decision

[82] See Contiades 1999, p. 199.

[83] Judgment 1117/2014, para. 16.

[84] See Kaithatzis 2010.

[85] See *Koufaki Ioanna and ADEDY v. Greece*, no. 57665 & 57657/2012, 7 May 2013.

[86] Judgments 668/2012, 1972/2012, 38/2013.

2010/320/EU, which constitutes the legal basis of the MoUs. This was despite the fact that a relevant preliminary reference question should have been raised, according to the criteria applied by the CJEU concerning the submission of preliminary references. At the same time, the Council of State has avoided making a preliminary reference with regard to the compatibility of specific measures laid down by the above-mentioned Council Decision, (e.g. wage cuts in the public sector) with specific provisions of the EU Charter of Fundamental Rights, for instance Arts. 20, 21(1) and 31(1). In general, as has been pointed out in Greek public law theory, the jurisprudence of the supreme courts tends to play down the importance of EU rules, which could contribute to the interpretation of the rules of the internal legal order, and has not yet developed a consistent constitutional policy regarding the relationship between the national constitution and EU law.[87]

We should also note that there has been a clear shift in the jurisprudence of the Council of State, which is based on an extension of the concept of public interest that now includes financial and service targets in order to avoid fiscal 'derailment' of the country. However, this is a choice made by the judges which is limited to the formative dimension of interpretation of legal provisions, without reaching the point of creating new rules of law by the court, in order to deal with situations that have not been foreseen by the legislator. It is significant that in a Council of State Decision[88] only a minority of three judges held that in cases involving the relationship of rights and the financial crisis, the constitutional provision (Art. 48 of the Constitution) which provides for the partial and temporary suspension of the Constitution due to national security reasons should be applied proportionately, even if the Constitution does not explicitly provide for the implementation of this provision in such a case. As far as the specific questions in Sect. 2.8 are concerned, we can make the observations below.

2.8.1 There is no statistical data concerning preliminary rulings addressed to the CJEU by the Greek Courts. It is commonly accepted that the Greek supreme courts were for a long time reluctant to submit preliminary rulings, which has changed over the last ten years, but is still not a well-established practice, as the recent case law concerning the loan agreements shows.

2.8.2–2.8.5 There is also no statistical data concerning the annulment of domestic acts on the grounds of their incompatibility with the Greek Constitution. In general, we can claim that the Council of State, at least after 1975, has been very active on rights protection, especially the protection of rights concerning individual autonomy, human dignity and the environment. The previous analysis also proves that the review of measures that implement EU law by the Greek courts does not demonstrate a sound doctrinal approach similar to that of the German Constitutional Court or the ECtHR. It is also obvious that such a lack of constitutional policy with regard to the relation between EU law and the Greek Constitution results in a gap in

---

[87] See Yiannakopoulos 2013, pp. 374–375.

[88] See Dissenting Opinion of three judges of the Council of State to Judgment 693/2011.

judicial review. The range of strategies followed by the Council of State, according to scholarly commentary,[89] varies from setting aside the Constitution in favour of EU law to setting aside EU law in favour of the Constitution. Both strategies lack consistency, since they do not provide us with sound criteria that are used constantly. Yet we should not come to the conclusion that setting aside EU law in favour of the Greek Constitution results in a more protective approach for the rights' holders, as the recent case law on austerity measures indicates.

2.8.6 As far as the question of reverse discrimination due to the implementation of EU law is concerned, the answer is that we can distinguish two distinct periods in the jurisprudence of the Greek courts. Since 2009, the relevant jurisprudence has changed and reverse discrimination due the implementation of EU law is considered to be unacceptable. The main doctrinal arguments which have led to this shift are founded on the equality principle provided by the Greek Constitution (Art. 4). However, this shift in the jurisprudence does not imply an automatic implementation of EU law with regard to Greek citizens. It only implies that the judge is obliged to examine whether or not the differential treatment between EU and Greek citizens can be justified according to the equality principle.[90]

2.9 *Other Constitutional Rights and Principles*

2.9.1 One of the consequences of the economic crisis is the further retreat of the justiciability of social rights, since their operation is completely dependent on available funding sources. Moreover, the case law of the Greek courts does not deny the normative content of social rights, but merely disputes the possibility to found claims for steady and fixed benefits on them.[91] Economic crisis further weakens this dimension of rights, so that they alone cannot provide sufficient basis for reviewing the constitutionality of measures taken, without recourse to constitutional provisions which can give rise to justiciable claims, such as the right to property.[92]

Another development in the protection of rights during the financial crisis concerns the transformation of the concept of public interest in the case law. According to recent jurisprudence, the measures taken are not merely intended to satisfy a simple public interest but a serious financial interest, which has two sides. On the one hand, its satisfaction is considered as a prerequisite for the state's ability to serve its basic functions under the Constitution. On the other hand, it is connected to the satisfaction of a fundamental interest of the EU, of which Greece is a member.

[89] Yiannakopoulos 2013, pp. 424–464.

[90] Ibid., pp. 342–348.

[91] See Ntouchanis 2007.

[92] Contiades and Fotiadou 2013, p. 31.

The Council of State and the Higher Special Court (*Anotato Eidiko Dikastirio*), in a series of judgments after 2012 that were not related to cuts in salaries, pensions or other measures taken to comply with the MoUs, have held that any measure which can help to prevent fiscal risk may provide an acceptable foundation for limitation of rights. These cases relate to the so-called 'privileges of the state', i.e. the short limitation periods for claims of citizens against the state and the lower rate of interest charged on such claims compared with the rate charged on claims of the state against individuals. Whereas until 2012, the case law of the Council of State, under the influence of the jurisprudence of the ECtHR, considered that these privileges were not compatible with the principle of equality (Art. 4 Constitution), the provisions of Art. 6 ECHR and Art. 1(1) of the First Additional Protocol to the ECHR, the case law changed after a decision by the Higher Special Court.[93] According to the rationale of the decision, the shorter limitation period for private claims against the government serves fiscal purposes, in particular the rapid resolution of cases with budgetary costs, which helps the state revenue-expenses balance. A similar shift was observed in the case law of the ECtHR in *Giavi v. Greece*.[94] The ECtHR, making a shift from earlier decisions,[95] held that the severe economic crisis can be an imperative reason of public interest, which imposes the restriction of rights arising from Art. 6 ECHR and Art. 1(1) of the Protocol. Therefore, with regard to Greece, we can claim that the economic crisis also affected a number of rights that do not belong to the category of social rights, but fall into the category of individual rights and rights of due process.

Apart from the above rights, another category affected by the economic crisis is rights regarding labour relations. The MoUs impose measures affecting the constitutionally guaranteed collective autonomy (Art. 22), reducing the role of trade unions in collective bargaining as well as the substance thereof, to the benefit of rules imposed unilaterally by the Greek legislature.[96] It is a choice that moves in the opposite trajectory from the ECtHR's jurisprudence on collective autonomy.[97] Moreover, the two MoUs tend to restrict or even eliminate the role of arbitration, by prohibiting increases in salaries and fees granted through arbitration.[98]

[93] Judgment 25/2012.

[94] *Giavi v. Greece*, no. 25816/2009, 3 October 2013.

[95] *Meidanis v. Greece*, no. 33977/06, 22 May 2008; *Zoumpoulidis v. Greece*, no. 36963/06, 25 June 2009.

[96] See Achtcioglou and Doherty 2014, pp. 219–240.

[97] See *Demir and Baykara v. Turkey*, no. 34503/97, 12 November 2008. For this reason, the strategic litigation followed by the applicants before the ECtHR in the case *Koufaki and ADEDY v. Greece* was criticised, on the grounds that the applications to the ECHR were limited only to salary cuts, without further developing the issues related to the changes in working relations, see Gavalas 2014.

[98] However, the Council of State in a recent Judgment (2307/2014) ruled that the relevant prohibition is contrary to Art. 22(2) of the Greek Constitution.

2.10 Common Constitutional Traditions

2.10.1 The question concerning whether the common constitutional traditions of the Member States can be an autonomous source of rights within the context of EU law cannot be answered definitively, since a convincing doctrine of sources from which fundamental rights are derived still remains elusive. However, the jurisprudence of the CJEU offers some guidelines which help us to determine the proper place of the constitutional traditions of the Member States within the context of EU law. On this issue, the jurisprudence of the CJEU on Art. 53 of the Charter is crucial (see Sect. 2.11 below). When the level of rights protection afforded by national constitutions is equivalent to that of the Charter, then common constitutional traditions can be a source of fundamental rights protection. In any other case, the CJEU focuses on whether or not the application of national standards touches upon the unity, primacy and effectiveness of EU law. The solution adopted by the CJEU is that rights protection under the Charter operates as a 'ceiling' for the afforded protection. Yet I consider the approach of the Advocate General in the *Melloni* case[99] to be more persuasive. Common standards of protection require common definitions. We should then 'differentiate between situations in which there is a definition at European Union level of the degree of protection afforded to a fundamental right ... and those in which that level of protection has not been subject to a common definition'.[100]

2.11 Article 53 of the Charter and the Issue of Stricter Constitutional Standards

2.11.1 We cannot examine the issue of stricter constitutional standards and the application of Art. 53 of the Charter without taking into account the CJEU's case law on the issue. According to the interpretation of Art. 53 given by the CJEU in the *Melloni* case, 'national authorities and courts remain free to apply national standards of protection of fundamental rights provided that ... the primacy, unity and effectiveness of EU law are not thereby compromised'.[101] Thus, national courts should apply national standards of protection of fundamental rights under the condition that they do not undermine the primacy, unity and effectiveness of EU law. The courts may only enforce more protective constitutional rights when the basic elements of EU law are not undermined. In other cases, the Charter displaces the national constitution and, as a consequence, the level of constitutional protection is lowered. Yet we have to take into account that there are still situations that

[99] Case C-399/11 *Melloni* [2013] ECLI:EU:C:2013:107.

[100] Opinion of AG Bot in Case C-399/11 *Melloni* [2013] ECLI:EU:C:2012:600, para. 124. On this issue see also Torres Pérez 2014, pp. 308–331, especially p. 326.

[101] Case C-399/11 *Melloni*, supra n. 99, para. 60.

are not entirely determined by EU law, situations where EU law leaves discretion to the Member States for the implementation of EU law. Arguably therefore, we might conclude that when a situation is entirely determined by EU law, the Charter displaces the level of protection afforded by national constitutions, whereas in cases that are not determined entirely by EU law a more flexible approach should be applied. For instance, there are cases in which the interpretation given to a constitutional right is considered, even by the CJEU, to be part of the national constitutional identity, which is being protected according to Art. 4(2) TFEU. In this regard, the possibility of applying a higher standard of protection provided by a national constitution should not be automatically excluded when the primacy, effectiveness and unity of EU law are involved. The wording of Art. 53 as such does not preclude an interpretation that incorporates a mandate for the CJEU to allow for higher levels of constitutional protection in specific cases, when there are no other rights or interests that should prevail.[102]

2.12 Democratic Debate on Constitutional Rights and Values

2.12.1–2.12.3 According to the above-mentioned analysis, we can claim that the main obstacle in Greece concerning the debate on constitutional rights and values within the EU legal order touches upon the restricted judicial review exercised by the Greek courts in cases in which the crucial legal issue is the compatibility of a rule of EU law with the Greek Constitution. The Greek courts systematically avoid examining the cases at issue from the viewpoint of the protection of the constitutional identity of a Member State or the breach of competence of the EU institutions, as is the case with the jurisprudence of other supreme courts. In the recent cases concerning the MoUs, the Greek courts have refrained from making preliminary references to the CJEU, and thus they have refrained from starting a dialogue between a national court and the CJEU that would be crucial for the development of common standards for rights protection.

Considering the restricted standing of private parties to request a review of EU legislation, such omission restricts the level of rights protection in combination with the national courts' lack of jurisdiction to examine the compatibility of EU law with the national constitution. Therefore, it would be necessary to develop mechanisms which would overcome such lacunae in rights protection. Thus, I fully agree that the suspension of the application of, and the carrying out of a review of EU measures, where an important constitutional issue has been identified by a number of constitutional courts, would be a measure to the right direction. This could strengthen

[102] Torres Pérez 2014, p. 327.

the federalist aspects of EU governance, while at the same time respecting a basic precondition for democracy, namely the constant re-evaluation of previous decisions.

2.13 Experts' Analysis on the Protection of Constitutional Rights in EU Law

2.13.1–2.13.3 Concerns about the reduction in the standard of protection and the rule of law in the context of the EU are fairly sound, but the whole issue is not a zero-sum game. As the Greek case indicates, the role of institutions that are entitled to protect rights is crucial. Greek courts have reviewed the measures taken under the bailout agreements only in respect of their compatibility with the Greek Constitution and the ECHR. Such omission is important if we consider that, since the inclusion of the Charter of Fundamental Rights in primary EU law, the whole constitutional structure of the EU has shifted from a constitutional order oriented towards the fulfilment of economic goals to a constitutional order in which a list of fundamental rights has an equal footing. Thus, it would be crucial for the whole system of rights protection in the EU to push the CJEU to rule on the normative content of the rights included in the Charter.

On the other hand, scholars such as De Witte have pointed out that the centralised and unitary form of review exercised by the CJEU in respect of EU law does not fit into the multilevel system of EU governance, since some cases may fall within the scope of application of the Charter and domestic law.[103] Thus, it would be helpful if there were some changes concerning the primacy of the review by the CJEU. A more proactive role for the national courts and other national institutions and a more relaxed approach by the CJEU concerning national standards of rights protection than currently taken would considerably contribute to moving in the right direction.[104]

3 Constitutional Issues in Global Governance

3.1 Constitutional Rules on International Organisations and the Ratification of Treaties

3.1.1 The Constitution of Greece sets the cornerstone of the relationship between Greece and international law in Art. 2(2), according to which, 'Greece adhering to the generally recognised rules of international law, pursues the strengthening of

[103] De Witte 2013, pp. 1523–1538, especially p. 1527.

[104] Ibid., pp. 1527–1533.

peace and of justice, and the fostering of friendly relations between peoples and States'. Thus, general objectives for Greek foreign policy and international co-operation are set.

The way in which rules of international law are integrated in domestic law either automatically or following ratification is regulated by Arts. 28 and 36 of the Constitution. Article 28(1) distinguishes between 'generally recognised rules of international law' and 'international conventions', a distinction which corresponds to the distinction between unwritten and written international law. Customary international law and general principles of international law are considered rules with general international recognition, which are automatically integrated in domestic law without any further need for ratification. International conventions become operative according to their respective conditions as of the time they are sanctioned by statute and become an integral part of domestic law.[105]

The legislature has the competence to ratify international treaties, placing them accordingly above statutes. The judiciary is responsible for classifying an international rule as a generally recognised rule, thus integrating it into domestic law. 'Controversies related to the designation of rules of international law as generally acknowledged' are settled by the Special Highest Court in accordance with Art. 100(1)(f) of the Constitution. The President of the Republic has competence to conclude certain categories of treaties in accordance with Art. 36(1) of the Constitution. Treaties of peace, alliance, economic cooperation and participation in international organisations or unions are ratified by the President of the Republic and published in the government gazette. However, it is the Government that bears responsibility for the political choices reflected in such treaties. Article 36(1) provides that the President of the Republic shall announce them to the Parliament with the necessary clarifications, whenever the interest and the security of the state thus allow.[106]

Furthermore, the Constitution explicitly provides in Art. 36(2) for certain categories of treaties that require ratification by statute voted by Parliament. These include conventions on trade, taxation, economic cooperation and participation in international organisations or unions and all others containing concessions for which, according to other provisions of the Constitution, no provision can be made without a statute or which may burden Greeks individually. *A contrario*, international treaties that do not fall into these categories may be concluded by the Government or by authorised diplomats. However, unless they are ratified by a statute, according to the aforementioned Art. 28(1) of the Constitution, they do not become part of domestic law.

Hence the Constitution explicitly addresses monist and dualist approaches. The Constitution primarily adopts dualism, however the influence of monist theory is detectable in the automatic integration of generally recognised international rules. International law is integrated into the internal hierarchy of legal norms, retaining

[105] Contiades and Fotiadou 2014, p. 720.

[106] Ibid.

its unique character. Generally recognised international rules and international conventions sanctioned by statute are placed beneath the Constitution and above statutes in the hierarchy of sources of law.[107]

3.1.2–3.1.3 Not applicable.

3.1.4 The Constitution provides an efficient legal framework for the participation of Greece in international organisations and the ratification of treaties. The above-mentioned recent, financial crisis-triggered discussion regarding concessions of sovereignty and the transfer of state competences to international organisations by the law incorporating the Memorandum, under Art. 28 of the Constitution, confirms that the Constitution provides the framework for dealing with concessions of sovereignty. Although Art. 28 was not employed by the Greek Parliament and the Council of State confirmed this choice, what was not questioned was the existence of constitutional paths to allow such concessions.

3.2 *The Position of International Law in National Law*

See Sects. 3.1 and 3.3.

3.3 *Democratic Control*

3.3.1–3.3.2 In Greece, international treaties and agreements relating to the areas noted in Sect. 3.1. of this report should be ratified by the Parliament. When such agreements make a concession of sovereignty and transfer state competences to international organisations (like the Troika), according to the Greek Constitution (Art. 28), a three-fifths, enhanced majority of the total number of Members of Parliament is required for ratification. An international agreement or treaty can be subject to referendum under to the Greek Constitution (Art. 44(2)); to be more precise, the relevant provision does not clearly provide for such option but also does not exclude it.[108] The Former Prime Minister proposed that a referendum could be used to ratify the loan agreements (see Sect. 1.4.2.). Yet even members of the Cabinet did not agree, and the referendum never took place.

---

[107] Ibid., p. 721.

[108] Article 44(2) 'The President of the Republic shall by decree proclaim a referendum on crucial national matters following a resolution voted by an absolute majority of the total number of members of the Parliament, taken upon the proposal of the Cabinet. A referendum on bills passed by Parliament, regulating important social matters with the exception of fiscal ones, shall be proclaimed by decree by the President of Republic, if this is decided by three-fifths of the total number of its members following a proposal of two-fifths of the total number of its members ...'

The constitutionality of the loan agreement was challenged before the Council of State. One of the arguments in support of the unconstitutionality of the loan agreement was that the agreement was integrated in the Greek legal order as a piece of legislation by a simple majority and not the qualified majority required for international treaties and agreements. In fact, the ratification of the loan agreement and its compatibility with the relevant constitutional provisions has been the subject of a vivid public deliberation which took place within the community of Greek public law lawyers. No other treaty ratification in the past has been discussed so widely.[109] However, the Greek Council of State rejected the argument of unconstitutionality, ruling that the MoU is merely a political programme, without any legally binding effects on its own.[110] Consequently, the existing constitutional provisions provide only for the formal ratification by Parliament of treaties and international agreements. Yet, the observance of the relevant provisions by Parliament is not under an intense review by the courts, since judicial review by Greek courts does not exceed the so-called *interna corporis* of the Parliament. Thus, considering the Greek judicial practice of the past years, which asserts the observation that the courts have been less active when issues concerning the ratification of a treaty are under review for constitutionality, it might prove helpful if the Greek Parliament were to obtain the means to exercise an intense control over the implementation of treaties and international agreements.

3.4 Judicial Review

3.4.1 The judicial review of the MoUs in terms of their compatibility with the Greek Constitution, EU law and the ECHR are discussed above in Sect. 2.8. The following further issues are worth mentioning here.

In Greece, the relevant rules concerning the review of international treaties are set out in Art. 28 of the Greek Constitution (see Sect. 3.1).

Article 28(3) of the Greek Constitution allows for the delegation of state powers to supranational organisations if this does not conflict with the democratic foundations of the Constitution and human rights. This procedure, according to Greek constitutional theory, serves as a quasi-constitutional revision process outside of the strict standard provided for in Art. 110, since the ratification of a treaty may result in an informal revision of the Constitution. Up until the loan agreements, all international treaties had been ratified by the vast majority of the MPs on the basis of Art. 28. Thus, there are two standards on which judicial review concerning the ratification of a treaty or an agreement can rely, i.e. the ratification process (see

[109] See for example Karavokyris 2014, Mantzoufas 2014 and DSA (Athens Bar Association) Essays on the MOU 2013.

[110] On the legal Status of the MoU, see Vlachou 2012.

above Sect. 3.3) and the content of the treaty, or the agreement in respect of the democratic foundations of the Constitution and human rights protection.

Thus, the critical question is whether the transfer of sovereignty inherent in the loan agreements and in being part of the European Monetary Union (EMU) affect the democratic system of government. The answer is based on an assessment made by the Parliament during the ratification of the relevant Treaty. As far as review by the courts of these matters is concerned, an assessment of the compatibility or otherwise of the Treaty on the Functioning of the EU or the loan agreements with the Greek Constitution would be a review with dubious legal consequences. If it were ruled that the TFEU was not compatible with certain articles of the Greek Constitution, the state would still be bound by the treaty and have legally binding obligations under the treaty. Such decision would not increase the credibility of the court, and would simultaneously reduce its legitimacy. So by the time the Greek judge ruled that the measures adopted in order to activate the European support mechanism are measures 'deriving from the status of Greece as a member of the EU and of its participation in the EMU',[111] the next step was to conclude that 'the measures are justified by invoking serious grounds of public interest which are objectives of common interest of the Member States of the EU',[112] (i.e. budgetary discipline and the stability of the euro area). The public interest has increasingly obtained an EU dimension and must be served by the policies of the countries participating in the EU. Further on, the question of whether participation in the EU raises issues of potential conflict between national constitutions and the provisions of EU law is only marginally considered by the Greek courts. Thus the national constitution is no longer the guarantor of popular sovereignty rooted in a political decision made by the people (popular sovereignty), but becomes a guarantor of a state's compliance with the obligations arising from participation in the EMU, regardless of a possible conflict between such obligations and policy decisions based on popular sovereignty.[113]

3.5 The Social Welfare Dimension of the Constitution

3.5.1–3.5.2 In Greece, the loan agreements have taken the form of MoUs and bilateral loans, in which the IMF is part of the Troika and thus one of the two 'signatories' parties. Consequently, the related public debate does not refer to the IMF as such or to the implication of its policies upon social rights. Instead, the discussion among public law theorists, the public debate in the press (including the

[111] See Judgment 668/2012, para. 35; see also the recommendation delivered by Judge E. Sarp on Judgment 668/2012, (in Greek) available at www.constitutionalism.gr. A recommendation is the proposal of one member of the judiciary on which the Court bases the judgment. Translation by the author.

[112] Ibid.

[113] See Drosos 2011, pp. 764–779, especially pp. 768–769.

Internet) and mass media, as well as the litigation in courts concerns the impact of the MoUs on social rights and the quality of democracy. However, we cannot ignore the fact that the austerity programme in Greece has a strong EU dimension, since it is related to the obligations undertaken by Greece due to participation in the EMU. Monetary integration is not the same as the general process of globalisation through trade liberalisation. The main difference is that it involves a deliberate institutional decision to give up national prerogatives over the exchange rate and interest levels for the sake of establishing a common currency. Within this context, democracy is affected only if we conflate democracy and state autonomy. If we escape such conflation, we should focus on the EU level and on the possible changes which should take place in order to make the EMU more compatible with democracy. In Greece, such a shift in the agenda is being proposed by political theorists dealing with European integration and less often by public law theorists. As far as the social rights agenda is concerned, a dimension often ignored in Greece is that the judicialisation of so-called mega-politics has had poor results.[114] The unprecedented recourse to the Greek courts has created hopes that austerity measures will be defeated in the courts. Yet, as mentioned above, the Greek supreme courts have been hesitant to intervene in the field of technocratic decision-making by the executive that is merely endorsed by the Parliament, since they feel that they are inadequately equipped to overturn such economic decisions. The most they could possibly ask from the governmental officials is a detailed cost-benefit analysis report justifying the necessity of adopted measures.[115]

3.6 Constitutional Rights and Values in Selected Areas of Global Governance

3.6.1 In all areas included in this section of the Questionnaire, there have been scholarly commentary and parliamentary debates. Yet, according to the analysis above, we can conclude that a prominent characteristic of the Greek case is that debates in the Parliament and scholarly commentary do not affect the practice of the courts, which seem to be very reluctant to review any measure that constitutes an obligation undertaken by Greece in the context of the EU with regard to its compatibility with the Greek Constitution or with EU law. Another observation we can make is that the jurisprudence of Greek courts during the crisis has put the boundaries of constitutional pluralism, as a main characteristic of European Public Law, to the test. Greek courts seem to be reluctant to engage in a dialogue with the CJEU; the dialogue between the Council of State and the European Court of Human Rights, which in the past has produced some fruitful results concerning rights

[114] Kaithatzis 2011.

[115] See dissenting opinion of Judge Karamanof to three judgments of the Council of State, 668/2012, 1972/2012, 38/2013.

protection, has turned into a monologue under the 'shadow' of the financial crisis. What the financial crisis has dredged up are the functional aspects of constitutional pluralism, namely the evasion of conflicts, and not the more substantial elements like the displacement of authority by arguments within the context of constitutional discourse.

References

Achtcioglou E., Doherty M. (2014) There Must be Some Way out of Here: The Crisis. Labour Rights and Member States in the Eye of the Storm. ELJ 20:219–240.

Amtenbrink F. (2012) The European Court of Justice's Approach to Primacy and European Consitutionalism – Preserving the European Constitutional Order? In: Hans Micklitz H.W., de Witte B. (eds.) The European Court of Justice and the Autonomy of the Member States. Intersentia, Cambridge, pp. 35–64.

Anagnostopoulos E. (2005) Η έννοια της «δίωξης» στα άρθρα 11 εδάφ. η και 12 εδάφ. Α του Ν. 3251/2004 (The notion of 'indictment' in art. 11 h' and 12 a' of Law No. 3251/2004). Poinika Chronika 9:855–7.

Anagnostopoulos E. (2011) Παρατηρήσεις σε ΟλΑΠ 1/2011 (Remarks on AP (Plenary) 1/2011, Poinika Chronika pp. 504–505.

Armstrong A. (2013) Towards a 'Genuine' Economic & Monetary Union: The New Governance of Fiscal Discipline (2013) Conference paper. The Constitutionalization of European Budgetary Constraints: Comparative and Interdisciplinary Perspectives. Tilburg Law School, Tilburg, 30–31 May 2013.

Baltas A. (2014) Παρατηρήσεις σε ΑΠ 241/2013 (Remarks on AP 241/2013). Poinika Chronika 4:287 et seq.

Brown C. (2003) Case C-112/00, *Eugen Schmidberger, Internationale Transport und Planzüge v Austria'* Judgment 12 June 2003. CML Rev. 40:1508 et seq.

Chiti E., Teixeira P.G. (2013) The Constitutional Implications of the European Responses to the Financial and Public Debt Crisis. CML Rev. 50:673–708.

Chryssogonos K. (2003) Constitutional law (in Greek). Sakkoulas, Athens.

Contiades X. (1999) The consolidating function of social rights. The social acquis paradigm (in Greek). Syntagma 2:199 et seq.

Contiades X, Fotiadou A. (2012) Models of Constitutional Change. In: Contiades X. (ed.) Engineering Constitutional Change. A Comparative Perspective on Europe, Canada and the USA. Routledge, Oxford, pp. 450 et seq.

Contiades X., Fotiadou A. (2013) How Constitutions Reacted to the Financial Crisis. In: Contiades X. (ed.) Constitutions in the Global Financial Crisis: A Comparative Analysis. Ashgate, Farnham, pp. 9–59.

Contiades X., Fotiadou A. (2014) The Hellenic Republic. In: Besselink L., Bovend'Eert P., Broeksteeg H., de Lange R., Voermans W. (eds.) Constitutional Law of the EU Member States. Kluwer Law International, Alphen aan den Rijn, pp. 718 et seq.

Contiades X., Tassopoulos I. (2012) Constitutional change in Greece. In: Contiades X. (ed.) Engineering Constitutional Change: A Comparative Perspective on Europe, Canada and the USA. Routledge, Abingdon, pp. 166 et seq.

Contiades X., Tassopoulos I. (2013) The Impact of the Financial Crisis on the Greek Constitution. In: Contiades X. (ed.) Constitutions in the Global Financial Crisis: A Comparative Analysis. Ashgate, Farnham, pp. 195–218.

De Witte B. (2013) Article 53. In: Peers S., Hervey T., Kenner J., Ward A. (eds.) The EU Charter of Fundamental Rights – A Commentary. Hart Publishing, Oxford, pp. 1523–1538.

Drosos Y. (2011) Constitutional discourse and financial crisis (in Greek). Efimerida Dioikitikou Dikaiou 6:764–779.

Fabrini F. (2014) The Euro Crisis and the Courts: Judicial Review and the Political Process in Comparative Perspective. Berkeley Journal of International Law 32:64–129.

Fytrakis E. (1998) Η απαγόρευση της αναδρομικότητας στην ποινική δικονομία (Non-retroactivity in criminal procedure). Ant. Sakkoulas, Athens.

Fytrakis E (2006) Το Ευρωπαϊκό Ένταλμα Σύλληψης σε εφαρμογή: Νέες εξελίξεις, νέες ανησυχίες (The EAW applied: new developments, new concerns). Poiniki Dikaiosini 2:210–220.

Gavalas N. 2014 Memorandum between the devil and the deep blue sea. From Council of State to the European Court of Human Rights (in Greek). http://www.constitutionalism.gr.

Kaiafa-Gbandi M. (2004) Το Ευρωπαϊκό Ένταλμα Σύλληψης: Οι ρυθμίσεις του Ν. 3251/2004 και η μετάβαση από τη έκδοση στην παράδοση (The EAW: The provisions of Law No. 3251/2004 and the transition from extradition to 'surrender'). Poiniki Dikaiosini 7:1294 et seq.

Kaithatzis A. (2010) The Judicial Review of Financial Policy Measures: Jurisprudential Tendencies and Adjustments in a Transitional Financial and Political Environment (in Greek). http://www.constitutionalism.gr.

Kaithatzis A. (2011) Megapolitics and weak judicial review: A comment on the strategics of observance of the Constitution in the era of memorandums (in Greek). http://constitutionalism.gr.

Kalfelis G. (2006) Το Ευρωπαϊκό Ένταλμα Σύλληψης (Μονοδιάστατη ενοποίηση των ευρωπαϊκών κατασταλτικών μηχανισμών;) (The EAW (One-sided unification of the European repressive mechanisms?)) Poiniki Dikaiosini 2:199–203.

Karaflos A. (2013) Ανακύπτοντα νομικά ζητήματα κατά την πρακτική εφαρμογή του ευρωπαϊκού εντάλματος σύλληψης (Emerging issues during the practical application of the EAW). Poinika Chronika 2:90–101.

Karavokyris Y. (2014) Constitution and crisis (in Greek). Kritiki, Athens.

Kedikoglou F. (2014) Ζητήματα έκδοσης και εκτέλεσης του Ευρωπαϊκού Εντάλματος σύλληψης (Questions concerning the issuing and execution of the EAW). A. Sakkoulas, Athens.

Lachana C. (2013) Quod ab initio non valet, in tractu temporis non convalescit: Νομική θεμελίωση της ασυμβατότητας της Οδηγίας 2006/24/ΕΚ προς το άρθρο 8 της ΕΣΔΑ με αναγωγή στα νομολογιακά προηγούμενα (stare decisis) του Δικαστηρίου του Στρασβούργου (Quod ab initio non valet, in tractu temporis non convalescit: Legal explanation of Directive's 2006/24/EC inconsistency with art. 8 ECHR in connection with the Strasbourg jurisdiction (stare decisis)). Poiniki Dikaiosini 12:1137–1153.

Mantzoufas P. (2014) The financial crisis and the Constitution (in Greek). Sakkoulas, Athens.

Mouzakis D. (2012) Πρακτικά προβλήματα από την εφαρμογή του Ν. 3251/2004 για το ευρωπαϊκό ένταλμα σύλληψης (Practical problems in the application of law 3251/2004 concerning the EAW). Poiniki Dikaiosini 1:57–67.

Mouzakis D. (2009) *Το Ευρωπαϊκό Ένταλμα Σύλληψης* (The European Arrest Warrant). Nomiki Bibliothiki, Athens.

Ntouchanis C. (2007) Lack of justiciability of social rights, as a matter of tracking their regulatory core (in Greek). In: Sotirelis G., Tsaitouridis C., Social rights and crisis of the welfare state (in Greek). Savvalas, Athens, pp. 220 et seq.

Papacharalambous, C. (2002) Το ποινικό δίκαιο του «εχθρού»: Ευρωπαϊκό ένταλμα σύλληψης, τρομοκρατία και έκτακτη αντιτρομοκρατική νομοθεσία στις ΗΠΑ (The penal law against the 'enemy': EU Arrest Warrant, terrorism and extraordinary counter-terrorism legislation in the USA). Poiniki Dikaiosini 2:189–195.

Poiares Maduro M., de Witte B., Kumm M. (2012) The Euro Crisis and the Democratic Governance of the Euro: Legal and Political Issues of a Fiscal Crisis. RSCAS Policy papers, 2012/08:8.

Spyropoulos P.C., Fortsakis T.P. (2009) Constitutional Law in Greece. Kluwer Law International, Alphen aan den Rijn.

Togias S. (2013) Ευρωπαϊκό ένταλμα σύλληψης και έκδοση αλλοδαπών. Επίκαιρες νομολογιακές τάσεις (The EAW and the extradition of aliens). Poiniki Dikaiosini 12:1154–1164.

Torres Pérez A. (2014) Melloni in Three Acts: From Dialogue to Monologue. EuConst 10:308–331.

Vasilakakis E. (2006) 9+1 σκέψεις για το ευρωπαϊκό ένταλμα σύλληψης (9+1 thoughts on the EAW). Poiniki Dikaiosini 2:204–209.

Vlachou I. (2012) Memoranda sunt Servanda? The legal status of the Memorandum of Understanding of the Greek bailout in the Hellenic, European and International legal order. L.L.M. Master's thesis, University of Leiden. http://studentthinktank.eu/wp-content/uploads/2012/11/THESIS_I.VLACHOU-11.pdf.14.

Voulgaris D. (2014) Παρατηρήσεις σε ΑΠ 117/2013 (Remarks on AP 117/2013). Poinika Chronika 4:285–286.

Vrioni K. (2011) Παρατηρήσεις σε ΑΠ 200/2011 (Remarks on AP 200/2011). Poiniki Dikaiosini 5:581–583.

Yiannakopoulos K. (2013) The influence of the EU on the review of constitutionality (in Greek). Sakkoulas, Athens.

4

The Constitution of Spain: The Challenges for the Constitutional Order Under European and Global Governance

Joan Solanes Mullor and Aida Torres Pérez

Abstract Although the constitutional text has remained nearly untouched – only twice has the Spanish Constitution been amended since its enactment in 1978 – global and European governance have deeply transformed the constitutional order. The impact of the process of European integration upon the Constitution is an open and evolving phenomenon, encompassing the challenge to constitutional supremacy, the incorporation of new sources of law, an imbalance between the legislative and executive powers, the enhanced role of the judiciary, the multilevel protection of fundamental rights and the transformation of regionalism as a model for organising the territorial power. First, this report will analyse the constitutional amendments regarding EU membership and the constitutional limits to European integration. Indeed, the only two constitutional amendments were both prompted by the EU. Secondly, the impact of EU integration upon the protection of constitutional rights will be critically examined, with special emphasis on the economic crisis. The obligations deriving from the EU might undermine the protection of constitutional rights, as the introduction of the European Arrest Warrant, the Data Retention Directive and the austerity measures adopted in the context of the economic crisis have shown. Thirdly and more generally, global governance has had constitutional implications, for instance regarding the strengthening of the executive power vis-à-vis the legislative, pressures on the welfare state, the fight against terrorism, the curtailing of powers of the Autonomous Communities and the response to immigration. In this context, it is necessary to recast the relationship

Joan Solanes Mullor is Lecturer of Constitutional Law at Pompeu Fabra University, Barcelona. e-mail: joan.solanes@upf.edu.

Aida Torres Pérez is Professor of Constitutional Law at Pompeu Fabra University, Barcelona. e-mail: aida.torres@upf.edu.

J. Solanes Mullor (✉) · A. Torres Pérez
Pompeu Fabra University, Barcelona, Spain
e-mail: joan.solanes@upf.edu

A. Torres Pérez
e-mail: aida.torres@upf.edu

between the Global-European spheres and the national constitutional order to ensure respect for the principles of the rule of law, the separation of powers and the protection of fundamental rights.

Keywords The Constitution of Spain · Constitutional amendments regarding European integration · The Spanish Constitutional Court · Constitutional review statistics · Fundamental rights · The rule of law as defined in Art. 9 of the Constitution · The principles of legal certainty and legitimate expectations European Arrest Warrant · Data Retention Directive · Privatisation of public services · European Commission and IMF austerity and restructuring programmes, social rights and trade union rights · Curtailing of the powers of autonomous regions

1 Constitutional Amendments Regarding EU Membership

1.1 Constitutional Culture

1.1.1 The Spanish Constitution of 1978 was drafted in the transitional period to democracy in the aftermath of Franco's dictatorship. General Francisco Franco died on 20 November 1975, putting an end to a long dictatorship established after the Civil War in 1939.[1] The Constitution was the outcome of a consensus among the main political parties represented in Parliament after the 1977 June elections.

The drafters were conscious of the need to reach a broad agreement about the basic structural principles of the newly established political order. The main goal was to design a stable democratic system and to ensure the protection of individuals' fundamental rights. The need to reach a consensus about highly controversial issues, such as the model of political decentralisation, on occasion led to ambiguous constitutional provisions in need of further interpretation and political negotiations. The Spanish Constitution was very much influenced by the German and Italian constitutions, regarding for instance the centralised model for the judicial review of legislation. Eventually, the Constitution was ratified in a referendum on 6 December 1978.

1.1.2 On the whole, the key elements of the rationale of the Constitution include (a) a system of representative democracy, separation of powers and the rule of law, (b) protection of constitutional rights and liberties and (c) the territorial decentralisation of political power in Spain. The model of territorial organisation was particularly contested and eventually a sort of quasi-federal state was established, i.e., the *Estado de las autonomías*. The allocation of powers between the central state and the autonomous communities has been a permanent source of conflict, and today this model is under pressure by the secessionist movement in Catalonia.

[1] See generally Ferreres Comella 2013a, pp. 1–24.

The Constitution managed to provide a framework for democratic political contestation and the protection of individual rights. Moreover, Art. 10(2), which indicates that constitutional rights need to be interpreted according to the Universal Declaration of Human Rights and other human rights treaties ratified by Spain, opened up the Constitution to international human rights law.

For a long time, the amendment of the Constitution was regarded as a 'taboo' since the priority was to secure the stability of the democratic system.[2] The fear was that any attempts to modify the Constitution would put the achievements of the democratic regime at risk, and the shadow of the dictatorship still loomed large. Nonetheless, after almost forty years since its enactment, there are more and more voices calling for an overall constitutional amendment regarding issues such as the territorial decentralisation of power, the Senate and the Crown.

1.2 Constitutional Amendments in Relation to the European Union

1.2.1 The Spanish Constitution has been amended only twice since its enactment in 1978. Both amendments were prompted by the process of European integration. Whereas these amendments were specific in their scope and nature, a more profound amendment of the Constitution in light of the constitutional transformations ensuing from EU membership has not yet taken place.[3] Indeed, only the amended Art. 135 explicitly refers to the EU in the whole constitutional text (see Sect. 1.2.3).

1.2.2 In terms of the process for constitutional amendment, the Spanish Constitution is rigid. There are two amendment procedures: the general procedure (Art. 167) requires a qualified majority of three-fifths of both parliamentary chambers (Congress and Senate), and a referendum is not compulsory. Nonetheless, a referendum shall be convoked if at least one-tenth of the representatives in Congress or in the Senate request it.

The Constitution provides for a more demanding procedure (Art. 168) in order to amend certain parts: the Preliminary Title – which includes provisions on the main principles of the constitutional order – basic fundamental rights, the Crown, and for the total revision of the Constitution. According to Art. 168, a qualified majority of two-thirds is required to support the initiative, a general election has to take place and, after the election, the support of a two-thirds majority of both chambers for the final text must be secured. Ratification by referendum is compulsory. In practice, the required qualified majorities generally involve the agreement of the two main political parties represented in Parliament (*Partido Popular*, PP and *Partido Socialista*, PSOE).

1.2.3 The first constitutional amendment took place in 1992 and was deemed to be necessary in order to ratify the Maastricht Treaty. The Maastricht Treaty

---

[2] Ferreres Comella 2000, p. 32.

[3] See Cruz Villalón 2006a, pp. 23–25.

represented a turning point from an economic to a political union and introduced EU citizenship. EU citizens were granted the right to vote and stand as candidates in local elections in their place of residence.

According to Art. 13(2) of the Spanish Constitution prior to 1992, foreigners could be granted the right to vote in local elections (*sufragio activo*), but were deprived of any right to stand as candidates (*sufragio pasivo*). After the Maastricht Treaty was signed and before its ratification, the Government asked the Constitutional Court (CC) about the compatibility of the Maastricht Treaty with the Constitution. The Constitution provides a special procedure for the constitutional review of international treaties prior to ratification.[4] If a treaty is found to be in breach of the Constitution, the treaty may only be ratified after a constitutional amendment. In this case, in Declaration No. 1/1992 of 1 July, the CC held that the Maastricht Treaty was incompatible with the Constitution with regard to the right of foreigners to stand as candidates in local elections.

Eventually, the amendment of Art. 13(2) was enacted on 27 August 1992. Actually, only two words ('*y pasivo*') were added to enable foreigners to stand as candidates in local elections.[5] No specific reference to EU citizens was included. The amendment took place through the general procedure (Art. 167) and without holding a referendum.

The second constitutional amendment was enacted in September 2011 in the context of the European crisis to incorporate the 'balanced budget' rule and limitations to the public debt and deficit in Art. 135 of the Constitution.[6]

---

[4] For a more detailed explanation about this procedure, see Sect. 3.1.

[5] After the amendment, Art. 13(2) of the Constitution reads as follows:

'Only Spaniards shall have the rights recognized in section 23, except in cases which may be established by treaty or by law concerning the right to vote and the right to be elected in municipal elections, and subject to the principle of reciprocity'. The English translation used in this report is available at: http://www.congreso.es/portal/page/portal/Congreso/Congreso/Hist_Normas/Norm/const_espa_texto_ingles_0.pdf.

[6] After the amendment, Art. 135 of the Constitution reads as follows:

'1. All public administrations will conform to the principle of budgetary stability.

2. The State and the Self-governing Communities may not incur a structural deficit that exceeds the limits established by the European Union for their member states.

An Organic Act shall determine the maximum structural deficit the state and the Self-governing Communities may have, in relation to its gross domestic product. Local authorities must submit a balanced budget.

3. The State and the Self-governing Communities must be authorized by Act in order to issue Public Debt bonds or to contract loans.

Loans to meet payment on the interest and capital of the State's Public Debt shall always be deemed to be included in budget expenditure and their payment shall have absolute priority. These appropriations may not be subject to amendment or modification as long as they conform to the terms of issue.

The volume of public debt of all the public administrations in relation to the State' gross domestic product may not exceed the benchmark laid down by the Treaty on the Functioning of the European Union.

4. The limits of the structural deficit and public debt volume may be exceeded only in case of natural disasters, economic recession or extraordinary emergency situations that are beyond the control of the State and significantly impair either the financial situation or the economic or social

The constitutional amendment was prompted by the so-called Euro-Plus-Pact, a package of measures adopted by the European Council in March 2011 to respond to the crisis and preserve financial stability,[7] and, more particularly, by the French-German summit held on 16 August 2011.[8] Several months after the constitutional amendment, the Treaty on Stability, Coordination and Governance in the Economic and Monetary Union (TSCG), signed on 2 March 2012, incorporated the so-called 'golden rule', i.e., the requirement that 'the budget position of the general government must be balanced or in surplus' (Art. 3(1)(a)). Moreover, according to Art. 3(2), there is an obligation to give effect to the financial provisions of Art. 3(1) in national law 'through provisions of binding force and permanent character, preferably constitutional, or otherwise guaranteed to be fully respected and adhered to throughout the national budgetary processes'.

The accelerated process through which Art. 135 of the Constitution was amended may well be contested in terms of democratic deliberation. Indeed, several scholars pointed out that the process had been carried out too quickly and without any public debate.[9] Article 135 of the Constitution was amended in a record time of thirteen days[10] by the end of the summer. Apparently, the President of the Government at the time, José Luis Rodríguez Zapatero, and the leader of the main opposition party, Mariano Rajoy, agreed on the constitutional amendment during a phone conversation.[11]

The amendment took place by means of the general procedure and without a referendum. The proposal for the constitutional amendment, submitted jointly by the PSOE and PP parliamentary groups, followed an urgent and special procedure

---

sustainability of the State, as appreciated by an absolute majority of the members of the Congress of Deputies.

5. An Organic Act shall develop the principles referred to in this article, as well as participation in the respective procedures of the organs of institutional coordination between government fiscal policy and financial support. In any case, the Organic Act shall address:

a The distribution of the limits of deficit and debt among the different public administrations, the exceptional circumstances to overcome them and the manner and time in which to correct the deviations on each other.
b. The methodology and procedure for calculating the structural deficit.
c. The responsibility of each public administration in case of breach of budgetary stability objectives.

6. The Self-governing Communities, in accordance with their respective laws and within the limits referred to in this article, shall take the appropriate procedures for effective implementation of the principle of stability in their rules and budgetary decisions.'

[7] European Council Conclusions, 20 April 2011, http://www.consilium.europa.eu/uedocs/cms_data/docs/pressdata/en/ec/120296.pdf.

[8] Ridaura Martínez 2012, p. 238.

[9] See, among others, Blanco Baldés 2011, pp. 12–15; Jimena Quesada 2012, pp. 350–353; Ridaura Martínez 2012, pp. 249–259; García-Escudero 2012, p. 165.

[10] This was the time from submission of the proposition to amend the Constitution on 26 August 2011 to approval by the Senate on 8 September 2011.

[11] Ferreres Comella 2013b, p. 233.

according to which the proposed amendment was only discussed and voted by the full chamber of the Congress and Senate (without being discussed in the respective parliamentary commissions), and the timelines were reduced. Consequently, the role of minority groups and the parliamentary debate were curtailed.[12]

Twenty-nine deputies and seven senators asked for a referendum, but they did not reach the minimum of one-tenth of all members as required by Art. 167 – which would have meant at least thirty-five deputies or twenty-seven senators.[13]

Hence, the constitutional amendment was not the outcome of an open and broad process of deliberation involving the people, but rather was enacted under pressure from other European governments and the markets.[14] The main goal was to signal Spain's commitment to the balanced budget rule and to the implementation of the ensuing austerity measures in accordance with the limits placed on public debt and deficit. The constitutional amendment was not an occasion for public debate, but the result of an agreement behind closed doors by the leaders of the two main political parties. Paradoxically, in November 2014, the current leader of the PSOE, Pedro Sánchez, announced that he was willing to amend Art. 135 again to ensure the protection of social rights and in particular public education, healthcare and pensions.[15]

1.3 Conceptualising Sovereignty and the Limits to the Transfer of Powers

1.3.1–1.3.2 Article 93 of the Constitution enables the transfer of powers 'derived from the Constitution' to international organisations. According to this Article, '[a]uthorization may be granted by an organic act for concluding treaties by which powers derived from the Constitution shall be transferred to an international organization or institution'. Despite the fact that the EU is not expressly mentioned, this provision was drafted with the future accession of Spain to the EU in mind.

Following this provision, the ratification of an international treaty that transfers sovereign powers to an international organisation needs to be approved by an organic law. This means that the transfer needs to be approved by an absolute majority of Congress. Hence, this clause merely sets the procedure in order to authorise the transfer of sovereign powers, but it does not include any substantive

---

[12] See García-Escudero 2012, p. 179. Indeed, two deputies of the parliamentary group ERC-IU-ICV submitted an individual complaint before the CC, but the complaint was found inadmissible.

[13] García-Escudero 2012, p. 172.

[14] Ferreres Comella 2013b, p. 233.

[15] Europa press 24 November 2014.

limits or requirements regarding the values, principles or objectives that should be respected by international organisations of which Spain is a member.

1.3.3 Nonetheless, the CC has interpreted this provision to contain implicit substantive limits to integration: the respect for state sovereignty, basic constitutional structures, and the system of values and fundamental principles enshrined in the Constitution, in particular fundamental rights.[16] In this decision, the CC established its counter-limits doctrine, following the lead of the German and the Italian Constitutional Courts.[17] The limits to integration were formulated rather broadly, since the Court did not spell out what 'basic constitutional structures' were considered to be or how to understand 'respect for state sovereignty' at a time in which this concept is constantly being revised and reshaped.

1.3.4 The foregoing decision was delivered in the context of the ratification of the Treaty Establishing a Constitution for Europe (TECE) in 2004, when the Spanish Government consulted the CC about the compatibility between the Constitution and the principle of primacy of EU law, expressly stated in the so-called European Constitution.[18] The CC resolved the potential conflict by crafting a distinction between the primacy of EU law and the supremacy of the Constitution. The CC found that the primacy of EU law did not impinge upon the supremacy of the Constitution, since the former referred to the applicability of domestic legislation clashing with EU law, whereas the latter referred to the validity of domestic legislation in light of the Constitution.[19] Following previous case law, the CC stated that the primacy of EU law was grounded on Art. 93, which allowed the transfer of powers to an international organisation. In turn, the CC declared for the first time that Art. 93 contained substantive limits to integration. Eventually, the CC concluded that the TECE was compatible with the Spanish Constitution and that no constitutional amendment was required. In the end, the process of ratification failed after the negative referendums in France and the Netherlands in 2005.

1.4 Democratic Control

1.4.1 The level of democratic control, in particular parliamentary oversight, over the ratification of EU treaties and the subsequent treaty amendments is rather low. As

---

[16] Declaration CC No. 1/2004, of 13 December, para. 2.

[17] Prior to 2004, scholars had criticised the formalist understanding of Art. 93 of the Constitution adopted by the CC, see Pérez Tremps 1994, pp. 36–37. After 2004 and the development of the counter-limits doctrine under Art. 93, scholars understood that the CC had given some teeth to this provision, see Saiz Arnaiz 2005, pp. 56–70.

[18] Article I-6 TECE.

[19] Previously, the Council of State (*Consejo de Estado*) – the supreme consultative body of the Government – had concluded that a conflict existed and the Constitution should have been amended to give priority to EU law. Council of State Report of 21 October 2004.

mentioned above, the ratification of EU treaties needs to be authorised through an organic law, which requires an absolute majority in Congress. The requirement of an absolute majority indicates the need to reach a broader consensus than is necessary to pass ordinary legislation. Still, this majority is lower than the majority for constitutional amendment (three-fifths pursuant to Art. 167 or two-thirds pursuant to Art. 168). In practice, the need to achieve an absolute majority has not prompted a more profound debate regarding the ratification of EU treaties.

Besides the ratification process, the Constitution does not attribute a specific role to Parliament in the European policymaking process or in monitoring the Government when acting at the European level. It is not constitutionally mandatory for the Government to consult or inform Parliament when dealing with EU affairs. The Council of State (*Consejo de Estado*) – the supreme consultative body of the Government – has advocated for a constitutional reform that would enhance the role of Parliament in European affairs.[20]

1.4.2 Moreover, a referendum is not compulsory and the ratification of EU treaties does not usually spur public debate. The Constitution provides for a consultative referendum in Art. 92. The President of the Government may decide to convoke a referendum of a non-binding nature regarding 'political decisions of special importance' with the authorisation of Congress. Indeed, the Government decided to call for a referendum regarding the TECE given the relevance of the constitutional treaty as a crucial moment in the European integration process.[21] In practice, the debate in other Member States and the potential failure of the Constitutional Treaty pushed the Spanish Government to hold a referendum – without much doubt regarding a positive outcome – in order to bolster the legitimacy of the European Constitution.

1.5 The Reasons for, and the Role of, EU Amendments

1.5.1–1.5.2 The only two constitutional amendments that have been made were prompted by the EU for the reasons elaborated in Sect. 1.2.3. The first amendment was due to the decision of the Constitutional Court that declared an incompatibility between the Constitution and the Maastricht Treaty regarding the right of EU citizens to stand as candidates in local elections. The second amendment took place in the context of the economic and financial crisis mainly with the goal of enhancing the trust of the markets and European institutions and leaders regarding the limits to the public debt and deficit in Spain. Thus, the constitutional amendments regarding the EU have been rather limited in their scope, and the EU is only explicitly mentioned in Art. 135.

---

[20] Council of State Report of 16 February 2006 on the amendment of the Spanish Constitution, pp. 108–113.

[21] See Sect. 3.3.

1.5.3 As a consequence of EU integration and the transfer of sovereign powers to the EU, national constitutions no longer regulate the exercise of public power within the state comprehensively. The scope and understanding of several constitutional clauses have been transformed, even though the wording remains the same.[22] EU integration has had a major impact on the constitutional legal order.[23] For instance, domestic judges have acquired the power to set aside legislation that clashes with EU law, whereas under the Constitution they are not allowed to review legislation and must make a reference to the Constitutional Court. The system of sources of law now incorporates EU law, which has primacy and direct effect. The powers of the executive have been expanded vis-à-vis the legislative power, since the Government participates in law-making at the EU level as part of the Council and has an important role in the implementation and execution of EU law. Finally, in the field of fundamental rights, the Charter applies alongside the constitutional bill of rights when national authorities implement EU law.

Given the relevance of the process of integration from a constitutional perspective, several authors have argued that the Constitution should incorporate a specific 'European integration clause'.[24] The current Art. 93 simply regulates the process for the ratification of international treaties, and it does not even explicitly mention the EU. A newly framed 'integration clause' might well include a procedural and a substantive prong. Procedurally, it would be advisable to reinforce the democratic legitimacy of the transfer of powers to the EU and the ensuing constitutional transformations by requiring a broader parliamentary majority and the holding of a referendum if a certain percentage of representatives ask for it. From a substantive standpoint, this clause might include the constitutional limits to integration and the basic principles of interaction with the EU.

2 Constitutional Rights, the Rule of Law and EU Law

2.1 The Position of Constitutional Rights and the Rule of Law in the Constitution

2.1.1 Title I of the Spanish Constitution, entitled 'Fundamental Rights and Duties', enshrines the Spanish bill of rights.[25] Title I is rather comprehensive since it

[22] Walter 2001, pp. 193–196; von Bogdandy 2001, pp. 212–213.

[23] For an analysis of the impact of integration upon the content of the Constitution, see Pérez Tremps 2004, pp. 112–120; Bustos Gisbert 2009, pp. 401–428.

[24] Solazabal Echavarría 2005, pp. 44–46; Albertí Rovira 2006, pp. 457–482; Alonso García 2006, pp. 557–561; Cruz Villalón 2006b, pp. 70–74; Escobar Hernández 2006, pp. 483–489; López Castillo 2006, pp. 501–532; Mangas Martín 2006, pp. 533–556. See also the Council of State Report of 16 February 2006, on the amendment of the Spanish Constitution, pp. 40–108 (with a proposal to amend the Constitution and to add a 'European integration clause').

[25] For this section, see Ferreres Comella 2013a, pp. 235–251.

includes civil, political and social rights. The level of protection granted to those rights, however, varies. From the perspective of the robustness of constitutional protection, one can identify three groups of rights: (i) rights included in Chap. II, Sect. 1; (ii) rights included in Chap. II, Sect. 2; and (iii) principles on social and economic policy included in Chap. III.

All rights and freedoms in Chap. II are deemed to be directly binding on all public authorities and thus they are directly enforceable by courts; additionally, the regulation of these rights is reserved to Parliament (*reserva de ley*; Art. 53(1)).

Among the rights listed in Chap. II, those included in Sect. 1, such as the right to life, physical integrity, free speech, privacy and association, the right to vote and fair trial, among others, are granted a heightened protection. In the case of an alleged violation of these rights, after exhausting the available judicial remedies before the ordinary courts, individuals may submit an individual complaint to the Constitutional Court (*recurso de amparo;* Art. 53(2)). Also, these rights need to be regulated by an organic law, which requires an absolute majority in Congress (Art. 81). Furthermore, they can only be amended following the extraordinary procedure set out in Art. 168 of the Constitution.

Finally, Chap. III includes the so-called principles on social and economic policy, such as the right to healthcare and the right to housing. These rights are not directly enforceable by courts and following Art. 53(3) 'they may only be invoked before the ordinary courts in accordance with the legal provisions implementing them'. The same provision lays down that '[r]ecognition, respect and protection of the principles recognised in Chapter shall guide legislation, judicial practice and actions by the public authorities'. They are thus interpreted as mandates to public authorities and must be taken into account upon the interpretation of other norms.

2.1.2 Even though there is no general constitutional provision stipulating the conditions under which restrictions on rights can be imposed, the Constitutional Court has addressed the issue in its case law. Although some rights, such as the right to be free from torture, might be regarded as absolute, rights can generally be restricted in order to protect other rights or general interests. Any restriction needs to be provided by law and justified under the proportionality principle. The principle of proportionality includes three steps according to which it is necessary to ask: 'first, whether the restriction is useful to achieve a legitimate goal; second, whether the restriction is necessary, in that no more moderate measure could be chosen to sufficiently satisfy that goal; third, whether the costs that the restriction entails are offset by the benefits that are to be achieved'.[26]

Besides the possibility of restricting rights, the Constitution allows the Government to suspend certain rights in specific circumstances (Art. 55). First, in the course of an investigation of 'armed bands or terrorist groups' three rights may be suspended under certain conditions: the right of the arrested person to be brought

[26] Ibid. p. 246.

before a judge no later than 72 hours after arrest; the right to privacy regarding one's home and the secrecy of communications. Secondly, when the Government declares a state of emergency or siege, a list of rights may be suspended, which is very exceptional and in practice has never happened.

In general, according to Art. 10(2) of the Constitution, constitutional rights need to be interpreted according to the Universal Declaration of Human Rights and other international human rights treaties ratified by Spain. This provision has been commonly used with regard to the European Convention on Human Rights (ECHR) and the corresponding European Court of Human Rights (ECtHR) case law.[27]

2.1.3 The principle of the rule of law is encapsulated in Art. 1(1) of the Constitution,[28] and further specified in Art. 9. In short, the principle requires that all public authorities abide by the law. Broadly, the principle requires respect of the separation of powers and the protection of individual rights. Indeed, Art. 9(1) confirms the binding nature of the Constitution upon public authorities and citizens, which was paramount after the dictatorship. As opposed to the constitutional tradition over the nineteenth century, the Constitution was no longer conceived as a political document of a programmatic nature, but rather as a binding norm at the top of the legal order.

More specifically, Art. 9(3)[29] lays down a set of techniques for the realisation of the rule of law principle. First, the hierarchical principle orders the norms in the legal system according to which superior norms prevail over inferior norms (*lex superior derogat legi inferiori*). Basically, the Constitution is at the top, followed by parliamentary legislation and finally governmental regulations. Respect for the hierarchical principle is a condition of validity of any legal provision.

Secondly, Art. 9(3) includes the principle of legal certainty and the principle of publicity. As such, a norm may only enter into force after publication. The main instrument for these purposes is an official bulletin called *Boletín Oficial del Estado*. Individuals cannot be bound by norms that are secret. Moreover, according to the principle of legal certainty, individuals need to be able to foresee what the applicable norms are and how they are going to be interpreted. The principle of legal certainty is key in the civil law tradition (see also Sect. 2.5).

Thirdly, the Constitution bans the retroactivity of norms that establish sanctions or restrict individual rights. Thus, the legislator may enact retroactive norms except in these circumstances. This ban on retroactivity is especially relevant in criminal

[27] Saiz Arnaiz 1999, pp. 156–169; Torres Pérez 2011, pp. 160–164.

[28] See Ferreres Comella 2013a, pp. 26–29.

[29] Article 9(3) reads as follows: 'The Constitution guarantees the principle of legality, the hierarchy of legal provisions, the publicity of legal statutes, the non-retroactivity of punitive provisions that are not favourable to or restrictive of individual rights, the certainty that the rule of law shall prevail, the accountability of public authorities, and the prohibition of arbitrary action of public authorities.'

law and is linked to the principle of *nulla poena sine lege*. Finally, public authorities must exercise their power according to the principle of responsibility and non-arbitrariness.

2.2 The Balancing of Fundamental Rights and Economic Freedoms in EU Law

2.2.1 In the last decade, the Spanish legislator has worked to enhance the economic freedoms recognised in EU law. This has generated tensions with the subnational territorial entities and some groups – such as professional associations – which have rooted their opposition in the constitutional text.

The context, however, is clearly imbalanced in favour of the economic freedoms of EU law against other constitutional principles. The transposition of the Services Directive[30] has altered the competences scheme of all levels of the public administration. The competences of subnational territorial entities, *inter alia*, to establish authorisations for private services and to regulate the protection of the environment regarding hazardous private activities, have been curtailed. The Law 20/2013 of 9 December on the Guarantee of the Internal Market has accelerated this trend and has implemented the freedom of services far beyond the requests of the Services Directive – to all kinds of 'economic activity', in the words of this legislation.[31] These initiatives have altered significantly the constitutional distribution of competences and the principles of political and administrative autonomy of Autonomous Communities and Municipalities.

Another example of these tensions is the debate surrounding the Draft Legislation on Professional Associations.[32] The Draft, based on the freedom of services at the EU level and aimed at bolstering the free movement of services and persons, sought to dismantle several Professional Associations and to reduce their capacity to regulate and intervene in the spheres of activity of their members. The Professional Associations claimed that Art. 36 of the Constitution provided a special recognition of such associations and that the restrictions of the Draft were thus unconstitutional. Finally, the pressure led the Spanish Government to announce the withdrawal of the Draft.[33]

[30] Directive 2006/123/EC of the European Parliament and of the Council of 12 December on services in the internal market, [2006] OJ L 376/36.

[31] Several constitutional complaints against Law 20/2013 have been lodged before the CC by the Autonomous Communities of Andalusia, Canarias and Catalonia.

[32] The Government issued a first Draft Legislation on 20 December 2013 and a second proposal on 11 November 2014.

[33] Cinco Días 15 April 2015.

2.3 *Constitutional Rights, the European Arrest Warrant and EU Criminal Law*

The Framework Decision on the European Arrest Warrant[34] (Framework Decision) was first implemented in Spain by Law 3/2003 of 24 March on the European Arrest Warrant. This law was later replaced by Law 23/2014 of 20 November on Mutual Recognition of Criminal Decisions in the European Union. Law 23/2014 includes a new general clause, according to which this law will be applied with respect for the fundamental rights, freedoms and principles enshrined in the Spanish Constitution, Art. 6 of the TEU, the Charter and the ECHR (Art. 3).

The relevant provisions in the Constitution are as follows:

> Article 17
>
> 1. Every person has a right to freedom and security. No one may be deprived of his or her freedom except in accordance with the provisions of this article and in the cases and in the manner provided by the law.
>
> 2. Preventive arrest may last no longer than the time strictly necessary in order to carry out the investigations aimed at establishing the events; in any case the person arrested must be set free or handed over to the judicial authorities within a maximum period of seventy-two hours.
>
> 3. Every person arrested must be informed immediately, and in a way understandable to him or her, of his or her rights and of the grounds for his or her arrest, and may not be compelled to make a statement. The arrested person shall be guaranteed the assistance of a lawyer during police and judicial proceedings, under the terms to be laid down by the law.
>
> 4. An habeas corpus procedure shall be provided for by law in order to ensure the immediate handing over to the judicial authorities of any person arrested illegally. Likewise, the maximum period of provisional imprisonment shall be determined by law.
>
> Article 24
>
> 1. All persons have the right to obtain effective protection from the judges and courts in the exercise of their rights and legitimate interests, and in no case may there be a lack of defense.
>
> 2. Likewise, all have the right to the ordinary judge predetermined by law; to defense and assistance by a lawyer; to be informed of the charges brought against them; to a public trial without undue delays and with full guarantees; to the use of evidence appropriate to their defence; not to make self-incriminating statements; not to plead themselves guilty; and to be presumed innocent.
>
> …

---

[34] Council Framework Decision of 13 June 2002 on the European arrest warrant and the surrender procedures between Member States (2002/584/JHA), [2002] OJ L 190/1.

Article 25

1. No one may be convicted or sentenced for actions or omissions which when committed did not constitute a criminal offence, misdemeanour or administrative offence under the law then in force.

...

3. The Civil Administration may not impose penalties which directly or indirectly imply deprivation of freedom.

2.3.1 The Presumption of Innocence

2.3.1.1 In Spain, the competent authority to issue a European arrest warrant (EAW) is any judge or court hearing a criminal case. Law 23/2014 has set some specific conditions for the issue of an EAW, in addition to the general requirements established in the Framework Decision. The conditions are as follows: first, the case needs to meet the requirements laid down in the Law on Criminal Procedure to hold a person in preventive imprisonment, or the requirements of Organic Law 5/2000 of 12 January on the Criminal Responsibility of Minors, to decide on detention as an interim measure; secondly, a judicial authority may only issue an EAW to enforce a sentence of imprisonment if the substitution or suspension of imprisonment is not possible; and finally, the judicial authority may issue an EAW only if the prosecutor or the private accusation consider it necessary (Art. 39). These additional requirements contribute to specifying the proportionality principle as it is applied at the moment of issuing an EAW and to a better protection of the presumption of innocence.

According to Law 23/2014, the competent court to execute an EAW is the *Juez Central de Instrucción de la Audiencia Nacional.* Thus, execution is centralised in a single court for the whole national territory.

2.3.1.2 The European Commission Report on the implementation of the EAW offers data on the number of EAWs that have been issued and executed by each Member State.[35] According to the latest report, between 2005 and 2009, on average, Spain issued 533.8 EAWs per year and executed 73.4 EAWs per year.

The Centre for European Policy Studies Special Report offers valuable quantitative information in this regard. In the period between 2005 and 2011,[36] Spain issued 3,766 warrants, which means that Spain issued the fifth largest number of EAWs of all the Member States. Only 563 resulted in effective surrender, which represents a success rate of 14%. The entry into force of Law 23/2014, which as

[35] Report from the Commission to the European Parliament and the Council of 11 April 2011 on the implementation since 2007 of the Council Framework Decision of 13 June 2002 on the European arrest warrant and the surrender procedures between Member States [COM(2011) 175 final]: http://ec.europa.eu/justice/criminal/files/eaw_implementation_report_2011_en.pdf.

[36] See Carrera et al. 2013, p. 6.

mentioned sets additional conditions for the issue of an EAW, might contribute to reducing the number of EAWs issued.

In turn, Spain received 8,702 requests for surrender (third largest number of EAWs received among the Member States), and 5,279 people were surrendered (in absolute terms, Spain is the state that has surrendered the largest number of people).[37] There is no provision for compensation due to surrender for people who are later acquitted.

The cases in which the execution of an EAW might give rise to the violation of fundamental rights might go unreported. NGOs and the media have denounced abuses in several countries. For instance, in Spain a documentary was launched about the case of Óscar Sánchez, who was accused of drug-trafficking and surrendered to Italy.[38] He spent 20 months in prison until it was discovered that he had been wrongly identified and he was eventually released. Cases such as this show that the right to the presumption of innocence might also be impinged upon as a consequence of the automaticity of the execution of EAWs.

2.3.2 *Nullum crimen, nulla poena sine lege*

No significant issues have arisen in Spain.

2.3.3 The Right to a Fair Trial and *In Absentia* Judgments

2.3.3.1 As it is widely known, the execution of the EAW for *in absentia* judgments has been a source of constitutional conflict in Spain. According to settled constitutional case law, the extradition of a person who has been convicted *in absentia* without making the surrender conditional on the opportunity to apply for a retrial violates the right to a fair trial (Art. 24(2) of the Constitution).[39]

This interpretation of the right to a fair trial clashed with the 2002 Framework Decision on the EAW, and even more clearly after its amendment in 2009. According to the Framework Decision, if the person had information about the trial or had been represented by an appointed lawyer, surrender may not be refused or subjected to conditions.

---

[37] See also the quantitative information provided by the Council of Europe, *Note from the General Secretariat to the Working Party on Cooperation in Criminal Matters (Experts on the European Arrest Warrant): Replies to questionnaire on quantitative information on the practical operation of the European arrest warrant – Year 2013.* 8414/2/14 REV 2 LIMITE COPEN 103 EJN 43 EUROJUST 70, Brussels, 31 July 2014: http://www.statewatch.org/news/2014/aug/eu-council-eaw-ststs-2013-8414-rev2-14.pdf.

[38] See: http://blogs.ccma.cat/senseficcio.php?itemid=53778.

[39] Judgment CC No. 91/2000, of 30 March, paras. 12–13 (this interpretation was contested within the Court, see the dissenting opinions).

In 2009, the CC was confronted with a case in which an English national, resident in Spain, had been sentenced in Romania to four years of imprisonment in his absence, although he had been represented by a lawyer of his choice. In its judgment, the CC held that the surrender of a person who has been condemned *in absentia* without making the surrender conditional on the possibility to obtain a retrial violates Art. 24(2) of the Constitution. Unfortunately for the applicant, he had already been surrendered by the time the CC decided the case.[40]

Two years later, in a similar case involving an Italian national who had been condemned *in absentia* to ten years of imprisonment for the crime of bankruptcy fraud in Italy, the CC decided to make a preliminary reference to the Court of Justice of the European Union (CJEU) for the first time ever. This is the well-known *Melloni* case. The reference included three questions about the interpretation and validity of the relevant provision of the EAW Framework Decision and the interpretation of Art. 53 of the Charter.[41]

In a nutshell, the CJEU upheld the validity of the Framework Decision in light of Arts. 47 and 48 of the Charter.[42] It did not even consider the CC's suggestion to interpret the Charter as providing a more extensive protection than the ECHR. The CJEU was satisfied with stating that the level of protection in the EU was compatible with the ECHR.[43] However, while states are allowed to provide for better protection than the ECHR, the CJEU rejected the possibility for the CC to grant a higher level of protection than the Charter in this case.[44]

Eventually, the CC overturned previous case law and revised the interpretation of Art. 24(2) of the Constitution regarding *in absentia* judgments with the consequence that the standard of constitutional protection was lowered.[45]

2.3.4 The Right to a Fair Trial

Within the domain of the right to a fair trial, the CC has held that, when a person has already consented to the execution of an EAW, the addition of new grounds for surrender without a previous audience amounts to a violation of the right to a fair

[40] Judgment CC No. 99/2009, of 28 September. See Izquierdo Sans 2010, pp. 218–225; Cedeño Hernán 2010, pp. 1–15; Fontanelli 2010, p. 372; Torres Pérez 2010, pp. 441–472.

[41] About the preliminary reference, see among others, Arroyo Jiménez 2011, pp. 1–25; Revenga Sánchez 2012, pp. 139–150; González Pascual 2012, pp. 161–178; Pérez Manzano 2012, pp. 311–345; Torres Muro 2013, pp. 343–370.

[42] Case C-399/11 *Melloni* [2013] ECLI:EU:C:2013:107. For comments on the CJEU preliminary ruling see, among others, De Boer 2013, pp. 1083–1104; Martín Rodríguez 2013, pp. 1–13; Skouris 2013, pp. 229–243; García Sánchez 2013, pp. 1137–1156; Groussot and Olsson 2013, pp. 7–35; Brkan 2013, pp. 139–145.

[43] For a critical appraisal of the CJEU reasoning regarding this issue, see Torres Pérez 2014, pp. 314–315; Diez-Hochleitner 2013, pp. 21.

[44] For the interpretation of Art. 53 of the Charter, see Sect. 2.11.

[45] Judgment CC No. 26/2014, of 13 February.

trial.[46] Also, the CC has held that the lack of a right to appeal the decision to execute an EAW does not violate the right to a fair trial, since this is not a decision about the merits of the case.[47]

For the statistics and individual cases reported, see Sect. 2.3.1.2.

2.3.5 The Right to Effective Judicial Protection: The Principle of Mutual Recognition

Regarding the tension between mutual recognition and constitutional rights see Sect. 2.3.3 about trials *in absentia.*

2.3.6 Other Aspects of EU Criminal Law – The Principle of *Ne Bis in Idem*

According to the Framework Decision, the principle of *ne bis in idem* can, depending on the circumstances, be a ground for either compulsory (Art. 3(2)) or optional (Art. 4(2), (3) and (5)) non-execution of an EAW.

In a case before the CC, the applicant argued that the EAW issued by France to enforce a sentence of 20 years of imprisonment regarded the same acts for which a petition of extradition had been rejected in 1989. At that time, the extradition had been rejected on the basis of the principle of reciprocity, since the person accused was a Spanish national. The CC held that decisions in extradition procedures do not have the effect of *res iudicata* and may, in certain circumstances, be replaced by others. In that case, the reason to refuse the execution had to do with the existing legal framework, which had been modified following the Framework Decision on the EAW. In addition, the reason to request the surrender was not the same, since extradition had first been sought to prosecute the person and the subsequent EAW was issued in order to enforce the sentence.[48]

2.4 The EU Data Retention Directive

2.4.1 The Constitution recognises the right to private and family life (Art. 18(1)), and provides as follows:

Article 18

1. The right to honour, to personal and family privacy and to the own image is guaranteed.

---

[46] Judgment CC No. 181/2011, of 21 November.

[47] Judgment CC No. 177/2006, of 5 June.

[48] Ibid.

> 2. The home is inviolable. No entry or search may be made without the consent of the householder or a legal warrant, except in cases of *flagrante delicto.*
>
> 3. Secrecy of communications is guaranteed, particularly regarding postal, telegraphic and telephonic communications, except in the event of a court order.
>
> 4. The law shall restrict the use of data processing in order to guarantee the honour and personal and family privacy of citizens and the full exercise of their rights.

Under this broad wording, the Constitution protects individuals from interferences by public authorities in the spheres of personal and family life. In addition, the Constitution enshrines two other more specific rights that are relevant in the overall constitutional debate about the EU Data Retention Directive.[49]

First, the Constitution guarantees the secrecy of communications, with the exception of searches and seizures previously authorised by a court order (Art. 18 (3)). In well-established case law, the CC has held that this right protects the act of communication itself, without a necessary link to private life.[50] In other words, this right offers a formal protection of the communication process regardless of its content. Secondly, the Constitution contains a clear mandate for the legislator to limit the use of data processing in order to protect the private and family life of individuals (Art. 18(4)). Although it is formulated as a mandate, the CC has interpreted this provision as a truly individual fundamental right similar to the other rights recognised in Chap. II, Sect. 1.

These constitutional provisions have conditioned the implementation of the EU Data Retention Directive in the period 2006–2014, but only in relation to the safeguards on the access to data. The rule of blanket data retention has not been disputed. In this regard, the legislator has considered that the constitutional protection of personal data is fulfilled with the obligation to obtain a court order in the context of a criminal investigation of a serious crime.[51] The legislator understands, in line with the spirit of the Directive, that the data to be retained do not reveal the content of the communications and, therefore, these are only circumstantial data. Nonetheless, and due to the specific formal protection of all types of communications guaranteed by Art. 18(3) of the Constitution, a court order is compulsory in the event of access to data by public authorities. Three exceptions to the compulsory court order regime should be highlighted: access to the International Mobile Subscriber Identity (IMSI) data regarding especially prepaid mobile phones;[52] the

---

[49] Directive 2006/24/EC of the European Parliament and of the Council of 15 March 2006 on the retention of data generated or processed in connection with the provision of publicly available electronic communications services or of public communications networks and amending Directive 2002/58/EC, [2006] OJ L 105/54.

[50] The landmark judgment is Judgment CC No. 114/1984, of 29 November.

[51] Article 7, Law 25/2007 of 18 October regarding the Retention of Telecommunications Data and Public Communications Networks.

[52] Single Additional Provision Law 25/2007. The IMSI data is a combination of algorithms which prevents telecommunications fraud (it allows the identification of the mobile phone). However, the IMSI itself does not allow the identification of the buyer of the phone or the content of the communication. A court order is required to access this information beyond the access of the mere

investigation of terrorism and organised crime,[53] and the possibility of suspension of these rights when a state of emergency or siege is declared.[54]

On the other hand, Spanish courts have only added a cautious interpretation of the scope of Law 25/2007 of 18 October implementing the EU Data Retention Directive. The legitimate aim of the access and use of the data retained, i.e. 'investigation, detection and prosecution of serious crime', must be determined case by case considering the nature of the offence and in accordance with the proportionality principle.[55] Spanish courts have declared that the expression 'serious crime' cannot automatically be interpreted in the sense of serious crimes as defined in criminal law (i.e. the formal definition under criminal law of a serious crime does not imply *per se* the existence of a legitimate aim for the purposes of Law 25/2007, which must be determined case by case). Yet ordinary courts have raised neither a constitutional challenge before the CC nor a preliminary reference to the CJEU. Only one, timid constitutional concern regarding Law 25/2007 has been voiced, *obiter dicta*, by the Spanish Supreme Court (SC), and this referred to the type of law regulating the data retention measures: since a fundamental right was at stake, the SC deemed an organic law to be more appropriate than an ordinary law.[56]

The annulment of the EU Data Retention Directive by the CJEU[57] has not led to the invalidation of Law 25/2007. This implementing measure is still in force. After the annulment of the EU Data Retention Directive in 2014, the legislator has only introduced minor amendments regarding the sanctioning measures and the procedure for access to data. The procedure shall operate through an electronic format and only government agents – police, customs surveillance and intelligence officers – are able to request 'essential information for the aims of the Law'.[58] There is no change to the rule of blanket data retention – or the data to be retained – and, therefore, in light of the inaction on the part of the Spanish legislator, it appears that the initiative of the EU legislator will be necessary to change the national law implementing the EU Data Retention Directive.

IMSI data, as well as to access the specific register of prepaid mobile phones created by the Single Additional Provision Law 25/2007 (Judgment SC No. 249/2008, of 20 May, para. 4).

[53] See Art. 55(2) of the Spanish Constitution and Art. 579(3) of the Law on Criminal Procedure, approved by the Royal Decree of 14 September of 1982.

[54] Article 55(1) of the Spanish Constitution allows the search and seizure of all types of communications in the case of a declaration of one of the two more serious exceptional situations (states of emergency and siege, but not the state of alarm). See also the Organic Law 4/1981 of 1 June regarding the States of Alarm, Emergency and Siege.

[55] Order of the Provincial Court of Madrid (Section 30) No. 572/2013, of 11 July, para. 2.

[56] Judgment SC No. 249/2008, of 20 May, para. 4. Under Art. 81 of the Constitution, an organic law is required to regulate the essential elements of some fundamental rights (rights under Art. 18 of the Constitution are included). As stated in previous sections, an organic law is a source of law with the force of legislation, which needs an absolute majority to be passed.

[57] Joined cases C–293/12 and C–594/12 *Digital Rights Ireland and Seitlinger and Others* [2014] ECLI:EU:C:2014:238.

[58] New Art. 6(2) Law 25/2007, as amended by Final Additional Provision 4(1) of Law No. 9/2014 of 9 May regarding Telecommunications.

The origin in EU law of the rule of blanket data retention may have well facilitated its incorporation into national law. It is uncertain whether an analysis based only on constitutional grounds would have led to a declaration of unconstitutionality. Arguably, the formal protection of communications, well established in the case law of the CC under Art. 18(3) of the Constitution, raises some doubts about the constitutionality of the rule. Ordinary courts, however, have not raised any constitutional challenge in the CC and, even for the cases in which a court order is not needed – in the case of the three exceptions mentioned above – they have upheld the measure.[59] It appears that for Spanish courts, the safeguard of a court order is enough to sustain the compatibly between the Constitution and the rule of blanket data retention. However, it should be pointed out that in the cases before the SC in which Law 25/2007 has been applicable, the SC has emphasised its nature as a national norm implementing EU law.[60] This nature has had an important impact on the reasoning of the SC and might have deterred it from submitting a constitutional challenge before the CC.

2.5 *Unpublished or Secret Legislation*

2.5.1 As seen in Sect. 2.1.3 on the rule of law, the publication of legal norms is a constitutional obligation established under Art. 9(3) of the Constitution. Moreover, Art. 2(1) of the Civil Code establishes that this general principle is applicable to all kinds of norms. This overall mandate is further reinforced by the Constitution with the obligation to publish State legislation (Art. 91) and international treaties (Art. 96 (1)). The legislation of Autonomous Communities must also be published according to each Autonomous Statute. Finally, administrative regulations with general and binding effects must also be published.[61]

Taking into account these constitutional and legislative references to the principle of publicity of norms, the CC has established a direct connection to the requirements of a democratic state.[62] The CC has declared that only the publicity of norms guarantees the subjection of citizens to the legal system and the exercise of

[59] See Judgment SC No. 249/2008, of 20 May.

[60] Ibid. This SC judgment covers all the EU legislative history and the ECHR Convention system approach in the field of personal data. It also confronts, in some way, the case law of the CC with the aforementioned standpoints. The SC ultimately relied heavily on the new framework of Law 25/2007 and the EU Data Retention Directive, and considered all the previous considerations to have been overcome.

[61] Article 52 of Law 30/1992 of 26 November of Rules on Public Administration and Administrative Proceedings. In October 2016, this provision will be derogated and replaced by a provision with identical effects: Art. 131 of Law 39/2015 of 1 October of Rules on Public Administrative Proceedings.

[62] Judgment CC No. 179/1989, of 2 November, para. 2.

their rights.[63] In practice, secret or unpublished legislation has not been an issue in Spain under the 1978 Spanish Constitution.

In view of the above, it seems plausible to say that secret norms and measures in Spain would be declared at least – in line with the CJEU decision on the *Heinrich* case – to be without general and binding effects on citizens. Moreover, in light of the well-established constitutional principle of publicity and the strong position of the CC, secret norms would be declared invalid.

2.6 Rights and General Principles of Law in the Context of Market Regulation: Property Rights, Legal Certainty, Non-retroactivity and Proportionality

2.6.1 In the last two decades Spain has faced the liberalisation of several markets on the impulse of the EU. The telecommunications, energy and transport markets are examples of the decisive influence of the EU. In this transition from public monopolies to liberal markets, property rights, and principles like non-retroactivity, legal certainty and proportionality have been affected, *inter alia*, by unexpected changes in the regulatory framework and the imposition of public service obligations on private companies, the alteration of property rights and new regulatory bodies. Indeed, these troubles are commonly shared by all European countries that have faced liberalisation on the impulse and under the supervision of the EU.[64]

As an example, changes in the legal framework of the renewable energy market have raised a huge debate in Spain. First, the elimination of the incentives to the renewable energy sector in 2012[65] and, secondly, the unexpected changes in the payment scheme of energy in 2014, which diminished the expected incomes of pre-existing renewable energy premises,[66] have led the renewable-energy sector to challenge these decisions before the Spanish courts alleging, *inter alia*, the infringement of the principles of legitimate expectations and legal certainty. EU law is at the forefront of this debate because these changes were made in order to implement Directive 2009/28/EC.[67] The resolution of this conflict, with the possible intervention of the European institutions, is still pending.[68]

---

[63] Ibid.

[64] For a general overview of the liberalisation of certain markets piloted by the EU and the issues of national reception – from the political, institutional, cultural and legal points of view – see the seminal work of Majone 1996.

[65] Royal Decree-Law 1/2012, of 27 January.

[66] Law 24/2013, of 26 December and Royal Decree 413/2014, of 6 June.

[67] Directive 2009/28/EC of the European Parliament and of the Council of 23 April 2009 on the promotion of the use of energy from renewable sources [2009] OJ L 140/16.

[68] Several Autonomous Communities have lodged constitutional challenges and conflicts of competence (Catalonia, Andalusia and Extremadura) before the CC. Also, renewable energy companies and environmental associations have brought several actions for judicial review of the

2.7 The ESM Treaty, Austerity Programmes and the Democratic, Rule-of-Law-Based State

2.7.1 The Treaty Establishing the European Stability Mechanism (ESM Treaty) imposes on Spain a mandatory contribution in the capital stock that amounts to 11.9037% of the total capital stock of the ESM.[69] Spain would be obliged to contribute 83,514 million EUR should the maximum calls allowed under the ESM Treaty be made. This corresponds to 19.73% of Spain's yearly budget for 2014 and 7.89% of its GDP in 2014.[70]

These data show that the ESM Treaty, if the calls were activated, would heavily determine the budget, and Spain's financial and expenditure obligations. The budgetary autonomy of the State, specially the prerogatives of the Government and Parliament regarding the drafting and approval of the State's general budget, as well as the financial autonomy of the Autonomous Communities, could be jeopardised by the capital calls from the ESM.[71] The ESM Treaty, the imposition of limits to the public debt and deficit (in the TSCG), the European Commission supervision of Member States' budgets prior to their approval (Two-Pack obligations) and the imposition of additional measures to fix macroeconomic imbalances (MIP framework) are factors which challenge the principle of financial autonomy of the Member States.

Despite this significant impact, a serious constitutional debate about the ESM Treaty provisions has not been launched. The possibility to submit this Treaty to an *ex ante* review by the CC –pursuant to Art. 95 of the Constitution – was not even raised, and the CC has not addressed the issue after the ratification and entry into force of the Treaty either. In the context of the debate about the TSGC, the CC has

administration (more than 100 have been heard by the SC since 9 September 2014). The Association to Support Renewable Energies (*Coordinadora de Apoyo a las Energías Renovables*), which includes more than 50 entities from this sector, has stated that it is preparing legal action at the EU level against the measures taken. Nonetheless, until now, the international strategy lead by international investors has been to present actions before international arbitrators under the Energy Charter Treaty: several actions have been brought before the International Centre for Settlement of Investment Disputes (ICSD), the Stockholm Chamber of Commerce (SCC) and the United Nations Commission on International Trade Law (UNICTRAL).

[69] Annex I ESM Treaty, Contribution Key for the Kingdom of Spain. The capital stock after the contributions of all the states amounts to 700,000 million EUR.

[70] The total amount of the yearly budget for 2014 is 423,231 million EUR (Law 22/2013 of 23 December regarding the General Yearly Budget for 2014). The yearly GDP for 2014 was 1,058,469 million EUR according to data provided by Eurostat and *Instituto Nacional de Estadística* (the Spanish Statistical Office).

[71] In Spain, the Government drafts the general state budget and Parliament approves it by passing a law. Parliament can amend the budget during the legislative process, but any amendments implying an increase of the expenditures or a decrease in the incomes must be approved by the Government (Art. 134 of the Constitution). In relation to the Autonomous Communities, the Constitution recognises their financial autonomy and they are entitled to draft and approve their own budgets (Art. 156 of the Constitution).

declared that the central Government – based on its coordination powers and competence on general economic planning – can intervene and supervise the Autonomous Communities' budgets, to guarantee budget stability, and that these powers do not unlawfully impinge upon the financial autonomy of the latter.[72]

In this regard, the incorporation of the fiscal compact golden rule (budget stability or surplus) in national law, 'preferably', in the words of the TSCG,[73] by means of a constitutional provision, is another example of a mandate coming from the EU without being preceded by a thorough constitutional and democratic debate as discussed in greater detail in Sect. 1.5.

The need to gain access to financial markets at reasonable interest rates moved Spain to go further in the introduction of the golden rule of budget stability. Instead of passing a bill, Spain established at the constitutional level the absolute priority of the payment of public debt over other national expenditures in the amendment to Art. 135 (see Sect. 1.2.3), which included para. 3 according to which: '… Loans to meet payment on the interest and capital of the State's Public Debt shall always be deemed to be included in budget expenditure and their payment shall have absolute priority. These appropriations may not be subject to amendment or modification as long as they conform to the terms of issue. …'.

Spain changed its priorities and expressed a strong payment commitment to the financial markets over other public expenditures, for instance in the social, education or welfare fields. Again, this important rule, meaning a shift in the balancing of the rights of citizens with those of the international creditor community, especially in the economic, social and cultural spheres, was introduced together with the incorporation of the golden rule and without a thorough constitutional and democratic debate.

In short, the severe impact of the economic and financial crisis in Spain have placed the country in a difficult position in negotiating and discussing the economic and financial measures to fight the crisis at the European Union level.

2.7.2 Other initiatives such as Eurobonds and the Banking Union were seen in Spain as alleviating measures to overcome the economic and financial crisis, especially to decrease dependence on the financial markets to get loans. For these reasons, the measures were generally uncontested from the constitutional perspective.

2.7.3 Nonetheless, some debates and contestation from the constitutional perspective have taken place in relation to certain austerity measures introduced by the Spanish Government. Despite the fact that Spain has not been subject to an official bailout, the banking rescue programme of Spanish financial institutions in 2012, the negative alert mechanism reports and the recommendations of the European Commission and the Council to carry out structural reforms have obliged Spain to launch several austerity programmes that have affected civil servants and other

---

[72] Judgment CC No. 215/2014, of 18 December.

[73] Article 3(2) TSGC.

public employees, and the quality, access and organisation of public services. Some of the measures and their origin will be addressed in greater detail in Sect. 3.5.

From the constitutional perspective, public employees have challenged the suspension of certain benefits before Spanish courts on the grounds of legitimate expectations and the prohibition of retroactivity. One of the contested measures was the suppression of the 'extra pay' of December 2012 by Royal Decree-Law 20/2012 of 13 July (the extra pay is included in the annual salary of an employee but is paid in two specific months, normally in December and June, together with the monthly payment). The decision was taken on 15 July and, therefore, the period between 1 June and 14 July could have generated a proportional payable right of the 'extra pay'. Lower judges and courts had decided differently on the issue, and finally several of them requested the CC to rule on the constitutionality of this measure. The Spanish Government and some Autonomous Communities had decided, before the resolution of the case by the CC, to reinstate this proportional amount of the 'extra pay'. Therefore, the CC declared the constitutional questions referred by the ordinary courts to be extinguished – without entering into the merits – since the object of the claims in these cases no longer existed.[74]

The reform of the labour market as a consequence of the austerity programmes has also had a special impact on public employees.[75] Most notable were the 5% reduction in the wages of public employees[76] and the possibility for the public administration to suspend or unilaterally modify collective agreements in the public sector for economic reasons.[77] Both measures have been contested based on arguments of their incompatibility with the right to collective bargaining and trade union freedoms (Arts. 28 and 37 of the Constitution). However, the CC upheld the decrease in salary,[78] and the new power of the public administration to suspend or modify collective agreements has only been condemned by the International Labour Organization (ILO).[79]

Finally, the healthcare reform introduced by the Government as part of its austerity measures has also been challenged before the CC.[80] The exclusion of illegal immigrants from the public healthcare system, except in cases of emergency situations, pregnancy and minors, and the pharmaceutical co-payment mechanism have been contested from the point of view of the constitutional right to

[74] Judgment CC No. 83/2015, of 30 April, regarding the extinction of the preliminary reference sent by the *Audiencia National* (National High Court). The other preliminary references will follow this same result.

[75] See Luz Rodríguez 2014, pp. 128–139.

[76] Royal Decree Law No. 8/2010, of 20 May.

[77] Article 32, Law 7/2007, of 12 April of the Basic Public Employees' Statute (as amended by Royal Decree Law n° 20/2012 of 13 July).

[78] Judgment CC No. 85/2011, of 7 June.

[79] 371st Report ILO, of 13–27 March 2014.

[80] Royal Decree Law No. 16/2012 of 20 April.

healthcare.[81] The European Committee of Social Rights has considered that such denial of access to healthcare for illegal immigrants is contrary to Art. 11 of the European Social Charter.[82] Moreover, several Autonomous Communities have decided to secure universal access to healthcare for illegal immigrants. The Government has challenged the norms adopted by the Basque Country and Navarra before the CC. The judgment is still pending but, in the meantime, the CC has lifted the suspension of these norms.[83] Also in relation to the healthcare system, the CC has declared unconstitutional the legislation of the Autonomous Communities of Catalonia and Madrid establishing the obligation to pay one euro per prescription.[84] However, this judgment should be read in light of a conflict of competences, i.e. the Autonomous Communities cannot impose extra charges in the healthcare system on their own (or without the intervention of the national Government).

2.8 Judicial Review of EU Measures: Access to Justice and the Standard of Review

2.8.1 Judicial review of EU measures in Spain through the preliminary ruling mechanism is, in practice, very limited due to the inaction of national judges. In the period 2006–2014, national courts submitted a total of 178 references for a preliminary ruling, out of which only one was a request for a preliminary ruling on the validity of an EU measure.[85] Lower courts have been the most active in submitting references about the interpretation of EU law, with the submission of a total of 140,[86] while the SC has submitted 37 requests. The sole submission of a request for a preliminary ruling on the validity of an EU measure was made by the CC in *Melloni* (see Sect. 2.3.3). These data show that Spanish courts are very reluctant to ask the CJEU to decide on the validity of an EU measure.

2.8.2–2.8.5 On the other hand, the CC has sustained a long-standing position of not assessing the legality of EU measures: conflicts between EU law and national law,

---

[81] To date, the only decisions of the CC are the Orders CC No. 239/2012, of 12 December and No. 114/2014, of 8 April, in which the CC partially lifted the suspension of the legislation of the Autonomous Communities of the Basque Country and Navarra on the ground that the benefits of the exclusion of illegal immigrants cannot outweigh the right to healthcare. See also Sect. 3.5.

[82] Conclusions XX-2 of the European Committee of Social Rights, November 2014.

[83] Order CC No. 239/2012, of 12 December; Order No. 114/2014, of 8 April.

[84] Judgments CC No. 71/2014, of 8 May and No. 85/2014, of 29 May.

[85] Data extracted from search in http://curia.europa.eu/ (Period of search: 1 January 2006 to 1 September 2014).

[86] The *Audiencia Nacional* (National High Court) has sent 3 references; the *Tribunales Superiores de Justicia* (High Courts of Justice of Autonomous Communities) 33; the *Audiencias Provinciales* (Provincial Courts) 22; *Juzgados de primera instancia de todos los órdenes jurisidiccionales* (Courts of First Instance) 80. Other administrative courts have sent 2 references.

and the validity of EU measures have been considered non-constitutional issues.[87] Therefore, these conflicts and their resolution have been left to the ordinary courts. In this line, the CC's recent case law shows an effort to emphasise the role of ordinary courts as EU judges. In this context, the CC has stated that the failure to submit a preliminary reference when mandatory and to disapply national law that is in conflict with EU law could amount to a violation of the constitutional right to a fair trial (Art. 24 of the Constitution).[88] Moreover, the CC has declared that, in certain cases, EU law has constitutional relevance and, therefore, the CC itself might submit a preliminary reference.[89] Notwithstanding these recent developments and the efforts of the CC, ordinary courts remain quite inactive in submitting preliminary questions regarding the validity of EU law.

It is difficult to compare the standard of national judicial review to the one deployed by the CJEU. There are neither official statistics nor scholarly work regarding the success rate of challenges against legislative measures brought before the CC. The data obtained from a statistical research carried out by the authors shows an indicative success rate of approximately 30% of challenges against legislative measures (period from 2006–2014).[90] This rate includes legislation declared partially or fully invalid or declared constitutional following a specific interpretation in conformity with the Constitution. This indicative success rate shows that the national standard of review is higher than the one sustained by the CJEU with regards to the annulment of EU law by the EU courts in 2001–2005 (success rates of 6.8% in the General Court and 16.1% in the CJEU).[91]

In relation to ordinary courts, there is also a lack of official statistical data and scholarly research regarding the standard of judicial review of administrative regulations and acts. Some studies suggest that the standard of judicial review varies depending on the field of administrative action. In areas like licensing or sanctions, ordinary courts exercise a strict scrutiny,[92] while in areas like economic regulation – telecommunications and the energy sectors – courts maintain a more deferential approach, with success rates of less than 25% against acts of the regulatory bodies.[93] These rates in the regulatory field could indicate a softer national judicial

[87] For all, see the judgments CC No. 28/1991, of 14 February; 64/1991, of 22 March; 147/1996, of 19 September; 13/1998, of 22 January.

[88] Judgments CC No. 78/2010, of 20 October (*Metropole* case) and No. 145/2012, of 2 July (*Iberdrola* case).

[89] Order CC No. 86/2011, of 9 June (preliminary reference to the CJEU, case *Melloni*) and the derived judgment of the CC on the merits No. 26/2014, of 13 February.

[90] This research has been carried out based on the Annual Reports and Statistics published by the CC. However, this data is partial and therefore the conclusions and the success rate calculated by the authors are not definitive and should be taken as mere indicators.

[91] Tridimas and Gari 2010, p. 170.

[92] Fernández Rodríguez 2009, pp. 34–79.

[93] Esteve Pardo 2009, pp. 899–902; Betancor Rodríguez 2012, pp. 619–620.

review standard than the one sustained by the General Court and the CJEU when reviewing the decisions of the European Commission (success rate of 35%).[94] However, the national standard of review cannot adequately be compared with the CJEU standard due to the lack of publicly available data. Thus, it is not possible to make a conclusive assessment of this issue.

2.8.6 No significant issues have arisen in Spain.

2.9 Other Constitutional Rights and Principles

2.9.1 The implementation of EU law has entailed challenges in Spain regarding the rule of law, the separation of powers doctrine and the territorial distribution of power. Three examples in this regard include: the obligation imposed by EU law to create independent regulatory bodies in certain markets, the increase of administrative regulations to implement EU measures and the weakening of the political autonomy of the Autonomous Communities.

In the energy and electronic communications sectors, the 2009 EU legislation has left no room for Member States to design their regulatory bodies: they must be separated and independent from the legislative and the executive powers.[95] In countries like Spain, unfamiliar with such administrative agencies outside the banking and financial sectors, the incorporation process of this new institutional design has been uneasy and has altered the traditional balance among the three branches of power. Several scholars have voiced concerns regarding the independence and judicial and parliamentary oversight of these regulatory bodies.[96] Following its creation, the European Commission expressed doubts about the independence and attribution of powers to the new Spanish super-regulator – with powers to regulate the energy, telecommunications, audiovisual, transport and postal sectors, as well as its monitoring and sanctioning powers to ensure effective competition in the market.[97] The Spanish Supreme Court has recently referred a

---

[94] Tridimas and Gari 2010, p. 170.

[95] Article 35(1)(4), Directive 2009/72/EC of the European Parliament and of the Council of 13 July 2009 concerning common rules for the internal market in electricity, [2009] OJ L 211/55; Art. 39(1)(4) Directive 2009/73/EC of the European Parliament and of the Council of 13 July 2009 concerning common rules for the internal market in natural gas, [2009] OJ 211/94; Art. 3 Directive 2009/140/EC of the European Parliament and of the Council of 25 November 2009 amending Directives 2002/21/EC on a common regulatory framework for electronic communications networks and services, 2002/19/EC on access to, and interconnection of, electronic communications networks and associated facilities, and 2002/20/EC on the authorisation of electronic communications networks and services, [2009] OJ L 377/37.

[96] Solanes Mullor 2014, pp. 443–463.

[97] Before 2013, Spain regulated these sectors through specialised and separate independent regulatory bodies. In 2013, Law 3/2013 of 4 June created the National Markets and Competition Commission (*Comisión Nacional de los Mercados y la Competencia*), which merged almost all the

case to the CJEU for a preliminary ruling on the compatibility of the creation of the new super-regulator with EU law in these fields.[98]

A similar problem arises also in relation to the increasing prominence of the executive vis-à-vis the legislative branch in implementing EU law. The obligation to comply with the deadlines for the implementation of directives and the necessity to directly apply EU regulations have justified the use of governmental regulations instead of legislative acts and, especially, the use of Royal Decree-Laws.[99] Royal Decree-Laws are in theory an exceptional legislative prerogative of the Government for 'extraordinary and urgent situations' (Art. 86 of the Constitution). A clear example of the misuse (and abuse) of Royal Decree-Laws is the implementation of the Services Directive by some Autonomous Communities whose Governments transposed it by Royal Decree-Law when the transposition deadline had already elapsed.[100]

The approval of several national legislative measures under the pressure of EU law has undermined the political autonomy of the Autonomous Communities. First, Organic Law 2/2012 of 27 April on Budget Stability and Financial Sustainability has regulated the implications of the golden rule incorporated in Art. 135 of the Constitution and limited the financial autonomy of the Autonomous Communities. Article 135 of the Constitution requires the Autonomous Communities to pass balanced budgets, limits their capacity to issue public debt and, overall, imposes the supervision of their financial system by the Central Government and European institutions. In addition, the material powers and competences of the Autonomous Communities have been constrained as a consequence of legislative measures at the central level such as Law 20/2013 of 9 December on the Guarantee of the Internal Market (see Sect. 2.2). Finally, some austerity measures launched by the Central Government have had an impact on the self-organisation and personnel of the Autonomous Communities. For instance, the Central Government has imposed a reduction of the salaries of the civil servants of the Autonomous Communities, and recently the CC has upheld this measure declaring that the Central Government is

existing specialised independent regulatory bodies (only the Stock Exchange Commission – *Comisión Nacional del Mercado de Valores* – was excluded). The European Commission raised doubts about the transition process and the independence of the appointed members of the existing regulatory bodies, which were dismissed before their mandate had expired. The powers of the new body were curtailed and some regulatory powers were reassigned to the Government. See in this regard the joint letter of the General Directorates of Competition, Energy, Telecommunications, Economy and Finance of the European Commission, sent to the Spanish Government on 29 November 2012, as well as the letter by Neelie Kroes, Vice-President of the European Commission, sent to José Manuel Soria, Spanish Minister of Industry, Energy and Tourism, on 11 February 2013.

[98] Order SC No. 5896/2015, of 3 July. The Spanish Supreme Court relied on the Hungarian case in which the CJEU decided that the dismissal of the appointed members of independent regulatory bodies before their mandate had expired was an attack against the independence of the regulators, and ruled that the creation of one super-regulator could not justify the dismissals (see Case C-288/12, *European Commission v. Hungary* [2014] ECLI:EU:C:2014:237).

[99] Sánchez Gutiérrez 2012, pp. 1–21; Alonso García 1990, pp. 297–302.

[100] Jiménez Asensio 2010, pp. 197–224.

entitled to take such measures and, therefore, to delve into the organisational structures of subnational entities.[101]

2.10 Common Constitutional Traditions

2.10.1 The CJEU has repeatedly declared that the constitutional traditions common to the Member States were one of the main sources of inspiration behind the interpretation of EU fundamental rights as general principles of EU law. Reference to the common constitutional traditions became a rhetorical clause that contributed to the legitimacy of sheer judicial activism in creating fundamental rights for the EU. The Lisbon Treaty retained the general principles of EU law as sources of fundamental rights 'as they result from the constitutional traditions common to the Member States' (Art. 6(3) TEU). Nonetheless, after the entry into force of the Lisbon Treaty, the Charter has displaced the general principles of EU law as the main source of EU fundamental rights in the CJEU case law. Still, Art. 52(4) of the Charter declares that '[i]n so far as this Charter recognises fundamental rights as they result from the constitutional traditions common to the Member States, those rights shall be interpreted in harmony with those traditions'.

2.10.2 The use that the CJEU has made of the comparative method has been sharply contested in the literature and regarded as discretionary and superficial.[102] Despite the erratic use of the 'common constitutional traditions' clause, taking into account the pluralist nature of the EU compound polity, the coexistence of the Charter and the national constitutions, and the supranational nature of the CJEU, there are good reasons to make use of the comparative method in order to give meaning to Charter rights. Without denying the autonomy of EU fundamental rights, the CJEU ought to take into consideration the existence of common trends and divergences regarding the interpretation of fundamental rights. As argued elsewhere,

> [t]his inter-state comparison would help to transcend superficial differences and to strengthen common understandings, while fostering an in-depth appraisal of pervasive particularities. In this way, the CJEU should seek to capture elements of commonality and assess elements of divergence in order to articulate an interpretation that reflects a synthetic understanding.[103]

In order to perform this comparative analysis, the CJEU could obtain the information needed from several sources, including the CJEU Service of Research and Documentation, the Advocate General Opinions; non-judicial actors in procedures before the CJEU such as the Commission, Member State Governments and the parties; and also judicial actors, such as the national courts and the ECtHR.[104]

---

[101] Judgment CC No. 81/2015, of 30 April 2015.

[102] Torres Pérez 2009, pp. 158–159; De Witte 1999, p. 878.

[103] Torres Pérez 2009, p. 168.

[104] Ibid., pp. 162–166.

2.11 *Article 53 of the Charter and the Issue of Stricter Constitutional Standards*

2.11.1 In *Melloni*, the CJEU had the chance to interpret Art. 53 of the Charter for the first time and held that:

> Article 53 of the Charter confirms that, where an EU legal act calls for national implementing measures, national authorities and courts remain free to apply national standards of protection of fundamental rights, provided that the level of protection provided for by the Charter, as interpreted by the Court, and the primacy, unity and effectiveness of EU law are not thereby compromised.[105]

Following the CJEU's interpretation of Art. 53 of the Charter, the chances to provide for more protective standards under national constitutions are rather limited.[106] Arguably, in situations not totally determined by EU law, such as in *Åkerberg Fransson*,[107] it might be possible to allow for better protection according to the national constitution, but only as long as the primacy, unity and effectiveness of EU law are not undermined, as the CJEU also stated in *Åkerberg Fransson*.

In practice, it will not always be easy to determine the margin of manoeuvre left to the Member States. Moreover, whether primacy, unity and effectiveness are compromised is a matter of interpretation. Indeed, we believe that the CJEU should not exclude the possibility for restrictions on those principles to be justified in certain circumstances, such as the need to respect national constitutional identity (Art. 4(2) TEU).

In cases where higher constitutional levels of protection are at issue, a more balanced and deferential approach by the CJEU would be advisable, instead of giving absolute preference to primacy, unity and effectiveness. Article 53 of the Charter could be interpreted as incorporating a mandate for the CJEU to allow for higher levels of constitutional protection, if there are no other rights or general interests that should prevail in the particular case.[108] A more deferential approach would allow the CJEU to accommodate diversity. For instance, the CJEU could have shown more deference in the review of affirmative action measures, such as in *Kalanke*[109] or *Abrahamsson*.[110]

In Spain, there are some instances in which EU law has had the effect of lowering the standards of rights protection. In addition to the EAW and the Data Retention Directive, in joined cases *ASNEF* and *FECEMD* for example,[111] the CJEU was questioned about the compatibility between the Data Protection

---

[105] See the *Melloni* case, supra n. 42, para. 60.

[106] Torres Pérez 2014, pp. 329–331, has criticised the CJEU's approach.

[107] Case C-617/10 *Åkerberg Fransson* [2013] ECLI:EU:C:2012:340.

[108] Torres Pérez 2014, p. 331.

[109] Case C-450/93 *Kalanke v. Frei Hansestadt Bremen* [1995] ECR I-03051.

[110] Case C-407/98 *Abrahamsson and Anderson* [2000] ECR I-05539.

[111] Joined cases C-468/10 and C-469/10 *ASNEF* [2011] ECR I-12181.

Directive[112] and a domestic provision according to which data had to appear in public sources in order for the processing of personal data to be allowed in certain circumstances. The CJEU declared that 'Member States cannot add new principles relating to the lawfulness of the processing of personal data to Article 7 of Directive 95/46 or impose additional requirements that have the effect of amending the scope of one of the six principles provided for in Article 7'.[113] In particular, the CJEU considered that the national provision was precluded by the Directive since 'it excluded in a categorical and generalised manner, the possibility of processing certain categories of personal data, without allowing the opposing rights and interests at issue to be balanced against each other in a particular case'.[114]

Thus, national legislation was precluded from providing better protection. The case did not reach the Constitutional Court, and it might actually be that the level of protection set by the EU legislator was compatible with the Constitution. Still, as a result of European integration, the level of protection of the right to privacy has been lowered.

Also, in the context of immigration, EU law might have had the effect of restricting certain fundamental rights. According to the Return Directive,[115] third country nationals can be detained up to 6 months while they are awaiting expulsion. This period may be extended for a further 12 months. Several Member States amended their respective legislation following the transposition of the Return Directive to increase the maximum length of detention, such as Greece, Italy, Spain and Hungary. In Spain, the maximum length of detention increased from 40 to 60 days. Greece and Italy went from 6 months and 3 months, respectively, to 18 months each. Thus, in some countries, the room for manoeuvre left by the Directive had the effect of worsening restrictions on the right to liberty.

Also, according to Art. 15(3) of the Return Directive: 'In every case, detention shall be reviewed at reasonable intervals of time either on application by the third-country national concerned or ex officio. In the case of prolonged detention periods, reviews shall be subject to the supervision of a judicial authority.' In the *Mahdi* case,[116] the CJEU held that 'EU law does not preclude national legislation from providing … that the authority which reviews the detention of a third-country national at reasonable intervals … must adopt, on the conclusion of each review, an express measure containing the factual and legal reasons justifying the measure adopted. Such an obligation would arise solely under national law'. Given the serious restriction on a fundamental right allowed by the Directive, revision should

---

[112] Directive 95/46/EC of the European Parliament and of the Council of 24 October 1995 on the protection of individuals with regard to the processing of personal data and on the free movement of such data, [1995] OJ L 281/31.

[113] Joined cases C-468/10 and C-469/10 *ASNEF*, supra n. 111, para. 32.

[114] Ibid. para. 48.

[115] Directive 2008/115/EC of the European Parliament and the Council of 16 December on common standards and procedures in Member States for returning illegally staying third-country nationals, [2008] OJ L 348/98.

[116] Case C-146/14 *Mahdi* [2014] ECLI:EU:C:2014:1320.

not be limited to rubber-stamping a previous decision to hold a person in custody. Indeed, a reasoned decision should be required as a matter of EU law, and this should not just be left to the Member States to decide. To be sure, in this context, the CJEU allowed for better protection at the Member State level, but it did not require it as a matter of EU law. This approach, however, might have an adverse effect and lead to a lowering of the standards of rights protection in other Member States.

2.12 Democratic Debate on Constitutional Rights and Values

2.12.1–2.12.3 The adoption (and implementation) of the Framework Decision on the EAW and the Data Retention Directive have not spurred a robust democratic debate, and public deliberation has been rather lacking. However, scholars have shown concern and adopted a critical position towards these instruments.[117]

In Spain, to our knowledge, there has been no situation in which constitutional issues have arisen and have been referred to the Constitutional Court at the stage of implementing EU law. In any event, we would support a recommendation to suspend the application and carry out a review of EU measures, if important constitutional issues were raised by a number of constitutional courts.

If an infringement proceeding has been initiated against a Member State and it alleges that implementation is hindered because an unconstitutionality has been identified in accordance with the domestic system of control of constitutionality, EU institutions should take this argument seriously and examine the possibility to embrace the interpretation of the fundamental right at stake at the EU level or rather to accommodate diversity, along the lines developed in the previous section. Moreover, the constitutional identity clause (Art. 4(2) TEU) may well have some bite in this context.

2.13 Experts' Analysis on the Protection of Constitutional Rights in EU Law

2.13.1 While EU law has contributed to furthering the protection of constitutional rights in certain fields, it has undermined the level of protection in others. On the one hand, for instance, the protection afforded by the Spanish Constitution to the right to non-discrimination has been enhanced by making reference to EU law

[117] Regarding the EAW, see Arangüena Fanego 2003, pp. 11–95; Fonseca Morillo 2003, pp. 69–95; De la Quadra-Salcedo Janini 2006, pp. 277–303. Regarding the Data Retention Directive, see Rodotà 2006, pp. 53–60; Vilasau 2006, pp. 1–15.

provisions and the CJEU case law. As such, the notion of indirect discrimination on grounds of sex is built on the CJEU case law and the relevant Directives.[118] Also, regarding non-discrimination on grounds of sexual orientation, which is not explicitly mentioned in the Constitution, the CC has referred to the Charter and several Directives that explicitly ban discrimination on this ground.[119]

Moreover, the CJEU case law has had an important impact regarding the protection of the right to housing in the context of the economic crisis and the creeping number of evictions in Spain. However, the CJEU has approached these cases from the perspective of consumer protection and the right to a fair trial, rather than the right to housing as such.[120]

On the other hand, EU integration might also have the effect of undermining the national standard of rights' protection. In Spain, the *Melloni* case stands out as a clear example of the lowering of standards of constitutional protection to fulfil obligations under EU law, since the CC had no choice but to overrule settled case law after the preliminary ruling.

Regarding the right to privacy and the protection of personal data, while the CC had made use of the Charter to reinforce the constitutional protection in certain cases, the implementation of the Data Retention Directive mandated the incorporation of the blanket data retention rule that has not been amended after the annulment of the Data Retention Directive by the CJEU. Also, as seen above, internal legislation providing for higher protection of personal data was declared incompatible with EU law. With regard to immigration, national legislation was amended to increase the maximum length of detention of third country nationals who are subject to return procedures under the umbrella of the Return Directive.

In the context of the economic and financial crisis, the adoption of austerity measures to fulfil obligations of budget stability has led to curtailing social rights,[121] such as the right to healthcare. The reform of the healthcare system has been challenged before the CC and the decision is still pending.

On the whole, there are several fields in which EU integration has led to a reduction of the levels of protection that individuals once enjoyed. In some cases, the lowering of standards has clashed with the Constitution. Nonetheless, even if the lower protection does not impinge upon the Constitution, it is disturbing that the level of rights protection is eventually reduced as a consequence of obligations derived under EU law.

---

[118] See, among others, judgments CC No. 147/1995, of 16 October; 240/1999, of 20 December; 253/2004, of 22 December; 3/2007, of 15 January.

[119] Judgment CC No. 41/2006, of 13 February.

[120] See Sect. 3.5.

[121] González Pascual 2014, pp. 117–120.

2.13.2–2.13.4 How could such an unwelcome result be avoided? Admittedly, EU integration might imply reducing the level of constitutional rights protection in some instances. The EU general interest or other competing rights might justify a restriction on the level of constitutional protection, but only when such an outcome is strictly necessary and cannot be avoided.

Within the domain of the EU, first of all, throughout the legislative process, the potential violation of the Charter or the need to give room to allow for better protection at the national level should be taken into consideration.[122] Once legislation has been adopted and a case reaches the CJEU, the Court should not disparage claims regarding constitutional protection for the sake of an absolute understanding of primacy and effectiveness. The CJEU might consider whether to embrace the constitutional understanding as the most adequate interpretation of the corresponding Charter right or accommodate diversity through the exercise of deference. The use of the comparative method by the CJEU in interpreting fundamental rights could be helpful for identifying common trends in the EU, as well as the adequate scope of deference.[123] In any event, and particularly if the outcome involves lowering the standards of rights protection, enhanced responsiveness to arguments grounded on the constitutional protection of fundamental rights would be advisable, given the pluralist nature of the EU and the pervasive contestation of its ultimate authority. For instance, in *Melloni*, one might agree that the countervailing interests and values, such as the need to effectively fight crime and protect victims' rights, in a context of mutual recognition, outweighed individual protection, as the person concerned had been informed and represented by lawyers of his choice. Nonetheless, a better articulation of the balancing of the conflicting rights and principles would have been welcomed, instead of an absolute understanding of primacy and effectiveness of EU law, since, in the end, the CJEU mandated the CC to lower the level of constitutional protection.[124]

In turn, a more proactive role for domestic courts, and particularly constitutional and supreme courts, in highlighting the standard of protection of constitutional rights through a robust use of the preliminary reference would facilitate the awareness of the impact of EU law on the constitutional system, and offer the CJEU the possibility to interpret the Charter accordingly or accommodate diverse interpretations. In the end, the building of a set of common rights can only successfully be achieved through the cooperation of domestic courts and the CJEU through a process of continuous dialogue, understood as the exchange of arguments in order to reach common understandings about the interpretation of fundamental rights.[125]

[122] De Witte 2013, pp. 1523–1538.

[123] Torres Pérez 2009, pp. 153–155.

[124] Torres Pérez 2014, p. 318.

[125] Torres Pérez 2009, pp. 179–184.

3 Constitutional Issues in Global Governance

3.1 Constitutional Rules on International Organisations and the Ratification of Treaties

3.1.1 The Government is charged with the negotiation and ratification of international treaties. However, in some cases, the prior consent of Parliament is necessary. According to the Spanish constitutional framework, international treaties are classified into three types taking into account the degree of participation of Parliament in the ratification process. First, international treaties that transfer constitutional powers to international organisations are subject to the consent of Parliament through an organic law, which requires an absolute majority (Art. 93 of the Constitution). Secondly, legislative consent by simple majority is required in the case of international treaties on specific matters, such as treaties that involve fundamental rights or financial obligations for Spain (Art. 94(1) of the Constitution).[126] Finally, in all other instances, the Government shall simply inform Parliament of the conclusion of international treaties and agreements (Art. 94(2) of the Constitution).

Besides the participation of Parliament in the process of ratifying international treaties, the Spanish Constitution also attributes a role to the CC. Prior to ratification, the Government or Parliament may consult the CC and seek a decision stating whether there is a conflict between the Spanish Constitution and the treaty (Art. 95(2) of the Constitution). In the case of a declaration of incompatibility, the treaty may only be ratified if the Constitution is amended accordingly. The CC's intervention prior to ratification is not mandatory, since the CC only intervenes at the request of the Government or Parliament; however, if an action for *ex ante* review of an international treaty is lodged, the decision of the CC is binding.

These provisions do not establish any explicit limit to the delegation of constitutional powers or the values, principles or objectives that should be respected by international organisations of which Spain is a member. Neither of these provisions contains a reference to any specific international organisation. Only in the context of the Spanish membership in the European Union and the implications of EU law for national law has the CC stated its position in relation to the limits of delegation of constitutional powers to international organisations. The legal scholarship has also debated this issue in connection with the EU debate.[127]

---

[126] The treaties are the following: '(a) of political nature; (b) of a military nature; (c) affecting the territorial integrity of the State or the fundamental rights and duties established under Part 1; (d) implying financial liabilities for the Public Treasury; (e) involving amendment or repeal of some law or requiring legislative measures for their execution'.

[127] See Sect. 1.3.

3.2 *The Position of International Law in National Law*

3.2.1–3.2.2 The Constitution establishes that international treaties shall be part of the internal legal system once officially published (Art. 96(1)). Thus, the Constitution encapsulates a sort of 'moderate monism', in the sense that only official publication is required for an international treaty to be binding domestically.

There is consensus about the position of international law in relation to domestic legislation (leaving aside the Constitution). Article 96(1) of the Constitution establishes that the provisions of an international treaty 'may only be repealed, amended or suspended in the manner provided for in the treaties themselves or in accordance with the general rules of international law'. Thus, it is understood that international law enjoys 'passive resistance' vis-à-vis domestic legislation in the sense that domestic legislation cannot modify international law. Consequently, Spanish judges are allowed to directly set aside domestic legislation in the case of incompatibility with international law. Yet, international treaties are not deemed to be hierarchically superior to legislative norms, since their interaction is established in terms of applicability rather than validity.

The position of international law with regard to the Constitution is still an open debate confronting constitutional and international law scholars. For constitutionalists, international law is subordinated to the Constitution[128] because: (i) Art. 95(1) of the Constitution requires the prior amendment of the Constitution in the case of ratifying a treaty that is incompatible with the Constitution; and (ii) the CC is able to declare an international treaty unconstitutional after its ratification.[129] For international lawyers and scholars, these reasons are inconclusive and they argue for the superiority of international law over the Constitution.[130]

Beyond this debate, the special status of international treaties on human rights ratified by Spain should be highlighted. According to Art. 10(2) of the Constitution, fundamental rights and freedoms recognised by the Constitution shall be interpreted in conformity with the Universal Declaration of Human Rights and other international treaties and agreements protecting human rights. These treaties, therefore, are considered to be a constitutional canon of interpretation.

3.3 *Democratic Control*

3.3.1 The Constitution does not give a decisive role to Parliament in the ratification and oversight of international treaties. The Government is in charge of the negotiations at the international level, while Parliament shall consent prior to the ratification by means of a simple or qualified majority depending on the type and

---

[128] See the seminal work of Pérez Royo 1998, pp. 167–172.

[129] Article 27(2)(c), Organic Law 2/1979 of 3 October on the Spanish Constitutional Court.

[130] For instance, see Marín López 1999, pp. 65–67.

content of the treaty.[131] In certain cases, the role of Parliament is reduced to a minimum and it must only be informed of the ratification of the treaty.

In the case of treaties falling under Art. 93 of the Constitution, there are no specific rules that qualify the legislative process for organic laws. In the case of treaties falling under Art. 94(1) of the Constitution, the authorisation does not have a legislative nature and the process contains some specificities (Art. 74(2) of the Constitution): the legislative initiative can only originate in Congress and, in the event of a disagreement between Congress and the Senate, a Mixed Committee will be constituted; if the disagreement persists, Congress will decide by qualified majority. These specific rules bolster the role of the Senate in comparison with its role in the ordinary legislative process, although Congress retains the last word.

Despite these rules, the effective involvement of and control by Parliament in the ratification process is doubtful. The Government has the 'qualification power', i.e. determines the type of treaty (i.e. decides whether Arts. 93, 94(1) or 94(2) is applicable to a treaty, see above) and therefore also decides on the level of participation of Parliament. In this decision, the Government has to request the opinion of the Council of State – the supreme consultative body of the Government – but this opinion is not binding.[132] Parliament, however, has reassessed the qualification on several occasions.[133] The Government also decides on the provisional application of a treaty, with the possibility to delay the submission of the treaty to Parliament for consent.[134] Most importantly, experience shows that parliamentary debates are without substance, being, in the vast majority of cases, a mere formality.[135]

The subsequent control mechanisms of Parliament for scrutinising the application of a treaty or the activities of the international organisation do not improve this poor initial role of Parliament. The Constitution does not foresee any special mechanism and the relevant international treaty determines the role of Parliament. We are only aware of special mechanisms in relation to the role of national parliaments in the European Union (Protocol No. 1 to the TFEU).

3.3.2 In line with the limited oversight of Parliament, referendum is scarcely used in Spain in the ratification process or subsequent oversight of an international treaty. There is neither a specific provision establishing the obligation to hold a referendum nor the ban of this instrument for this purpose. As stated above, Art. 92 of the Constitution allows the Government to call a consultative referendum on 'political decisions of special importance'. This kind of referendum, which is not binding, has been used only twice, precisely regarding international treaties. These two experiences have shown that the referendums were used for strategic political decisions

---

[131] See Sect. 3.1.

[132] Article 5(1)(e), Law 50/1997 of 27 November on the Government and Art. 22(1), Organic Law 3/1980 of 22 April on the Council of State.

[133] Izquierdo Sans 2002, pp. 24–27.

[134] Ibid. p. 19.

[135] Ibid., pp. 29–30.

rather than to enhance the democratic legitimacy of the ratification of a particular treaty.

Spain became a member of the North Atlantic Treaty Organization (NATO) on 30 May 1982, in the context of strong social and political contestation against it. In October 1982, the recently elected socialist Government had advocated for Spain's withdrawal from NATO. However, international commitments and alliances made the new Government change this initial position. In 1986, the Spanish Government decided to call a referendum to enable citizens to have a say on the continuity of the country's membership to NATO.[136] The Government mounted a political campaign in favour of remaining in NATO. The referendum was used on this occasion to legitimise a controversial change of the Government's position rather than to enhance democratic legitimacy.

The second and last referendum was held in 2005 by the Spanish Government prior to the ratification of the Treaty Establishing a Constitution for Europe, as mentioned before.[137] Again, the referendum was used strategically to achieve political purposes at EU level – to bolster the EU Constitution against more sceptical countries – rather than to exclusively enhance democracy in the national sphere where the positive outcome could be clearly anticipated before the referendum. The turnout was rather low (42.32% of the voters).

3.4 *Judicial Review*

3.4.1 The CC is in charge of reviewing the constitutionality of international treaties. According to Art. 95(2) of the Constitution, the CC can be consulted on whether an international treaty is compatible with the Constitution prior to its ratification (*ex ante* judicial review). In the case of no prior consultation, a ratified treaty can also be declared unconstitutional according to Art. 27(2) of Law 2/1979 of 3 October (*ex post* judicial review).

In practice, the CC has hardly ever reviewed the constitutionality of an international treaty. Only on two occasions – in 1992 and 2004 – was the CC consulted prior to ratification, first in relation to the Maastricht Treaty and secondly with regard to the Treaty Establishing a Constitution for Europe, which were discussed in Sects. 1.2.3 and 1.3.

The judicial review of international law is even more limited due to the fact that ordinary courts are not entitled to review international treaties. As mentioned above, a conflict between domestic legislation and a treaty should be resolved in favour of the treaty, which entails the disapplication of domestic legislation ('passive resistance' of treaties). In the case of the suspected incompatibility of a treaty with the Constitution, the judge should submit a question of constitutionality to the CC. In

[136] Royal Decree 214/1986 of 6 February.

[137] Royal Decree 5/2005 of 14 January.

any event, if the CC were to find that the Constitution and a treaty were incompatible, it would declare the respective international legal provision to be unconstitutional, but it would not have the power to annul it. Consequently, that provision could not be applied internally, and Spain might incur responsibility under public international law.

3.5 The Social Welfare Dimension of the Constitution

3.5.1–3.5.2 The 1978 Spanish Constitution encapsulates economic, social and cultural rights, but provides a lower level of protection for them than in the case of civil and political rights (see Sect 2.1.1). Most of these rights are categorised as 'principles governing economic and social policy' (Title I, Chap. III).[138] Only some social rights, such as the right to education, are placed in the section providing maximum protection within the Constitution. This lower level of protection for the majority of social rights means that an individual complaint before the CC is not available and, most importantly, that the legislator enjoys more leeway when regulating economic, social and cultural rights. In short, constitutional constraints and barriers are weaker in this field.[139]

Despite the lower level of constitutional protection, Spain has developed a strong social welfare state, including a universal public healthcare system, a solid social security system (with unemployment benefits, public pensions and disability pensions), strong social services and, finally, a public educational system in all levels (primary, secondary and higher education). Globalisation and, in particular, the consequences of the global economic and financial crisis have had a negative impact on the Spanish social welfare state, which has been subject to strong pressure. Financial markets, international organisations, the EU and the IMF at the forefront have pressed Spain to adopt an agenda of structural reforms, i.e. a severe austerity reform programme.[140]

In April 2009, the European Commission initiated an excessive deficit procedure against Spain.[141] Moreover, Spain has been signalled as a country with

---

[138] *Inter alia*, within Chap. III, the Spanish Constitution recognises the right to social security (Art. 41), the right to healthcare (Art. 43), the right to environment (Art. 45) and the right to housing (Art. 47).

[139] See Art. 53(3) of the Constitution for the diminished protection of economic, social and cultural rights that are recognised in Chap. III. For a common understanding amongst the Spanish scholarship of social rights as non-enforceable rights, see Díaz Crego 2012, pp. 17–20.

[140] The Spanish Governments have taken measures in all fields, *inter alia*, the reduction of protection in the case of unemployment, the reform of public pensions and cutting funding to the public education and the healthcare systems. For the implications for the Spanish constitutional system, see González Pascual 2014, pp. 116–127.

[141] Council Decision 2009/417/EC of 27 April 2009 on existence of an excessive deficit in Spain. The Council's Recommendations 15764/09 ECOFIN 775 UEM 301; 12171/12 ECOFIN 669 UEM 252; 10560/1/13 ECOFIN 478 UEM 173 OC 361 to Spain with a view to bringing an end to the situation of an excessive government deficit, follow upon the procedure.

macroeconomic imbalances by the Alert Mechanism Report (AMR).[142] Following this mechanism, Spain was subject to an in-depth review and, as a result, was requested to adopt reforms in the labour market and the social security scheme (with special attention to the pension system). Finally, despite the fact that Spain has not been subject to a formal bailout, the banking rescue programme for Spanish financial institutions in 2012 has implied, in practice, an international intervention in several Spanish financial institutions. The memorandum of understanding signed between Spain and the Troika (the European Commission, the European Central Bank and the IMF) has imposed obligations on financial institutions, but the State is the ultimate accountable party and has to accept the austerity reform programme as a condition for access to the financial assistance granted by the Troika. Precisely, based on the reports of the Troika and the financial assistance provided to the Spanish financial institutions, the Government has challenged several Autonomous Communities' laws protecting the right to housing in the CC, alleging that these laws can jeopardise financial stability;[143] these have been declared unconstitutional[144] or temporarily suspended by the CC.[145] In short, Spain has launched a massive austerity programme that has impacted all areas of the welfare state. *Inter alia*, health and education expenditures along with social assistance to dependents have been reduced, and the conditions for receipt of public pensions have been made more restrictive.[146]

The austerity reform programme has been widely contested politically by the leftist parties and socially by NGOs and other platforms. Yet, with some exceptions,[147] ordinary courts and the CC have not been able to confront the challenges to the social welfare state. So far, the CC has remained a passive spectator.

---

[142] Alert Mechanism Report 2014 COM (2013) 790 final of 13 November 2013 (Spain was signalled as a country with 'excessive imbalances', the worst classification) and Alert Mechanism Report 2015 COM (2014) 904 final of 28 November 2014 (the Commission reclassified Spain as a country with only 'imbalances', recognising the improved position of the country).

[143] Law 4/2013 of 1 October on Measures to Protect the Social Function of Housing of the Autonomous Community of Andalusia and Law 24/2013 of 2 July on Urgent Measures to Guarantee the Right to Housing of the Autonomous Community of Navarra. *Inter alia*, this legislation provides for the temporary suspension of evictions.

[144] In a recent judgment, the CC has declared unconstitutional some housing measures launched by the Andalusian Government through Decree-Law 6/2013 of 9 April. This Decree-Law included some measures that were subsequently incorporated in Law 4/2013 of 1 October, now temporarily suspended by the CC. The declared unconstitutionality is based on the use of the Decree-Law (this instrument cannot be used to regulate the right to property) and the lack of competence of the Autonomous Communities to expropriate inhabited houses in the context of an eviction procedure. Again, the CC has not approached the right to housing from a substantive point of view and has only faced it indirectly in light of a source of law issue or a conflict of competences between territorial entities. See Judgment CC No. 93/2015, of 14 May 2015.

[145] Order CC No. 69/2014, of 10 February and No. 115/2014, of 8 April.

[146] See González Pascual 2014, pp. 117–120.

[147] See Sect. 2.7.

Moreover, for instance, the CC struck down a law passed by the Autonomous Community of Andalusia to enhance the right to housing.[148]

Paradoxically, in certain cases, protection in the social welfare area has come from the CJEU, the ECtHR and the Committee on Economic, Social and Cultural Rights (CESCR). Facing the inaction of the CC, in the last years ordinary courts have turned towards the CJEU seeking collaboration to deal with some of the negative effects of the economic crisis.[149] For instance, the CJEU gave protection to Spanish citizens against evictions, declaring the Spanish mortgage law unfair for the consumer.[150] The Spanish legislation did not allow, in mortgage enforcement proceedings, for the debtor to claim the existence of unfair terms or for the competent court to stay this kind of proceeding to adopt interim measures.[151] Moreover, a debtor against whom mortgage enforcement proceedings were brought was precluded from lodging an appeal against any decision of the judge of first instance to dismiss his objection to enforcement.[152] The decisions of the CJEU in the *Aziz* and *Sánchez Morcillo* cases, declaring the Spanish legislation incompatible with EU law (based, *inter alia*, on incompatibility with Art. 47 of the Charter), have had a significant impact in the context of the economic crisis and have led to the amendment of Spanish mortgage law. On the other hand, the ECtHR is timidly providing protection also in this field through interim measures aimed at paralysing evictions.[153] Finally, in the first decision taken under the individual communication mechanism provided by the Optional Protocol, the CESCR concluded that Spain violated the right to housing (Art. 11 of the International Covenant on Economic, Social and Cultural rights, in conjunction with Art. 2.1) because its courts failed to take all reasonable measures to adequately notify Ms. I.D.G that the lending institution had filed a mortgage foreclosure against her.[154]

[148] See supra n. 144.

[149] Gómez Pomar and Lyczkowska 2014, pp. 7–10.

[150] See Iglesias Sánchez 2014, pp. 955–974.

[151] Case C-415/11 *Aziz* [2013] ECLI:EU:C:2013:164.

[152] Article 695(4), of Law 1/2000 of 7 January on Civil Procedure; Case C-169/14 *Sánchez Morcillo and Abril García* [2014] ECLI:EU:C:2014:2099.

[153] Interim measures taken by the ECtHR in the *A.M.B. and others* case on 12 December 2012, the *Mohamed Raji and others* case on 31 January 2013 and in the *Salt* case on 15 October 2013. However, the ECtHR has not decided on the merits of either case. In *A.M.B. and others* the ECtHR lifted the interim measures and declared inadmissible the complaint because of the non-exhaustion of domestic remedies (case *A.M.B and others v. Spain*, no. 77842/12, decision of 28 January 2014). In relation to the *Mohamed Raji* case, the ECtHR struck the application from its list of cases (case *Mohamed Raji and others v. Spain*, no. 3637/13, decision of 16 December 2014) because the Madrid city council decided not to enforce the demolition and eviction proceedings. In the *Salt* case, on 6 November 2013, the ECtHR lifted the interim measures because the Spanish authorities gave guarantees of alternative housing for the families concerned.

[154] Decision CESCR on the individual communication No. 2/2014, of 17 June 2015 (reference E/C.12/55/D/2/2014).

3.6 Constitutional Rights and Values in Selected Areas of Global Governance

Global governance has influenced and transformed certain values of the Spanish constitutional framework. The fight against terrorism – global and national – and the phenomenon of immigration are only some examples.

First, the transformations of Spanish criminal law on terrorism and organised crime should be highlighted. Beyond the EAW, these transformations have implied serious challenges to the rule of law and the principle of proportionality. These changes include the criminalisation of new conducts such as the extension of the concept of terrorist crime to mere collaboration with the aim to constitute a terrorist organisation (Art. 576(1) of the Criminal Code, approved by Organic Law 10/1995 of 23 November), the 'individual terrorism' conduct without connection to a criminal organisation (Art. 577 of the Criminal Code), or the mere defence of terrorism (Art. 578 of the Criminal Code). In connection to this, the close relationship of Spain with the United States in fighting terrorism has raised strong criticism in relation to the collaboration of Spain in the secret detention and unlawful inter-state transfers of suspected terrorists.[155]

Secondly, also in the context of the fight against terrorism, the law adopted in Spain to ban political parties (Organic Law 6/2002 of 27 June on Political Parties) is still contested. The right of association (Art. 22 of the Constitution) and the right to vote (Art. 23 of the Constitution) are at the forefront of the debate. The measures introduced by Organic Law 6/2002 were highly controversial, including, *inter alia*, the regulation of a specific procedure of illegalisation before a specialised section of the SC (Art. 11), the effects of the illegalisation decision for future associations (Art. 12), and the detailed clauses for illegalisation of a political party (Art. 9). This has led to the characterisation of Spain as a militant democracy. Yet in several judgments, the ECtHR has endorsed these measures.[156] Moreover, the so-called *Parot* doctrine adopted by the SC in 2006, aimed at extending the sentence of terrorists whose convictions are about to end, raised serious issues in relation to legal certainty, unexpected changes in the case law and the principle of non-imposition of heavier penalties than the ones that were applicable at the time that the criminal offence was committed. Eventually, this doctrine was declared incompatible with the ECHR by the Strasbourg Court.[157]

---

[155] Marty, D. *Alleged secret detentions and unlawful inter-state transfers of detainees involving Council of Europe member states.* Report of the Parliamentary Assembly of the Council of Europe (Committee on Legal Affairs and Human Rights), 12 June 2006.

[156] See for instance, case *Etxeberria and Others v. Spain*, nos. 35579/03, 35613/03, 35626/03, 35634/03, judgment of 6 November 2009.

[157] In 2006, the SC ruled that for crimes committed before the current Criminal Code came into effect in 1995, reductions would no longer apply to the accumulative maximum sentence of 30 years, but to the absolute total term of the sentence (judgment SC No. 197/2006, of 20 February). The CC ratified and declared constitutional this interpretation by the SC (judgment CC No. 114/2012, of 24 May). The ECtHR declared a violation of Arts. 5(1) and 7 of the ECHR (see *Del Río Prada v. Spain* [GC], no. 42750/09, judgment of 21 October 2013).

Finally, the global phenomenon of immigration, combined with the economic and financial crisis, has also produced tensions in relation to welfare rights, the right to a fair trial, the right not to be discriminated against and, above all, the more basic principle of human dignity. Several humanitarian crises on Spanish borders – the attempt by immigrants to surpass the fences of Ceuta and Melilla – have been a constant in the last years. The refortification of the fences, the treatment of the incoming immigrants by the police – reported deaths and mistreatments on the fences – and the deportations by public authorities are some of the challenges for the more basic human rights on Spanish soil. Along the same line of fighting illegal immigration, a 2003 reform established a mechanism for the automatic expulsion from Spanish territory of illegal immigrants sentenced to prison for less than six years.[158] The law does not provide for proportionality or a balancing test for taking into account all the personal and general interests in a particular case. The SC, however, reinterpreted this article in a constitutional spirit and introduced a balancing test.[159]

As it has been put, the Spanish constitutional system is 'under stress'.[160] European and global governance, and particularly the economic and financial crisis, have had a deep impact on basic constitutional values and principles such as the welfare state, the territorial distribution of power and the democratic legitimation of governmental powers. The consequences of this new scenario are hard to predict and might result in social contestation against the transformed constitutional framework. Indeed, there are already social and political signs in this direction, such as the emergence of new political parties and groups deeply opposed to the austerity measures. In any event, it seems necessary to recast the relationship between the Global-European spheres and the national constitutional order so as to reinforce basic principles such as democracy, the rule of law and a high level of protection of fundamental rights.

References

Albertí Rovira E. (2006) La cláusula europea en la Reforma de la Constitución española (The European integration clause in the reform of the Spanish Constitution). In: Álvarez Junco J., Rubio Llorente F. (eds.) El Informe del Consejo de Estado sobre la reforma constitucional: texto del informe y debates académicos (The Report of the Council of State about the constitutional reform: text of the report and academic debates). Centro de Estudios Políticos y Constitucionales/Consejo de Estado, Madrid, pp. 457–482.

[158] Article 89 of the Criminal Code, as amended by Organic Law 11/2003 of 29 September.

[159] See for all, judgment SC No. 588/2012, of 29 June.

[160] González Pascual 2014, pp. 116–127.

Alonso García R. (1990) Sobre la posibilidad de desarrollo del Derecho comunitario a través de la técnica del Decreto-Ley (The possibility of applying EU law through royal decree-laws). Revista de Administración Pública 123:297–302.

Alonso García R. (2006) Reforma constitucional: la recepción en la Constitución del proceso de construcción europea (Constitutional reform: the reception of European integration in the Constitution). In: Álvarez Junco J., Rubio Llorente F. (eds.) El Informe del Consejo de Estado sobre la reforma constitucional: texto del informe y debates académicos (The Report of the Council of State about the constitutional reform: text of the report and academic debates). Centro de Estudios Políticos y Constitucionales/Consejo de Estado, Madrid, pp. 557–561.

Arangüena Fanego C. (2003) La orden europea de detención y entrega. Análisis de las leyes 2 y 3 de 14 de marzo de 2003, de transposición al ordenamiento jurídico español de la decisión marco sobre la 'Euroorden' (The EAW. Analysis of Laws 2 and 3 of 14 May 2003, regarding the transposition of the EAW framework decision into the Spanish legal system). Revista de Derecho Penal 10:11–95.

Arroyo Jiménez L. (2011) Sobre la primera cuestión prejudicial planteada por el Tribunal Constitucional. Bases, contenido y consecuencias (About the first preliminary reference of the Spanish Constitutional Court. Bases, content and consequences). Indret, Revista para el análisis del derecho, 4:1–25.

Betancor Rodríguez A. (2012) Regulación: Mito y Derecho. Desmontando el mito para controlar la intervención de los reguladores económicos (Regulation: myth and law. Dismantling the myth of reviewing the decisions of regulatory agencies). Civitas, Cizur Menor.

Blanco Baldés R. (2011) La reforma de 2011: de las musas al teatro (The reform of 2011: from contemplation to action). Claves de la razón práctica 216:8–18.

Brkan M. (2013) L'arrêt *Melloni*: nouvelle pierre dans la mosaïque de la protection des droits fondamentaux dans l'Union européenne. Revue des affaires européennes 1:139–145.

Bustos Gisbert R. (2009) Integración europea y constitución española: ¿Tancredismo, desnudez o invisibilidad? (European integration and the Spanish Constitution: Risk, nudity or invisibility?). In: García Roca J., Albertí Rovira E. (eds.) Trenta años de Constitución (30 years of the Constitution). Tirant lo Blanch, Valencia, pp. 401–428.

Carrera S., Guild E., Hernanz N. (2013) Europe's most wanted? Recalibrating Trust in the European Arrest Warrant System. CEPS paper in Liberty and Security in Europe 55:1–46.

Cedeño Hernán M. (2010) Vulneración indirecta de derechos fundamentales y juicio en ausencia en el ámbito de la orden europea de detención y entrega, a propósito de la STC 199/2009, de 28 de septiembre (Indirect violation of fundamental rights and *in absentia* trials in the context of the EAW: a commentary to the judgment CC 1999/2009, of 28 September). Revista General de Derecho Europeo 20:1–15.

Cruz Villalón P. (2006a) Europeanización de la Constitución española: una introducción al problema (Europeanisation of the Spanish Constitution: an introduction to the problem). In: Cruz Villalón, P. (ed.) Hacia la europeización de la Constitución española. La adaptación de la Constitución española al marco constitucional de la Unión Europea (Towards the Europeanisation of the Spanish Constitution: The adaptation of the Spanish Constitution to the constitutional framework of the European Union). Fundación BBVA, Bilbao, pp. 23–48.

Cruz Villalón P. (2006b) La cláusula general europea (The European general clause). In: Cruz Villalón P. (ed.) Hacia la europeización de la Constitución española. La adaptación de la Constitución española al marco constitucional de la Unión Europea (Towards the Europeanisation of the Spanish Constitution: The adaptation of the Spanish Constitution to the constitutional framework of the European Union). Fundación BBVA, Bilbao, pp. 51–74.

De Boer N. (2013) Addressing Rights Divergences under the Charter: *Melloni*. CML Rev. 50:1083–1104.

De la Quadra Salcedo Janini T. (2006) El encaje constitucional del nuevo sistema europeo de detención y entrega (Reflexiones tras la STC 177/2006, de 5 de junio) (The constitutionality of the EAW (Notes after the judgment CC No. 177/2006 of 5 June)). Revista española de derecho constitucional 78:277–303.

De Witte B. (1999) The Past and Future of the European Court of Justice in the Protection of Human Rights. In: Alston, P. (ed.) The EU and Human Rights. Oxford University Press, Oxford, pp. 859–898.

De Witte B. (2013) Article 53. In: Peers S., Hervey T., Kenner J, Ward A. (eds.) The EU Charter of Fundamental Rights. A Commentary. Hart Publishing, Oxford, pp. 1523–1538.

Díaz Crego M. (2012) Derechos sociales y amparo constitucional (Social rights and the individual constitutional complaint). Revista vasca de administración pública 94:17–47.

Díez-Hochleitner J. (2013) El derecho a la última palabra: ¿Tribunales constitucionales o Tribunal de Justicia de la Unión? (The right to the last word: Constitutional Courts or the CJEU?). WP IDEIR 17:1–38.

Escobar Hernández C. (2006) La cláusula europea en la Constitución española: algunas reflexiones para una eventual reforma constitucional (The European integration clause in the Spanish Constitution: some thoughts for a possible constitutional reform). In: Álvarez Junco J., Rubio Llorente F. (eds.) El Informe del Consejo de Estado sobre la reforma constitucional: texto del informe y debates académicos (The Report of the Council of State about the constitutional reform: text of the report and academic debates). Centro de Estudios Políticos y Constitucionales/Consejo de Estado, Madrid, pp. 483–499.

Esteve Pardo J. (2009) La revisión judicial de las decisiones de las autoridades reguladoras (Judicial review of decisions of regulatory agencies). In: Muñoz Machado S., Esteve Pardo J. (eds.) Derecho de la regulación económica (Regulatory Law). Iustel, Madrid, pp. 881–921.

Fernández Rodríguez T. (2009) De la arbitrariedad de la administración, 3ª ed (About the arbitrariness of the public administration, 3rd edn.). Civitas, Cizur Menor.

Ferreres Comella V. (2000) Una defensa de la rigidez constitucional (A defense of the constitutional rigidity). Cuadernos de filosofía del derecho, Doxa 23:29–43.

Ferreres Comella V. (2013a) The Constitution of Spain. A Contextual Analysis. Hart Publishing, Oxford.

Ferreres Comella V. (2013b) Amending the National Constitutions to Save the Euro: Is This the Right Strategy? Texas International Law Journal 48:223–240.

Fonseca Morillo F. (2003) La orden de detención y entrega europea. (The EAW). Revista de Derecho Comunitario Europeo 14:69–95.

Fontanelli F. (2010) How Interpretation Techniques Can Shape the Relationship between Constitutional Courts and the European Union: A comment on the Spanish Tribunal Constitutional's Judgment No. 199/2009 and the Czech Constitutional Court's judgment No. 29/2009. King's Law Journal 21:371–392.

García-Escudero P. (2012) La acelerada tramitación parlamentaria de la reforma del artículo 135 de la Constitución (The quick parliamentary approval of the reform of article 135 of the Constitution). Teoría y Realidad Constitucional 29:165–198.

García Sánchez B. (2013) ¿Homogeneidad o estándar mínimo de protección de los derechos fundamentales en la Unión Europea? (Homogeneity or a minimum standard for the protection of fundamental rights in the European Union?). Revista de Derecho Comunitario Europeo 46:1137–1156.

Gómez Pomar F., Lyczkowska K. (2014) Spanish Courts, the Court of Justice of the European Union, and Consumer Law. Indret, Revista para el análisis del derecho 4:1–34.

González Pascual M. (2012) Mutual Recognition and Fundamental Constitutional Rights: The First Preliminary Reference of the Spanish Constitutional Court. In: Claes M., De Visser M., Popelier P. (eds.) Constitutional Conversations in Europe: Actors, Topics and Procedures. Intersentia, Cambridge, pp. 161–178.

González Pascual M. (2014) Austerity measures and welfare rights: the Spanish constitutional system under stress. EJSL 1–2:116–127.

Groussot X., Olsson I. (2013) Clarifying or Diluting the Application of the EU Charter of Fundamental Rights? – The Judgments in Åkerberg and Melloni. Lund Student EU Law Review 2:7–35.

Iglesias Sánchez S. (2014) Unfair Terms in Mortgage Loans and Protection of Housing in Times of Economic Crisis: Aziz v. Catalunyacaixa, Judgment of the Court of Justice (First Chamber) of 14 March 2013. CML Rev. 51:955–974.
Izquierdo Sans C. (2002) Intervención parlamentaria en la celebración de tratados internacionales en España (Spanish parliamentary oversight on ratification of international treaties). Revista Electrónica de Estudios Internacionales 4:1–46.
Izquierdo Sans C. (2010) Conflictos entre la jurisdicción comunitaria y la jurisdicción constitucional española (en materia de derechos fundamentales) (Conflicts between the European judiciary and the Spanish Constitutional Court (in the field of fundamental rights)). Revista Española de Derecho Europeo 34:193–233.
Jimena Quesada L. (2012) La reforma del artículo 135 de la Carta Magna Española (la superación de los clichés del tabú y la rigidez constitucionales) (The reform of Art. 135 of the Spanish Constitution: overcoming the taboo and cliché of amending the Constitution). Teoría y Realidad Constitucional 30:335–356.
Jiménez Asensio R. (2010) La incorporación de la Directiva de Servicios al derecho interno (Transposition of the services directive into the Spanish national legal system). Instituto Vasco de Administración Pública (IVAP), Oñati.
López Castillo A. (2006) A propósito de la proyectada articulación de una cláusula europea en la Constitución española: propuestas y apuntes para el debate (In relation to the proposal of introducing a European integration clause in the Spanish Constitution: some proposals and thoughts for the debate). In: Álvarez Junco J., Rubio Llorente F. (eds.) El Informe del Consejo de Estado sobre la reforma constitucional: texto del informe y debates académicos (The Report of the Council of State about the constitutional reform: text of the report and academic debates). Centro de Estudios Políticos y Constitucionales/Consejo de Estado, Madrid, pp. 501–532.
Luz Rodríguez M. (2014) Labour rights in crisis in the Eurozone: the Spanish case. EJSL 1–2:128–139.
Majone G. (1996) Regulating Europe. Routledge, London and New York.
Mangas Martín A. (2006) La reforma del artículo 93 de la Constitución española (The reform of article 93 of the Spanish Constitutuion). In: Álvarez Junco J.; Rubio Llorente F. (eds.) El Informe del Consejo de Estado sobre la reforma constitucional: texto del informe y debates académicos (The Report of the Council of State about the constitutional reform: text of the report and academic debates). Centro de Estudios Políticos y Constitucionales/Consejo de Estado, Madrid, pp. 533–566.
Marín López A. (1999) Orden jurídico internacional y Constitución española (International law and the Spanish Constitution). Revista de Derecho Político 45:35–67.
Martín Rodríguez P. (2013) Crónica de una muerte anunciada: comentario a la sentencia del Tribunal de Justicia (Gran Sala), de 26 de febrero de 2013, Stefano Melloni, C-399/11 (Chronicle of an announced death: a commentary to the judgment of the CJEU (Grand Chamber), of 26 February 2013, Stefano Melloni, C-399/11. Revista General de Derecho Europeo 30:1–13.
Pérez Manzano, M. (2012) El Tribunal Constitucional español ante la tutela multinivel de derechos fundamentales en Europa. Sobre el ATC 86/2011, de 9 de junio (The Spanish Constitutional Court before the multilevel protection of fundamental rights in Europe. About the constitutional court ruling No. 86/2011, 9 June). Revista Española de Derecho Constitucional 95:311–345.
Pérez Royo J. (1998) Las fuentes del derecho (The sources of law). Tecnos, Madrid.
Pérez Tremps P. (1994) Constitución Española y Comunidad Europea (The Spanish Constitution and the European Community). Fundación Universidad Empresa/Civitas.
Pérez Tremps P. (2004) Constitución española y Unión Europea (The Spanish Constitution and the European Union). Revista española de derecho constitucional 71:103–121.
Revenga Sánchez M. (2012) Rectificar preguntando. El Tribunal Constitucional acude al Tribunal de Justicia (ATC 86/2011, de 9 de junio) (Rectifying through asking. The Spanish Constitutional Court goes to the CJEU (Order CC No. 86/2011, of 9 June)). Revista Española de Derecho Constitucional 41:139–150.

Ridaura Martínez J. (2012) La reforma del artículo 135 de la Constitución española: ¿pueden los mercados quebrar el consenso constitucional? (The reform of article 135 of the Spanish Constitution: Can the markets break the constitutional consensus?). Teoría y Realidad Constitucional 29:237–260.

Rodotà S. (2006) La conservación de los datos de tráfico en las comunicaciones electrónicas (The conservation of data in electronic communications). IDP. Revista de Internet, Derecho y Política (UOC) 3:53–60.

Saiz Arnaiz A. (1999) La apertura constitucional al derecho internacional y europeo de los derechos humanos: el artículo 10.2 de la Constitución española (The constitutional gate to international and European human rights law: article 10.2 of the Spanish Constitution). Consejo General del Poder Judicial, Madrid.

Saiz Arnaiz A. (2005) De primacía, supremacía y derechos fundamentales en la Europa integrada: la Declaración del Tribunal Constitucional 1/2004 de 13 de diciembre de 2004 y el Tratado por el que se establece una Constitución para Europa (Primacy, supremacy and fundamental rights in the European integration process: Declaration CC No. 1/2004, of 13 December 2004). In: López Castillo A., Saiz Arnaiz A., Ferreres Comella V. (eds.) Constitución Española y Constitución Europea (The Spanish Constitution and the European Constitution). Centro de Estudios Políticos y Constitucionales, pp. 51–71.

Sánchez Gutiérrez M. (2012) Los Decretos-Leyes como instrumento de transposición de directivas comunitarias (Royal decree-laws as tools for transposing EU directives). Revista General de Derecho Administrativo 31:1–21.

Skouris, V. (2013) Développements récents de la protection des droits fondamentaux dans l'Union européenne: les arrêts *Melloni* et *Akerberg Fransson*. Il diritto dell'Unione Europea 2:229–243.

Solanes Mullor J. (2014) La introducción del Estado regulador y la administración independiente en España. El impulso del Derecho de la Unión Europea y las transformaciones del Derecho Público español (The introduction of the regulatory state and independent agencies in Spain: an innovation of the European Union and the transformation of Spanish public law). Doctoral dissertation, Universitat Pompeu Fabra.

Solazabal Echavarría J. (2005) El Tratado Constitucional europeo y la reforma de la Constitución española (The Treaty establishing a Constitution for Europe and the reform of the Spanish Constitution). Revista del Ministerio de Trabajo y Asuntos Sociales 57:33–47.

Torres Muro I. (2013) La condena en ausencia: unas preguntas osadas (ATC 86/2011, de 9 de junio) y una respuesta contundente (Sentencia del Tribunal de Justicia de la Unión Europea de 26 de febrero de 2013) (The sentence in absentia: courageous questions (Order CC nº 86/2011, of 9 June) and one conclusive answer (Judgment of the CJEU of 26 February 2013). Revista Española de Derecho Constitucional 97:343–370.

Torres Pérez A. (2009) Conflicts of rights in the European Union. A theory of supranational adjudication. Oxford University Press, New York.

Torres Pérez A. (2010) Euroorden y conflictos constitucionales: A propósito de la STC 199/2009, de 28.9.2009 (EAW and constitutional conflicts: a commentary of the judgment CC 199/2009, of 28 September 2009). Revista Española de Derecho Europeo 35:441–472.

Torres Pérez A. (2011) The judicial impact of European Law in Spain: ECHR and EU Law compared. Yearbook of European Law 30(1):159–179.

Torres Pérez A. (2014) *Melloni* in three acts. EuConst 10(2):308–331.

Tridimas T., Gari G. (2010) Winners and losers in Luxembourg: A statistical analysis of judicial review before the European Court of Justice and the Court of First Instance (2001–2005). E.L.Rev. 35(2):131–173.

Vilasau M. (2006) La Directiva 2006/24/CE sobre conservación de datos del tráfico en las comunicaciones electrónicas: seguridad v. privacidad (Directive 2006/24/EC regarding the retention of data: security v. privacy). IDP. Revista de Internet, Derecho y Política (UOC) 3:1–15.

Von Bogdandy A. (2001) La integración europea a la luz de la Constitución alemana: una reflexión entorno a la Sentencia del Tribunal Constitucional Federal sobre el caso Maastricht (The European integration in light of the German Constitution: thoughts about the judgment of the German Federal Constitutional Court in the *Maastricht* case). Cuadernos de Derecho Público 13:195–213.

Walter C. (2001) Constitutionalizing (Inter)national Governance. Possibilities and Limits to the Development of an International Constitutional Law. German Yearbook of International Law 44:170–201.

5

Ireland: The Constitution of Ireland and EU Law: The Complex Constitutional Debates of a Small Country

Gerard Hogan

Abstract The 1937 Constitution of Ireland draws on the following three main influences: (1) the US Constitution as regards judicial review of legislation; (2) UK common law heritage regarding the fused Westminster style legislative/executive model; and (3) a variety of continental constitutions regarding some fundamental rights. The report observes that apart from constitutional guarantees on fair trial and *habeas corpus*, most fundamental rights provisions are expressed at a high level of generality. A distinctive feature is that the Constitution can only be amended by a referendum, and this is indeed frequently done, including with regard to EU law. The central EU amendment is the so-called 'necessitated obligations' clause (Art. 29.4.(6)), which has the effect of overriding all other constitutional provisions. The Constitution is a key part of the political debate, and extensive constitutional issues have also arisen in relation to EU law. Three of the most important data retention cases that have come before the ECJ have all originated from Ireland. Another notable case is *Pringle*, where an MP raised concerns about the large size of the financial liabilities undertaken by the ESM Treaty. With regard to the European Arrest Warrant, whilst the Irish courts carry out more extensive judicial review, the automaticity involved in mutual recognition has nevertheless been a constant source of concern for judges. The rule of parliamentary reservation of law has led to extensive adjudication, e.g. in relation to the introduction of indictable offences by governmental regulations under EU measures, and in relation to the ratification of an IMF loan agreement and an extradition treaty.

Keywords The Constitution of Ireland · The Supreme Court of Ireland
Constitutional amendments regarding EU and international co-operation
The 'necessitated obligations' clause/Article 29(6) · Fundamental rights

---

G. Hogan (✉)
European Court of Justice, Luxembourg, Luxembourg
e-mail: gerard.hogan@curia.europa.eu

Digital Rights Ireland and the Data Retention Directive · Schrems
European Arrest Warrant, mutual recognition, automaticity of extraditions, defence rights and judicial review · *Pringle* and the ESM Treaty · *Meagher*, *Maher*, indictable offences and parliamentary reservation of law · Property rights
Crotty and referendums · Ratification of an IMF loan agreement and an extradition treaty by governmental regulations

1 Constitutional Amendments Regarding EU Membership

1.1 Constitutional Culture

1.1.1 The Constitution of Ireland entered into force on 29 December 1937 following its approval at a referendum which was held on 1 July 1937.[1] Since June 1941 the Constitution can only be amended by means of a referendum. It replaced the Constitution of the Irish Free State 1922, although key elements of that Constitution were preserved. That Constitution itself was the product of the Anglo-Irish War of 1919–1921 and the subsequent Treaty of December 1921.

Despite the (relative) frequency with which the Constitution has been amended, its basic structure has remained unchanged. In general, it may be said that the majority of the amendments have been designed either to delete the more nationalistic[2] or specifically Roman Catholic inspired provisions[3] or to deal with the various amendments to EU Treaties. Several amendments deal with the vexed question of abortion. Perhaps the single biggest institutional change has been the creation of a new Court of Appeal in October 2014 and the (de facto) re-constitution of the Supreme Court along US lines.[4]

1.1.2 The Constitution mandates a (relatively) strict separation of powers, save that it follows the fused legislative/executive model in the Westminster style. It is also quite prescriptive in terms of matters such as parliamentary privilege, elections,

[1] See generally, Hogan 2012.

[2] Thus, for example, the territorial claim to Northern Ireland contained in the original Art. 2 and Art. 3 of the Constitution was deleted by the 19th Amendment of the Constitution Act 1998, which also gives effect to aspects of the Belfast Agreement between the UK and Ireland. See generally Hogan 2000.

[3] Thus, for example, the 5th Amendment of the Constitution Act 1972 deleted the reference to the 'special position' of the Roman Catholic Church 'as guardian of the faith professed by the great majority of the citizens', along with the named recognition of other religious denominations and 'the Jewish Congregations'.

[4] By the 33rd Amendment of the Constitution (Court of Appeal) Act 2013 which came into effect on 28 October 2014. The practical effect of this was that all appeals now go from the High Court to the Court of Appeal. The decision of that Court is final save for those cases where the case either raises a point of law of exceptional importance or the interests of justice so require. There is also provision for 'leapfrog' appeals directly from the High Court to the Supreme Court, also confined to exceptional cases.

legislative procedure, executive powers and the powers of the (largely ceremonial) President. It gives strikingly impressive powers of judicial review of legislation to the High Court, Courts of Appeal and the Supreme Court. The Constitution also contains elaborate protections for a range of civil and political rights, including trial in due course of law, equality before the law, the protection of life, person, good name and property rights, liberty and habeas corpus, the home, free speech and assembly. The right to family life, the protection of children and the right to education are contained in Art. 41, Art. 42 and Art. 42A. Freedom of religion is also protected.[5]

While the Constitution is often unfavourably – and, in many respects, quite unfairly – compared with the European Convention on Human Rights (ECHR) by political activists and non-governmental organisations, it has nonetheless succeeded in becoming a key part of the political debate and is increasingly seen as a badge of national identity. In many respects its longevity and the vast corpus of important case law thereby generated, along with the fact that it can only be amended by referendum, have all contributed to this development.

1.2 The Amendment of the Constitution in Relation to the European Union

1.2.1–1.2.4 As is by now (relatively) well known, the Irish rules governing the transfer or delegation of powers to the European Union are complicated and, in many respects, quite singular. While the recent decision in *Pringle v. Government of Ireland*[6] has in some respects presaged a significant change in direction, in practice every significant treaty change over the last forty years or so has had to be enacted by referendum. Why is this so?

The Constitution of Ireland of 1937 is relatively 'rigid' in that since June 1941 it can *only* be amended by means of a referendum. If, therefore, it is considered that the ratification of an EU Treaty requires a constitutional amendment, then this can be achieved *only* by means of a referendum. Articles 46 and 47 of the Constitution require that a special Bill must be passed in both Houses of the Oireachtas (Parliament). The Bill must then be submitted to referendum and the amendment is carried if a simple majority vote in its favour. The Constitution has been amended in this manner on 29 occasions, but there have also been 11 occasions where such a proposal has been defeated. The referendum procedure is regarded as the

[5] See generally Kelly 2003; and Casey 2000.

[6] [2012] IESC 47, [2013] 3 IR 1.

quintessence of the overriding principle contained in the Constitution itself, namely that of popular sovereignty.[7] The Supreme Court has twice rejected the notion that there are implied limits to the capacity of the People to amend the Constitution.[8]

There have been nine referendums in respect of European treaties:

1.	1972	Entry into the EEC
2.	1987	Single European Act
3.	1992	Maastricht
4.	1998	Amsterdam
5.	2001	Nice I (defeated)
6.	2002	Nice II (successful)
7.	2008	Lisbon I (defeated)
8.	2009	Lisbon II (successful)
9.	2012	Fiscal Treaty

These referendums have led to the inclusion of several constitutional amendments that authorise the ratification of the relevant EU treaties, including the following clauses in Art. 29.4:

> 4° Ireland affirms its commitment to the European Union within which the member states of that Union work together to promote peace, shared values and the well-being of their peoples.
>
> 5° The State may ratify the Treaty of Lisbon ..., and may be a member of the European Union established by virtue of that Treaty. ...
>
> 7° The State may exercise the options or discretions –
>
> i to which Article 20 of the Treaty on European Union relating to enhanced cooperation applies,
>
> ii under Protocol No. 19 on the Schengen acquis ..., and
>
> iii under Protocol No. 21 on the position of the United Kingdom and Ireland in respect of the area of freedom, security and justice ....,
>
> but any such exercise shall be subject to the prior approval of both Houses of the Oireachtas.
>
> 8° The State may agree to the decisions, regulations or other acts –
>
> i under the Treaty on European Union and the Treaty on the Functioning of the European Union authorising the Council of the European Union to act other than by unanimity,
>
> ii under those treaties authorising the adoption of the ordinary legislative procedure, and
>
> iii under subparagraph (d) of Article 82.2, the third subparagraph of Article 83.1 and paragraphs 1 and 4 of Article 86 of the Treaty on the Functioning of the European Union, relating to the area of freedom, security and justice,
>
> but the agreement to any such decision, regulation or act shall be subject to the prior approval of both Houses of the Oireachtas.

[7] See *Pringle v. Government of Ireland* [2012] IESC 47, [2013] 3 IR 1, 101–103 *per* O'Donnell J.

[8] *Re Art. 26 and the Regulation of Information Bill 1995* [1995] 1 IR 1, *Riordan v. An Taoiseach*

9° The State shall not adopt a decision taken by the European Council to establish a common defence pursuant to Article 42 of the Treaty on European Union where that common defence would include the State.

10° The State may ratify the Treaty on Stability, Coordination and Governance in the Economic and Monetary Union … .[9]

The Constitution is, of course, the quintessential product of orthodox nationalist thinking about the nation state. It proceeds on the assumption that state sovereignty resides in one of the three organs of state, namely, the executive, legislative and judiciary. Thus, even to this day, Art. 15.2.1 of the Constitution makes the following claim that:

> The sole and exclusive power of making laws for the State is hereby vested in the Oireachtas [Parliament]: no other legislative authority has power to make laws for the State.

This latter claim is, of course, quite unrealistic in the context of EU membership, but broadly similar claims are also made in the context of both the executive and judicial powers. How, then, can these constitutional provisions be reconciled with EU membership? The short answer is that they cannot in themselves be so reconciled.

Faced with this problem on entry to the (then) EEC in 1972, the device was adopted by the Third Amendment of the Constitution Act 1972, whereby Art. 29 of the Constitution, which deals with international relations, was amended to permit entry. The effect of this general amendment,[10] which was expressed to override all other constitutional provisions, was that (a) Ireland was empowered to join the European Economic Community, and (b) no law or administrative act which was 'necessitated' by Ireland's Community law obligations could be found unconstitutional ('the necessitated obligations' clause). The 'necessitated obligations' clause, now contained in Art. 29.4.6, provides as follows:

6° No provision of this Constitution invalidates laws enacted, acts done or measures adopted by the State, before, on or after the entry into force of the Treaty of Lisbon, that are necessitated by the obligations of membership of the European Union …, or prevents laws enacted, acts done or measures adopted by –

[9] For the text of the Constitution, see http://www.irishstatutebook.ie/eli/cons/en.

[10] Originally numbered as Art. 29.4.3. It has subsequently been renumbered on several occasions to accommodate a variety of constitutional amendments. Following on the 28th Amendment of the Constitution Act 2009 (which permitted the ratification of the Lisbon Treaty), it is now numbered as Art. 29.4.6. A version of the 'necessitated obligations' clause in relation to legislation enacted pursuant to obligations imposed by the Fiscal Treaty is contained in Art. 29.4.10 following the enactment of the 30th Amendment of the Constitution Act 2012 (which permitted the ratification of the Fiscal Treaty).

i the said European Union ... institutions thereof,
ii the European Communities or European Union existing immediately before the entry into force of the Treaty of Lisbon, or institutions thereof, or
iii bodies competent under the treaties referred to in this section, from having the force of law in the State.

The formula contained in what was then Art. 29.4.3 of the Constitution worked relatively well until its limitations were highlighted by the Supreme Court's decision in April 1987 in *Crotty v. An Taoiseach.*[11] The plaintiff in this case had challenged the decision of the Government to ratify the Single European Act (SEA) by means of parliamentary legislation only, without a referendum. The Supreme Court ultimately held that ratification of Title II of the SEA (dealing with the creation of the single market) was within the scope of the 1972 constitutional amendment, since it did no more than attempted to give effect to market integration policies which had been contained in the original 1957 EC Treaty. The Court took a different view of Title III (which provided for formalised common foreign policies rules), holding that a constitutional amendment was necessary to ratify this aspect of the Treaty.

The Supreme Court's reasoning may be summarised thus:

(a) There was no Community *legal* – as distinct from political – obligation to ratify the SEA. Ratification by parliamentary legislation was therefore not protected from constitutional attack by the 'necessitated obligations' clause in the 1972 amendment.
(b) Without the protection of the 'necessitated obligations' clause, ratification was unconstitutional, since Title III of the SEA curbed an essential feature of state sovereignty. In the Court's view the power to conduct the foreign affairs of the state was an essential part of sovereignty, and the Government could not by a binding Treaty commitment agree to transfer that power to other states or to the Community.

While the reasoning and ultimate decision in *Crotty* remain controversial, it has been nonetheless accepted by successive Governments of the day. A special referendum was then passed in May 1987[12] allowing ratification of the Single European Act. But the long-term implications have also been significant. In practice, this means that the ratification of every Treaty change involving any further appreciable transfer of sovereignty or the creation of new competences for the Union has required – or at least has been thought to require – a referendum.[13]

[11] [1987] IR 713. ('An Taoiseach' are the Irish words for 'the Prime Minister'). For the background to this important decision and its implications, see generally, Hogan 1987; Bradley 1987; and Temple Lang 1987.

[12] 10th Amendment of the Constitution Act 1987.

[13] Of course, there have been several instances where Ireland has ratified Treaty changes without the necessity for a constitutional amendment, not least in the case of Treaty changes required to permit accession by new Member States.

One of the difficulties with *Crotty* is that it is a single, isolated judgment from the Supreme Court which is by now over twenty-five years old. Not surprisingly, the composition of that Court has changed completely in the intervening years. Moreover, both Irish constitutional law and European Union law have developed significantly in the last thirty years.

A more nuanced view emerged from the Supreme Court's decision in *Pringle v. Government of Ireland*.[14] In *Pringle*, the plaintiff's case was that the ratification of the European Stability Mechanism Treaty was such a momentous decision on the part of the Government that, following *Crotty*, it required approval by a referendum. The plaintiff pointed to the fact that it involved a potential liability of up to 11.1454 billion EUR by way of contribution to a fund totalling some 700 billion EUR for the express purpose of securing the stability of the eurozone in circumstances where the allocations from the fund could, at least in certain circumstances, be made by a qualified majority of the contracting states, which might not include Ireland, either because Ireland disagreed with the allocation or was excluded from voting.

O'Donnell J. put the matter well when he stated:

> There can be little doubt that if the essence of sovereignty, at least as contemplated by the Irish Constitution, is to be understood as meaning that Ireland fetters its sovereign right to decide by joining any organisation which acts collectively, or at least one in which Ireland does not retain a veto (and therefore the right to say no), then the ESM Treaty would be of dubious constitutional validity, along with, it must be said, many other important international agreements.[15]

Following a very close analysis of the relevant provisions of Art. 28 and Art. 29 of the Constitution dealing with executive responsibility to Dáil Éireann (the lower House of Parliament) and the executive's powers in the field of foreign affairs, respectively, O'Donnell J. went on to point out that

> [f]rom these provisions may be drawn the unremarkable conclusion that the Constitution contemplates that the conduct of the State's foreign relations will necessarily involve the making of binding agreements with other states, which agreements could have financial consequences for the State, and on occasions require an alteration of its domestic law. … It can be deduced from these constitutional provisions, at a minimum, that the Constitution clearly anticipated the Executive power could and would involve the making of binding agreements with other nations, and that Ireland might become involved in disputes which themselves might be resolved by a process involving a binding determination by which Ireland would be obliged to abide. … This again contemplates that the business of the conduct of foreign affairs might necessarily involve the making of agreements with foreign States, cooperation with, and membership of, international bodies, and occasionally, and regrettably, the possible occurrence of disputes including the commitment of the State to a war.

O'Donnell J. then stressed the extent to which judicial review of the executive function in the sphere of foreign affairs remained limited:

---

[14] [2012] IESC 47, [2013] 3 IR 1.

[15] [2013] 3 IR 1, 104.

> The courts' function in this regard is to enforce those boundaries of, and limitations to, the exercise of the Executive power in foreign relations which are either express in, or to be implied from, the constitutional text, and at the same time to reject any attempt to impose limitations on Governmental conduct of foreign relations not justified by the Constitution. ... Since it is to the Government alone that the conduct of foreign affairs is consigned by the Constitution, it follows that such international relations must be conducted by the Government, which cannot abdicate, alienate, transfer or subordinate its functions to any other State or body.

O'Donnell J. stressed the extent to which membership of international organisations – such as, for example, the United Nations or the International Monetary Fund – was regarded as the very exercise of sovereignty and not a restriction upon its exercise. What was critical, therefore, was whether the power to conduct foreign affairs had been transferred or alienated to another body. Short of that, the fact that the Government had made a momentous decision with potentially profound consequences was in itself irrelevant.

It is hard to disagree with the conclusion of many observers that the effect of *Pringle* has been to neutralise at least part of the earlier decision in *Crotty*, which dealt with restrictions on the executive power of the state.[16] One should not, however, deduce from this that the Government now has a free hand, because the other aspect of *Crotty* – namely, that a proposal to amend an EU treaty does not enjoy constitutional immunity for the purposes of Art. 29.4.6 of the Constitution because it is not (yet) an obligation of EU law – continues to hold sway. There will thus continue to be constitutional objections where an EU Treaty imposes specific obligations on Member States over and above any perceived restrictions on the right to conduct foreign policy. Accordingly, even if the decision in *Pringle* had been delivered before the dates of both the Lisbon Treaty and the Fiscal and Stability Treaty, it is hard to see how a referendum would still not have been required in both instances. In the case of the Lisbon Treaty, the decision to accord Treaty status to the Charter of Fundamental Rights would probably have required a constitutional amendment, given the uncertain reach and scope of the Charter and the manner in which it might potentially overreach some of the corresponding fundamental rights provisions of the Irish Constitution. The same is true in respect of the Fiscal Treaty: the specific obligations in relation to fiscal discipline and budget deficits would cut across the autonomy of Dáil Éireann in relation to such matters granted by the Constitution.

The provisions of Art. 29.4.7 and Art. 29.4.8 have their origins in the variable geometry provided for in the aftermath of the Amsterdam Treaty. Given that the United Kingdom had secured opt-outs from the Schengen agreement and in the entire area of justice and home affairs, it was for practical purposes necessary for Ireland to do likewise, as otherwise the entire common travel arrangements with the United Kingdom (and specifically free access over the land border with Northern Ireland) would have been placed in jeopardy. From a constitutional perspective it

[16] See in particular the important articles written by two former members of the Supreme Court: Keane 2014, pp. 195–213; and Geoghegan 2014, pp. 213–219.

was considered that the 'necessitated obligations' clause would break down in the face of the adoption of measures in respect of which Ireland later elected to opt in and which were thus plainly optional in the sense just described. Article 29.4.7 and Art. 29.4.8 are accordingly designed to give democratic legitimacy to such decisions by securing the prior assent of both Houses of the Oireachtas. In practice, however, this generally amounts to giving parliamentary assent to matters which have already been diplomatically agreed in principle at EU level, and there is no real sense in which the negotiating hand of the executive has been constrained by the need to secure subsequent parliamentary approval.

1.3 The Supremacy of EU Law

1.3.1–1.3.4 The constitutional provisions and court judgments regarding sovereignty are outlined in the preceding section.

Regarding supremacy, Ireland may be regarded as a classic example of a dualist state on the basis of Art. 29.6 of the Constitution (see Sect. 3.2). However, the situation is very clearly otherwise in the case of European Union law, since the effect of Art. 29.4.6 of the Constitution, the wording of which was provided in the preceding section, is to confer supremacy on EU law over the domestic law and Constitution to the extent that this is necessitated by the obligations of EU membership. To date, application of the supremacy clause has been largely unproblematic. It is nonetheless clear that from the standpoint of Irish law, EU law is supreme within its proper sphere of application because Art. 29.4.6 of the Constitution says it is, and not because of some autonomous, freestanding notion of European Union law which the Irish courts feel obliged to apply independently of this constitutional provision.

1.4 Democratic Control

1.4.1 While Art. 15.2.1 of the Constitution provides that the exclusive lawmaking power resides in the Oireachtas,[17] it has on the whole performed poorly as a law making institution. In practice, legislation is drafted by specialist teams within the Attorney General's Office, who in turn take their instructions from the civil service departments that sponsor the measure. Very few measures which have been drafted or prepared otherwise than with the approval of the Government become law. To

[17] I.e., the Parliament which consists of Dáil Éireann (the lower House), Seanad Éireann (the upper House) and the President.

that extent, therefore, the Oireachtas might better be regarded as 'a law-declaring rather than a law-making body'.[18]

Added to this is the fact that, at least in the past, legislation was often drafted in wide and loose terms, such that in many instances the underlying policy was really to be found in the statutory instrument giving effect to the legislation. Admittedly, Art. 15.2.1 of the Constitution has been deployed on a number of occasions to invalidate legislation which has been held to confer open-ended powers on members of the Government (and, in some cases, other bodies) to make ministerial orders on the basis that the powers so delegated were essentially legislative in nature.[19] This important development notwithstanding, the basic problem remains that of weak parliamentary oversight of the legislative drafting process.

This problem was especially acute in the context of the transposition of European Union directives, as the European Communities (Amendment) Act 1973 permitted the relevant minister to give effect to a directive by means of a statutory instrument. In essence, the weak parliamentary oversight at Union level[20] was magnified by even weaker legislative scrutiny at national level, so that important legislative measures are transposed into national law without really any effective parliamentary scrutiny at all. The constitutionality of this system was upheld by the Supreme Court in *Meagher v. Minister for Agriculture*[21] and *Maher v. Minister for Agriculture*[22] with few, if any, reservations in respect of its implications for a democratic system of government.

The present system can, however, be defended on the very practical ground that it ensures that directives are transposed into national law in a timely fashion:

> The ever-increasing number of directives requiring implementation within strict deadlines inevitably puts pressure on members of the Irish executive to implement directives by statutory instruments even in circumstances where enactment by statute might otherwise have been more appropriate.[23]

A key limitation on the power to implement Union law by regulation was contained in Sect. 3(3) of the European Communities Act 1972: an indictable offence may not be created by regulation. However, apparently sensible – and eminently justifiable – judicial intervention here, aimed at upholding the rule of law, has had unforeseen consequences. The issue arose in *Browne v. Attorney General*,[24] where the applicant had been charged with violating a ministerial order

[18] Chubb 1974, p. 65.

[19] See, e.g., *McGowan v. Labour Court* [2013] IESC 21, [2013] 2 ILRM 376, *Bederev v. Ireland* [2015] IECA 38, [2015] 1 ILRM 301.

[20] Even if post-Lisbon the power of co-decision at European Parliament level has been strengthened and enhanced.

[21] [1994] 1 IR 329. See generally Fahey 2010, pp. 51–69 for a very helpful overview of the case law.

[22] [2001] 2 IR 139.

[23] Tomkin 2004, p. 150.

[24] [2003] 3 IR 205.

which restricted drift-net fishing. The restriction was required by a Council regulation. Indeed, the ministerial order had expressly recited that it was being promulgated in order to permit the enforcement of a Council regulation. In order to circumvent the prohibition in the 1972 Act, the respondent claimed that he possessed the authority to create an indictable offence under Sect. 223A of the Fisheries (Consolidation) Act 1959 (as amended), under which he could 'prescribe and adopt either or both of the following measures, namely, measures of conservation of fish stocks and measures of rational exploitation of fisheries'. The Supreme Court held that the power to make regulations could not be used to circumvent this statutory prohibition:

> There is no indication whatever in the language of section 223A that it was envisaged by the Oireachtas that the second respondent could give effect to principles and policies which had never been considered or adopted by the Oireachtas by means of a statutory instrument under that section which effectively circumvented the prohibition on the creation of indictable offences in section 3(3) of the Act of 1972.[25]

The effect of *Browne* was reversed by the European Communities Act 2007, in which the Oireachtas permitted the creation of indictable offences by secondary legislation implementing Community law.[26] Section 4 of the 2007 Act also allows the minister to exercise the power to make a statutory instrument for the purposes of implementing an EU act, if the 'obligations imposed on the State under the European act concerned relate, in whole, to matters to which that [power] relates'. Other legislative innovations increasing the armoury of the executive in Community law matters have followed. For example, Sect. 4 of the Communication Regulations (Amendment) Act 2007 inserted a new Sect. 46A into the Communication Regulations Act 2002, which now allows the minister to create indictable offences by regulation in order to give effect to various provisions of Community law. Thus, worries about the democratic deficit aside, an unfortunate – and entirely unforeseen – consequence of the Supreme Court decision in *Browne* has been that instead of compelling the Oireachtas to introduce new criminal offences by primary legislation with the full panoply of political safeguards, there has been an increase in the number of areas in which a minister can introduce new indictable offences by regulation. The requirement of the rule of law that statutory requirements be public and precise has been undermined somewhat by these developments.[27]

In addition, the principle of legal certainty, central to the rule of law, has been undermined by the sheer volume of Community law that is put on the statute books:

[25] Ibid., p. 220, per Keane C.J.

[26] European Communities Act 1972, s. 3(3), as substituted by European Communities Act 2007, Sect. 2.

[27] *Cf. Quinn v. Ireland* [2007] IESC 16, [2007] 3 IR 395, where Denham J. held that regulations having statutory effect (Sect. 4 of the European Communities Act 1972 having given birth to such strange creatures) cannot themselves be amended by subsequent regulations.

> There is no official publication that gives up to date information as to whether or not a particular statutory instrument has been amended or revoked. In fact, the only certain way of establishing as to whether or not a particular statutory instrument is in force, is by going through every subsequent statutory instrument manually, and checking to see if another statutory instrument under a different name, amends the earlier statutory instrument.[28]

1.4.2 On EU referendums in Ireland, see Sect. 1.2.

1.5 Waning Constitutional Influence?

1.5.1–1.5.3 While concerns have been frequently expressed that the on-going expansion of the scope and reach of European Union law might ultimately lead to a waning of the influence of the Constitution of Ireland, this has not (as yet, at least) happened. These concerns were particularly voiced during the two Lisbon referendums, as it was suggested that by 'constitutionalising' the Charter of Fundamental Rights and by the ever expanding potential reach of EU law, key decision-making on aspects of fundamental rights by the Irish judiciary (and especially by the Irish Supreme Court) might be supplanted in practice by the Court of Justice.

It has to be said that there is no immediate sign of this, partly because of the absolute centrality of the Constitution to Irish political, social and legal discourse. In addition, the fact that the People have an important role in key decision-making via the referendum process reinforces this legal and cultural tendency. This was immediately visible in the recent same-sex marriage referendum on 22 May 2015.

The striking scenes of popular joy and celebration in Dublin as the referendum results were announced were remarkable, even astonishing.[29] While some disagree as to the wisdom of the referendum process in relation to matters of this kind,[30] what is undeniable is that a decision of this sensitivity brought about in this fashion is likely to have greater long-term democratic acceptability even by comparison with a purely legislative change or a change imposed by either the Irish Supreme Court, the Court of Justice or the European Court of Human Rights.

---

[28] Tomkin 2004, p. 152.

[29] See e.g. O'Hanlon, G (2015, June 1) Scenes of joy in Dublin Castle on May 23rd felt like a kind of secular Pentecost. The Irish Times.

[30] See e.g. Weeks, L. (2015, June 2). Rule by way of referendum is not the best way to make decisions. The Irish Times.

2 Constitutional Rights, the Rule of Law and EU Law

2.1 *The Position of Constitutional Rights and the Rule of Law in the Constitution*

2.1.1 Articles 40 to 44 of the Constitution of Ireland are headed 'Fundamental Rights' and deal with what might be regarded as standard civil and political rights: thus the principle of equality, life, person, good name, property rights, personal liberty, habeas corpus, inviolability of the dwelling, free speech and assembly, family and children, education and freedom of religion are all protected. In addition, Art. 38.1 of the Constitution guarantees that '[n]o person shall be tried on any criminal charge save in due course of law', and Art. 38.5 guarantees the right to jury trial. In some cases the guarantees are detailed and specific: this is true, for example, of the procedure to be followed in habeas corpus applications.[31] In most other cases, however, the guarantees are expressed at a high level of generality.[32]

Two specific features of these fundamental rights provisions should, however, be noted. First, the courts have developed a doctrine of unenumerated or implied rights designed to capture standard fundamental rights which are not otherwise expressly provided for in Arts. 40 to 44: rights protected under this heading include free movement and travel, the right to fair procedures, the right to marry and the right to privacy. Secondly, Art. 45 contains a list of what would nowadays be described as socio-economic rights which are not 'cognisable by any Court under any provision of this Constitution'.[33]

Over and above the specific constitutional provisions lie the general principles of law – such as proportionality, non-retroactivity and legal certainty – some of which have a specific constitutional grounding. Thus, for example, Art. 5 of the Constitution describes the State as a democracy, and this provision is increasingly cited by the courts to justify decisions supporting the rule of law.[34] Article 15.5.1

---

[31] Article 40.4.1 provides that '[n]o citizen shall be deprived of his personal liberty save in accordance with law'. Para. 2 continues as follows: 'Upon complaint being made by or on behalf of any person to the High Court or any judge thereof alleging that such person is being unlawfully detained, the High Court and any and every judge thereof to whom such complaint is made shall forthwith enquire into the said complaint … and the High Court shall … after giving the person in whose custody he is detained an opportunity of justifying the detention, order the release of such person from such detention unless satisfied that he is being detained in accordance with the law.'

[32] Thus, for example, Art. 40.5 provides: 'The dwelling of every citizen is inviolable and shall not be entered save in accordance with law.'

[33] Thus, for example, Art. 45.4.2 provides: 'The State shall endeavour to ensure that the strength and health of workers, men and women, and the tender age of children shall not be abused and the citizens shall not be forced by economic necessity to enter avocations unsuited to their sex, age or strength.'

[34] See e.g. *Mallak v. Minister for Justice* [2012] IESC 59 (The Minister does not enjoy an absolute discretion with regard to a naturalisation application if by this is meant that he or she is free to act in an autocratic or arbitrary fashion, since this would be the antithesis of the guarantee contained in Art. 5); *Waterville Fisheries Development Ltd v. Acquaculture Licensing Appeals Board (No.2)*

expressly forbids the enactment of legislation 'which declare[s] acts to be infringements of the law which were not so at the date of their commission'.

2.1.2 The Constitution itself uses different language to describe the rights it protects and sometimes employs different language to set out the circumstances in which the right can be curtailed or restricted. Although some rights are described as 'inviolable' or 'inalienable', this is not universally the case. Similarly, while the power of the State 'to delimit the exercise of constitutionally protected rights' is expressly given in some cases and not referred to at all in others, this does not mean 'that, where absent, the power does not exist'.[35]

For the best part of twenty years, however, the Irish courts have employed a standard proportionality doctrine in assessing the validity of legislative restrictions on the exercise of constitutional rights. The classic test remains that articulated by Costello J. in *Heaney v. Ireland*:[36]

> The objective of the impugned provision must be of sufficient importance to warrant overriding a constitutionally protected right. It must relate to concerns pressing and substantial in a free and democratic society. The means chosen must pass a proportionality test. They must:
>
> (a) be rationally connected to the objective and not be arbitrary, unfair or based on irrational considerations,
> (b) impair the right as little as possible, and
> (c) be such that their effects on rights are proportional to the objective.

This test has been consistently applied and it has helped to provide an objective template whereby the legitimacy of such restrictions on the exercise of constitutional rights can be assessed.[37]

2.1.3 Irish courts frequently employ the concept of the rule of law, although this is sometimes no more than a rhetorical makeweight. Nevertheless, the rule of law principles reflect the idea that the State is described as a democracy in Art. 5 of the Constitution and that Art. 34 of the Constitution commits the administration of justice to the judiciary. Among the key ideas contained in the rule of law decision making found in the Irish jurisprudence are the following:

– The principle of legality: every decision affecting legal rights must have an appropriate legal basis.

[2014] IEHC 381 ('absolute discretion' given by statute does not mean that the Board was not obliged to give reasons for its decisions).

[35] *Murray v. Ireland* [1985] IR 532, 538, *per* Costello J.

[36] [1994] 3 IR 593, 607, *per* Costello J. The test was expressly borrowed from a then contemporary decision of the Supreme Court of Canada: *Chaulk v. R.* (1990)3 SCR 1335–1336.

[37] See, e.g., *Daly v. Revenue Commissioners* [1996] 3 IR 1 *Re Art. 26 and the Health (Amendment) Bill (No.2)* [2005] IESC 7, [2005] 1 IR 105 , *King v. Minister for Environment (No.2)* [2006] IESC 61, [2007] 2 IR 296. See generally: Hogan 1997, Foley 2010 and Kenny 2014

- The executive cannot constitutionally be given the power by statute to act in an arbitrary or autocratic fashion.[38]
- The right of access to the courts: legislation which restricts the right of access to the courts will be construed narrowly.[39] Legislation which unfairly restricts access to the courts will be found to be unconstitutional.[40]
- The law must be certain and accessible.[41]
- Legislation cannot retroactively create new criminal offences or other legal wrongs.[42]
- Fundamental rights should not be affected adversely by legislation save through the use of clear language.[43]
- Legal penalties cannot be created by the use of oblique language in a statute. It is, for example, a 'cardinal principle in the judicial interpretation of statutes that the range of criminal liability should not be held to have been statutorily extended except by clear, direct and unambiguous words'.[44]

---

[38] *Mallak v. Minister for Justice* [2012] IESC 59; *Waterville Fisheries Development Ltd. v. Acquaculture Licensing Appeals Board (No.2)* [2014] IEHC 381.

[39] *Murphy v. Greene* [1990] 2 IR 560, *Re MJBCH* [2013] IEHC 256, [2013] 1 IR 407.

[40] *Macauley v. Minister for Posts and Telegraphs* [1966] IR 345, *Blehein v. Minister for Health and Children* [2008] IESC 40, [2009] 1 IR 275.

[41] But note the decision of the Supreme Court in *Minister for Justice and Equality v. Adach* [2010] IESC 33, [2010] 3 IR 402. The background to that case was that the European Arrest Warrant Act 2003 had been amended by legislation enacted by the Oireachtas (Parliament) and duly signed by the President on 21 July 2009. Notice of this had been published in the official gazette in the manner required by Art. 25 of the Constitution. The amending legislation required that no appeal would be taken in European Arrest Warrant cases save with leave of the High Court. In October 2009 the requested person, Mr. Adach, purported to appeal without leave of the High Court, contending that the new legislation had not been officially published until November 2009. This was admitted – a translation into Irish had been awaited – but the Supreme Court noted that the appellant and his advisers were fully aware of the effect of the new provision and they had been advised of its terms by the trial judge. The Court rejected arguments that case law such as Case C-345/06 *Heinrich* [2009] ECR I-01659 had any relevance to this question, since the matter was governed entirely by the publication requirements of Art. 25 of the Constitution. While Hardiman J. acknowledged the importance 'of accessibility, clarity and foreseeability when considering laws mandating the deprivation of a person's liberty', this was not such a case, as the legislation in question was essentially a law prescribing new procedural rules.

[42] *Doyle v. An Taoiseach* [1986] ILRM 693. See also *The People v. Geraghty* [2014] IECA 2.

[43] See e.g. *Albatross Feeds Ltd v. Minister for Agriculture and Food* [2006] IESC 52, [2007] 1 IR 271.

[44] *Director of Public Prosecutions v. Flanagan* [1979] IR 265, 280 *per* Henchy J. Additionally, laws which create unclear or arbitrary offences have been held to be unconstitutional: see, e.g., *King v. Director of Public Prosecutions* [1981] IR 233, *Douglas v. Director of Public Prosecutions* [2013] IEHC 343, [2014] 1 IR 510.

2.2 The Balancing of Fundamental Rights and Economic Freedoms in EU Law

2.2.1 During the referendums on the Lisbon Treaty, certain decisions of the Court of Justice of the European Union (CJEU), such as *Laval* and *Viking*,[45] prompted concerns about the EU prioritising economic liberties over traditional human rights, and that the CJEU imposed significant limitations on the right of workers to take collective action where the exercise of that right interfered with the freedom of establishment and freedom to provide services.[46] This issue has, however, simply not arisen in practice, and it remains to be seen how the Irish courts would endeavour to reconcile traditional liberties with the free movement objectives which were prioritised in *Laval* and *Viking*.

2.3 Constitutional Rights, the European Arrest Warrant and EU Criminal Law

Introduction: Implementation of the European Arrest Warrant (EAW) in Ireland and the main principles in its judicial application The European Arrest Warrant Act 2003 (as amended) (the 2003 Act) has given effect to the EAW Framework Decision.[47,48] The system mandated by the 2003 Act requires that all applications be made to the High Court, generally under the supervision of a specially assigned judge. Since 2009, leave is required before an appeal can be taken from the High Court to the Supreme Court.[49] Following the establishment of the new Court of Appeal in October 2014, appeals now lie (with leave) to the Court of Appeal. In exceptional cases the Supreme Court can grant leave to hear an appeal from the Court of Appeal.

A further consideration is that prior to 1 December 2014, no Irish court had jurisdiction to make a reference to the CJEU in respect of the interpretation of a framework decision. Article 10(3) of Protocol No. 36 to the Treaty of Lisbon provided for jurisdiction to make a reference after a five-year transitional period. The Lisbon Treaty entered into force on 1 December 2009, and the transitional period expired on 1 December 2014. Given the sheer volume of case law which the

---

[45] Case C-341/05 *Laval* [2007] ECR I-11767 and Case C-438/05 *Viking Line* [2007] ECR I-10779.

[46] Kiernan et al. 2012, p. 539.

[47] Council Framework Decision of 13 June 2002 on the European arrest warrant and the surrender procedures between Member States (2002/584/JHA), [2002] OJ L 190/1.

[48] See generally, Fahey 2010, pp. 107–128 and more generally, Farrell and Hanrahan 2011.

[49] Section 16(11) of the 2003 Act (as substituted by Sect. 10 of the EAW (Application to Third Countries and Amendment) and Extradition (Amendment) Act 2012).

2003 Act has generated to date,[50] one may expect – should this trend continue – that a steady stream of references will be made by the Irish courts over the next number of years.

Indeed, this case law has been such that it could not be said that the Irish courts have largely acted as 'rubber stamps', since the Irish courts have paid particular attention to the procedural safeguards prescribed by the 2003 Act. Accordingly, applications for surrender which have not specified with 'unambiguous clarity … the number and nature of the offences for which the person sought is so sought'[51] or have not clearly indicated whether the warrant sought is in respect of a conviction *in absentia*[52] will be rejected. There is likewise no prospect of surrender if the foreign offence does not 'correspond' to an offence known to Irish law.[53] The High Court has nonetheless provided a very complete explanation of the difference between the EAW system and the former system of extradition in *O'Sullivan v. Irish Prison Service*,[54] which admirably sums up the prevailing judicial attitude to the EAW regime:

> Despite superficial similarities between extradition and surrender, namely that both can result in the forcible departure, by compulsion of law, of a person from this State, the EAW regime must be considered as a regime different, separate and distinct from extradition. The principles upon which each rests are materially different: one driven by executive motivation, the other by mutual judicial trust and respect. The EAW regime was developed to solve many notable and renowned problems, which developed with the extradition system which existed previously. The former regime, and indeed the one which still regulates our relationship with the vast majority of States worldwide, was technical, slow, and lacked reciprocal judicial trust and respect. Without the latter it is incumbent on both the State and its Courts to apply a heightened level of scrutiny in relation to those being extradited; many of the world's legal systems do not uphold the same principles or rule of law or democracy which we enjoy here, the risk of wrongful conviction or *mala fides* prosecution are therefore much greater outside of the EU. Even with our more developed neighbours, procedural safeguards and concepts of justice and punishment may be at significant variance with our own. A more thorough investigative procedure is therefore both justified and required, so as to safeguard the rights of those whose extradition is sought … .
>
> The EAW regime and the Framework Decision upon which it is based are the result of ever-increasing cooperation in criminal and judicial matters, particularly with regards to extradition … within the Union, which was necessitated by the opening up of the free market. … This has meant the removal of a number of traditional exceptions for extradition, for example with regards to the political offence exception and the non-extradition of nationals.

---

[50] The Supreme Court appears to have given some 40 written judgments on diverse aspects of the EAW.

[51] *Minister for Justice and Equality v. Connolly* [2014] IESC 34, [2014] 2 ILRM 241, 253, *per* Hardiman J.

[52] *Minister for Justice and Equality v. Palonka* [2015] IECA 69.

[53] 2003, Sect. 38(1)(b) and see generally *Minister for Justice and Equality v. Marjasz* [2012] IEHC 233. Differences in terminology between domestic and foreign offences do not, however, generally lead to a lack of correspondence: see *Minister for Justice v. Szall* [2013] IESC 7, [2013] 1 IR 470.

[54] [2010] 4 IR 562.

> Therefore it cannot be accurate to assimilate, ideologically or practically, the case law or mind-set of extradition into those of *intra*-Union surrender. … I am satisfied that this represents an entirely new system. Surrender is not extradition. There is no hearing into the merits of the prosecution, pending or anticipated in the requesting jurisdiction; nor should there be; and the Executive no longer has a role. There is a special relationship between the Member States of the Union. By virtue of this unity there is increased judicial co-operation between Members. However there is necessarily a great level of trust that the other Member State will act in accordance with the highest and fundamental principles of the Union; namely rule of law, peace, freedom and democracy. Nonetheless, there may be circumstances where certain Member States may be lacking in this regard. It is for this reason that procedural safeguards are placed within the Framework Decision.[55]

In addition, as will be seen, some hugely complicated EAW cases have come before the Irish courts. Two in particular – *Minister for Justice v. Tobin* and *Minister for Justice v. Bailey* – require elaborate consideration. But before examining this case law, a number of special features and safeguards of the 2003 Act should be noted.

First, Sect. 38 of the 2003 Act contains important safeguards in terms of the correspondence of the offence and the seriousness of the offence. Section 38(1)(b) of the 2003 Act provides:

> Subject to *subsection* (2), a person shall not be surrendered to an issuing state under this Act in respect of an offence unless (a) the offence corresponds to an offence under the law of the State, and
>
> (i) under the law of the issuing state the offence is punishable by imprisonment or detention for a maximum period of not less than 12 months, or
>
> (ii) a term of imprisonment or detention of not less than 4 months has been imposed on the person in respect of the offence in the issuing state, and the person is required under the law of the issuing state to serve all or part of that term of imprisonment or (a) the offence is an offence to which paragraph 2 of Article 2 of the Framework Decision applies or is an offence that consists of conduct specified in that paragraph, and under the law of the issuing state the offence is punishable by imprisonment for a maximum period of not less than 3 years.

Secondly, the provisions of Sect. 37 include the following safeguards that will be of importance to the cases that follow:

> (1) A person shall not be surrendered under this Act if:
>
> (i) …
>
> (a) his or her surrender would constitute a contravention of any provision of the Constitution (other than for the reason that the offence specified in the European arrest warrant is an offence to which *section 38(1)(b)* applies[56]),

---

[55] [2010] 2 IR 562 at 597–598, *per* McKechnie J.

[56] This is a technical provision to ensure that applicants cannot resist extradition on the ground that they would be deprived of their right to jury trial for serious offences punishable for more than one year in the requesting state.

(b) there are reasonable grounds for believing that:

(i) …

(ii) in the prosecution or punishment of the person in the issuing state, he or she will be treated less favourably than a person who:

(I) is not his or her sex, race, religion, nationality or ethnic origin,

(II) does not hold the same political opinions as him or her,

(III) speaks a different language than he or she does, or

(IV) does not have the same sexual orientation as he or she does,

or

(ii) were the person to be surrendered to the issuing state:

(I) he or she would be sentenced to death, or a death sentence imposed on him or her would be carried out, or

(II) he or she would be tortured or subjected to other inhuman or degrading treatment.

Section 37 of the 2003 Act may be thus be said to give effect to Recital 12 of the Framework Decision, which provides that the EAW procedure does not:

> [p]revent a Member State from applying its own constitutional rules relating to due process, freedom of association, freedom of the press and freedom of expression in other media.

In fact, Sect. 37 of the 2003 Act probably goes a good deal further than this by protecting the full panoply of constitutional rights and not just those reflecting due process and freedom of speech.[57] In the course of the parliamentary debates on the 2003 Bill, the sponsoring minister justified Sect. 37 of the 2003 Act on the ground that it would ensure that 'no state in the European Union [would] have a higher degree of real and substantial protection for those who seek the protection of the [Irish] courts'.[58]

It is perhaps not altogether surprising that these provisions have generated a good deal of case law. While it might seem that the Irish courts are under a particular duty to treat surrender applications under the EAW procedure in 'a most serious fashion', the 'practical operation of the Act of 2003 has not matched the

---

[57] The Commission Staff Report Document, Annex to the Report from the Commission on the implementation since 2005 of the Council Framework Decision of 13 June 2002 on the European arrest warrant and the surrender procedures between Member States (2007), at pp. 5–6 commented adversely on this development:

'… EL, IE, IT and CY have transposed the text into their legislation in such a way that it goes beyond the Framework Decision and therefore creates the risk that a EAW will be refused on the basis of grounds not envisaged in the Framework Decision. In addition to referring to the European Convention on Human Rights, IE and IT require refusal where surrender would breach their national constitutions. Although this may cover situations arising under both Art. 6 TEU and Recital 12 (such as rules on due process), it nevertheless goes beyond the Framework Decision, in particular as Art. 6 TEU refers only to those constitutional principles common to Member States.'

[58] 577 *Dáil Debates* Col. 10 (17 December 2003).

ideal and the role of Sect. 37 has been "read down" dramatically through judicial interpretation'.[59]

In *Minister for Justice v. Altaravicius*[60] the Supreme Court stressed that the 2003 Act must be interpreted in the light of the objectives of the Framework Decision, which include 'to remove the complexity and potential for delay inherent' in the pre-existing extradition arrangements between the Member States (Preamble) and to ground the EAW procedure on the principle of mutual recognition of judicial decisions (Recital 6 and Art. 1(2)) and 'on a high level of confidence between Member States' (Recital 10). It was against that background that the Supreme Court stressed that the residual power to refuse surrender contained in Sect. 37(1)(b) of the 2003 Act must be understood: this provision was a residual power which was to be confined to exceptional cases. As Murray C.J. stated, it could not constitute a breach of the Constitution to effect a surrender 'simply because [the foreign] legal system of trial differed from ours as envisaged by the Constitution'.[61]

---

[59] Fahey 2010, p. 110. For a similar view, see Walsh 2009.

[60] [2006] IESC 23, [2006] 3 IR 148.

[61] [2007] 3 IR 732, 743. The Chief Justice had earlier stated ([2007] 3 IR 732, 741):

'The effect of such an argument is that an order for surrender under the Act of 2003, and indeed any order for extradition, ought to be refused if the manner in which a trial in the requesting State including the manner in which a penal sanction is imposed, does not conform to the exigencies of our Constitution as if such a trial or sentence were to take place in this country. That can hardly have been the intention of the Oireachtas when it adopted s. 37(1) of the Act of 1973 since it would inevitably have the effect of ensuring that most requests for surrender or extradition would have to be refused. And indeed if that were the intent of the Framework Decision ... and other countries applied such a test from their own perspective, few, if any, would extradite to this country ... .

The manner, procedure and mechanisms according to which fundamental rights are protected in different countries will vary according to national laws and constitutional traditions. The checks and balances in national systems may vary even though they may have the same objective such as ensuring a fair trial. There may be few, if any, legal systems which wholly comply with the precise exigencies of our Constitution with regard to these matters. Not all for example will provide a right to trial by jury in exactly the same circumstances as our Constitution does in respect of a trial for a non-minor offence. Rules of evidence may differ. The fact that a person would be tried before a judge and jury in this country for a particular offence could not in my view, be a basis for refusing to make an order for surrender solely on the grounds that in the requesting State he or she would not be tried before a jury. ...

That is not by any means to say that a Court, in considering an application for surrender, has no jurisdiction to consider the circumstances where it is established that surrender would lead to a denial of fundamental or human rights. There may well be egregious circumstances such as a clearly established and fundamental defect in the system of justice of a requesting State where a refusal of an application for surrender may be necessary to protect such rights. It would not be appropriate in this case to examine further possible or hypothetical situations where this might arise. The sole matter which I wish to make clear here is that the mere fact that a trial or sentence may take place in a requesting State according to procedures or principles which differ from those which apply, even if constitutionally guaranteed, in relation to a criminal trial in this country does not of itself mean that an application for surrender should be refused pursuant to s. 37(2) of the Act.'

This trend was continued in the subsequent decision of the Supreme Court in *Minister for Justice v. Stapleton.*[62] Here the question was whether the respondent could invoke undue delay as a ground to resist surrender to the UK under Sect. 37 of the 2003 Act. In effect, the argument was that if he were to face trial in Ireland at that time, he could invoke the jurisprudence arising from the due process provisions of Art. 38.1 in order to demonstrate that such trial would infringe his constitutional rights due to undue delay. Proceeding from that premise, the applicant then argued that his surrender to the UK would amount to an infringement of his constitutional rights.

In his judgment for the Supreme Court, Fennelly J. observed that the principle of 'mutual confidence' in the respective legal systems was broader and went further than the systems of mutual political and judicial trust which were contained in the European Convention on Extradition 1957 and, in our own legal system, the Extradition Act 1965, as it 'encompasses the system of trial in the issuing member state'.

Fennelly J. further noted that the question of whether there had been any undue delay could be best resolved within the context of the legal system of the requesting state. The mere fact that there was a difference in criminal procedure between the two jurisdictions was not in itself enough. Fennelly J. then stated:

> I cannot see that any of the differences discerned by the trial judge between the right to seek prohibition of trial in the English courts and our own could amount to the establishment of an infringement of the right to fair trial, or fair procedures, whether by reference to the [European] Convention [on Human Rights] or to the Constitution. They certainly do not amount, to repeat the words of Murray C.J. [in *Brennan*], to 'a clearly established and fundamental defect in the system of justice of [the] requesting State'.
>
> On the facts of this case, there is available to the respondent a procedure which will enable him, on surrender to the issuing Member State to seek a remedy based on the very long period of time which has elapsed since the alleged commission of the offences. Moreover, on the facts of the case, it is demonstrably more efficient and more convenient that those matters be debated before the courts of the country where the respondent is to be tried. The prosecuting and police authorities as well as other witnesses are available to and amenable to the jurisdiction of the courts of that country. Documentary evidence, of the type demanded by the respondent, will be more readily available there. If not, its absence may be more readily explained. There may, in addition, be arguments or points of domestic law, whether based on precedents or otherwise, which the respondent can advantageously argue or rely upon which may not be available to him in this jurisdiction and of which an Irish court might not necessarily be aware.[63]

It is accordingly clear from this case law that Sect. 37(1)(b) of the 2003 Act can only be successfully invoked by a respondent if it can be demonstrated that the very act of surrender would either itself *ex facie* amount to an unconstitutionality in the circumstances or where the Court, acting on the clearest of evidence, has significant grounds for apprehending that the requested person would, if surrendered, face a

---

[62] [2007] IESC 30, [2007] 1 IR 669.

[63] [2007] 1 IR 669, 691–692.

manifestly unfair trial which does not meet contemporary minimum standards presupposed by the Framework Decision itself.

There appears to be only two cases where the Court has refused to sanction surrender in the light of the provisions of Sect. 37. In *Minister for Justice and Equality v. Nolan*,[64] the requested person was facing surrender to the UK to serve out the balance of a sentence which had been imposed by a British court. Aspects of that particular sentencing regime had already been held by the European Court of Human Rights (ECtHR) to be contrary to Art. 5.1 of the ECHR insofar as it provided for detention beyond the tariff stipulated by the trial judge.[65] The Supreme Court held that to surrender the applicant in these circumstances would amount to a breach of Sect. 37(1)(a)(i) of the 2003 Act, since it would be contrary to the state's obligations under the ECHR. In effect, therefore, the Court refused the surrender of the respondent where he would be delivered up to complete the balance of a sentence which had been held to be non-ECHR compliant. In the other case, *Minister for Justice and Equality v. Rostas*,[66] the High Court refused to sanction the surrender of a Romanian of Roma ethnicity in respect of a conviction for robbery in 1995, where there were clear and detailed reasons to suggest that the conviction represented a miscarriage of justice.[67]

The decision in Tobin and abuse of process The Irish courts have also been obliged to deal with some particularly difficult EAW cases, of which the Tobin litigation is perhaps the paradigm example. In *Minister for Justice v. Tobin (No. 1)*,[68] an Irish national[69] had been arrested in Hungary following the death of two young children in a road traffic accident. He was then permitted by the authorities to leave Hungary, but was subsequently convicted in his absence by the Hungarian courts. The Supreme Court ultimately refused to sanction his surrender from Ireland under the EAW procedure on the basis that it had not been shown that he had 'fled' Hungary in the manner then required by Sect. 10 of the 2003 Act.

---

[64] [2013] IESC 54.

[65] See *James, Wells and Lee v. the United Kingdom*, nos. 25119/09, 57715/09 and 57877/09, 18 September 2012.

[66] [2014] IEHC 391, [2015] 1 ILRM 1.

[67] Edwards J. noted ([2015] 1 ILRM 1, 58–59) while the trial took place 'in a very different Romania to today's Romania', nevertheless:

> 'while it is impossible to determine definitively whether the respondent in fact received a fair trial, there is sufficient supporting evidence demonstrating the consistency of her narrative with what is known to have been commonplace in Romania and its criminal justice system at the material time, and concerning the manner in which persons of Roma ethnicity were frequently ill-treated and discriminated against by police and officials within that system, to give the court substantial grounds for believing that there is a real risk that the respondent has suffered a flagrant denial of justice in the requesting country.'

[68] [2008] IESC 3, [2008] 4 IR 42.

[69] Later described by Hardiman J. as a person of 'unblemished character' who 'has had a distinguished career in an Irish public company': *Minister for Justice v. Tobin (No. 2)* [2012] 4 IR 147, 266.

While Fennelly J. accepted that the 'fleeing' requirement was not compatible with the requirements of the Framework Decision, he concluded that in view of the express language of the 2003 Act, it could not be construed in a manner compatible with the Framework Decision without giving the Act an interpretation which would be *contra legem.*

The Oireachtas subsequently enacted the European Arrest Warrant (Amendment) Act 2009, Sect. 6 of which deleted the 'fled' requirement. At that point, the State sought a fresh surrender of Mr. Tobin. A majority of the Supreme Court ultimately refused the request. The two judges of the minority, Denham C. J. and Murray J., took the view that the State was obliged to alter the law in order to ensure that it conformed with the requirements of the Framework Decision, and that obligation effectively superseded any issue concerning the rights of the accused. The majority could not accept this approach and, in lengthy and passionate judgments, they concluded that the surrender would amount to an abuse of process by re-opening a final decision and interfering with vested rights.[70]

2.3.1 The Presumption of Innocence

2.3.1.1–2.3.1.2 The automaticity underlying the EAW system has been a constant source of judicial concern for the Irish courts. This can be seen in two important

[70] Note, for example, that some members of the majority went to pains to stress that they were entitled to rely on a fundamental legal principle of domestic law – namely abuse of process – in the context of the interpretation of the Framework Decision, provided that the application of these rules did not infringe the principle of non-discrimination or effectiveness. As Fennelly J. observed ([2012] 4 IR 147, 212):

'The legislation was then amended by this State. Indeed this had to be done in order to bring Irish law into conformity with the Framework Decision. That is cold comfort for the appellant. He is the only person whose surrender had been refused by reason of the 'fled' provision. The amendment … exposed him to the possibility that a second European Arrest Warrant would be issued, which is indeed what has occurred. If the legislation had been enacted originally in conformity with the Framework Decision, he would at least have had his case decided on appropriate grounds. He would either have been surrendered to Hungary or he would have succeeded on appeal on one of the other grounds advanced in *Tobin (No. 1).* He would not have been subjected to the same judicial process twice.

The consequence of the amending legislation was that the appellant has faced a second process of arrest, objection, High Court hearing and appeal. All this is the result of what appears to have been a legislative error followed by its correction. None of this was the responsibility of the appellant. … [T]his is quite different from cases where an earlier proceeding has failed by reason of defects in a warrant. In those cases it will be apparent that the surrender … is the result of a particular defect in the warrant and that … the error can be remedied and a new warrant can be issued without the defects.

These are in essence the reasons why I agree … that the appeal should succeed on the ground of abuse of process. The principle of national procedural autonomy permits the courts of the Member States to apply national procedural rules so long as they do not infringe either the principle of non-discrimination or of effectiveness.'

recent Supreme Court decisions in *Minister for Justice and Equality v. Bailey*[71] and *Minister for Justice and Equality v. Ostrowski.*[72]
In *Bailey* the applicant, a British national, had been a suspect in the murder of a noted French actress, Sophie Toscan du Plantier, in rural west Cork in December 1996. This murder was one of the most controversial murder cases in Irish criminal justice history. The Director of Public Prosecutions decided not to prosecute Mr. Bailey who had been identified as a suspect in the crime.[73] Section 42(c) of the 2003 Act as originally enacted had provided that no surrender could take place where the Director of Public Prosecutions had already decided not to prosecute the suspect for the crime in question, but this prohibition was later deleted in 2005.[74]

At that point the French authorities issued an EAW request for Mr. Bailey, but this was ultimately refused by the Supreme Court for two fundamental reasons. First, the Court concluded that it was implicit in Art. 4(7)(b) of the Framework Decision that it imported a requirement of reciprocity. A murder committed outside of Ireland is a crime in Irish law only if committed by an Irish citizen, so that, for example, a court in Ireland could not seek the surrender of a British national in respect of a murder committed in France. It followed that Ireland could not surrender a British national to France in respect of a murder committed in Ireland. Secondly, it was also clear that Mr. Bailey was being sought for the purposes of a preliminary investigation and that no decision had yet been taken to charge the person whose surrender had been sought.[75]

In *Ostrowski* the surrender of a Polish national was sought on the ground that he was found in possession of 0.72 g of marijuana. In the High Court, Edwards J. refused to order surrender on the ground that this was wholly disproportionate, not least as the accused was most unlikely to receive a prison sentence in respect of this offence. This decision was, however, reversed on appeal by the Supreme Court. Denham C.J. stressed that once the offence met the minimum gravity test[76] specified by the 2003 Act, the High Court had no further role in the matter in assessing any question of proportionality. She also took the view that the Irish courts had no role in assessing what type of sentence the offender was likely to

[71] [2012] IESC 16, [2012] 4 IR 1.

[72] [2013] IESC 24.

[73] This has always been a matter of considerable controversy. It is sufficient perhaps to state that in the course of the EAW proceedings evidence emerged to show that the Director of Public Prosecutions considered that the police inquiry 'into the case was "prejudiced" against [Mr. Bailey] and flawed': *Minister for Justice v. Bailey* [2012] 4 IR 1, 65, *per* Hardiman J.

[74] Criminal Justice (Terrorist Offences) Act 2005, Sect. 83.

[75] Article 1(1) of the Framework Decision requires that the warrant must be 'for the purpose of conducting a criminal prosecution or executing a custodial sentence or detention order.' Section 21A of the 2003 Act requires the High Court to refuse to order the surrender where the Court is satisfied 'that a decision has not been made to charge the person with and try him or her for the offence specified in the warrant'. See also to same effect, *Minister for Justice v. McArdle* [2005] IESC 76, [2005] 4 IR 260 and *Minister for Justice v. Olsson* [2011] IESC 1, [2011] 1 IR 384.

[76] In this case the offence carried a maximum penalty of three years imprisonment.

receive in the requesting state. It is interesting, however, that two other members of the Court, McKechnie J. and MacMenamin J., while concurring in the result, expressed deep unease at this result. Both intimated that the EAW system required revision to ensure that the proportionality of any request was assessed both by the requesting and, indeed, the surrendering state.

2.3.2 *Nullum crimen, nulla poena sine lege*

2.3.2.1 It may seem surprising, given the extensive litigation regarding the EAW, that the issue of *nullum crimen sine lege* has not featured prominently in Ireland. This is probably because of the protections contained in Sect. 38 of the 2003 Act, the wording of which was provided in the introduction to Sect. 2.3. In the vast majority of cases the requesting state will be required to show that the offence in question has a corresponding Irish offence.

2.3.3 Fair Trial and *In Absentia* Judgments

2.3.3.1 The issue of *in absentia* judgments has also proved troubling. Section 45 of the 2003 Act contained a general prohibition on surrender for such purposes, but this prohibition has itself been re-cast on two separate occasions.[77] In the present form, Sect. 45 provides that '[a] person shall not be surrendered under this Act if he or she did not appear in person at the proceedings resulting in the sentence or detention order in respect of which the European arrest warrant was issued, unless the European arrest warrant indicates the matters required by points 2, 3 and 4 of point (d) of the form of warrant in the Annex to the Framework Decision as amended by Council Framework Decision 2009/299/JHA … '.

It should be noted, however, that the Sect. 45 prohibition is not absolute, reflecting the exceptions expressly provided in Art. 5 of the Framework Decision.[78] It does not apply to persons who have had adequate notice of the trial but who elect not to participate.[79] To that extent it may be that Sect. 45 of the 2003 Act is not inconsistent with the decision of the Court of Justice in *Melloni.*[80] At the same time, these safeguards are real. Thus, for example, it is inappropriate to order surrender

[77] Section 45 of the 2003 Act was first replaced by Sect. 20 of the Criminal Justice (Miscellaneous Provisions) Act 2009. That substitution was itself replaced by Sect. 23 of the European Arrest Warrant (Application to Third Countries) and Extradition (Amendment) Act 2012.

[78] *Minister for Justice and Equality v. McCague* [2008] IEHC 154, [2010] 1 IR 154, *per* Peart J.

[79] *Minister for Justice and Equality v. McCague* [2008] IEHC 154, [2010] 1 IR 154 (the accused who discharged his legal team in advance of a scheduled trial date cannot contend that he was sentenced *in absentia*, even where the accused contended that he was ill and feared for his life if he attended the trial).

[80] Case C-399/11 *Melloni* [2013] ECLI:EU:C:2013:107.

where the accused did not appear at the trial, unless the requesting authority has actually completed and filled in the table contained in Sect. 45 of the 2003 Act.[81]

2.3.4–2.3.5 The Right to a Fair Trial/The Right to Effective Judicial Protection

See matters covered in previous sections.

2.3.6 Proportionality and EU Criminal Law

As can be seen from this brief discussion, the Irish courts have expressed unease with aspects of the operation of the EAW system, particularly its automaticity and lack of proportionality. While there is no doubt that the Oireachtas sought to provide the greatest level of protection possible when enacting the 2003 Act, the courts have struggled to fully live up to these expectations,[82] as they have felt obliged to give effect to the language and objects of the Framework Decision,[83] save where to do so would be plainly *contra legem*.[84] It should also be noted that the courts have at times expressed unease regarding aspects of the lack of proportionality inherent in the EAW system[85] and the automaticity involved in giving effect to foreign prosecutorial and judicial decisions.[86]

2.4 The EU Data Retention Directive

2.4.1 As it happens, three of the most important data protection cases which have either recently come before the CJEU or are pending before that Court have come

[81] *Minister for Justice and Equality v. Palonka* [2015] IECA 69.

[82] See e.g. the very narrow reading given to the 'protecting constitutional rights' provisions of Sect. 37 of the 2003 Act as demonstrated in cases such as *Stapleton* and *Brennan*.

[83] The principle of *interprétation conforme* as expressed in cases such as Case C-105/03 *Pupino* [2005] ECR I-05285 features prominently in the Irish EAW jurisprudence. As one might expect, the effect has been in nearly every case to dilute the specific *national* safeguards contained in the 2003 Act in favour of a more standardised interpretation which conforms with the requirements of the Framework Decision: see generally the comments of Murray J. in *Minister for Justice and Equality v. Tokarski* [2012] IESC 61.

[84] As happened with respect to the 'fleeing' provisions discussed in *Minister for Justice v. Tobin (No.1)* [2008] IESC 3, [2008] 4 IR 42. See generally, *Minister for Justice v. Palonka* [2015] IECA 69, *per* Finlay Geoghegan and Peart JJ.

[85] See, e.g., the comments of Denham C.J., McKechnie and MacMenamin J.J. in *Minister for Justice v. Ostrowski* [2013] IESC 24.

[86] See, e.g., the disagreement even among the majority in *Minister for Justice v. Tobin (No. 2)* [2012] 4 IR 147 as to whether the Irish courts could look behind the merits of the Hungarian conviction.

from Ireland: *Ireland v. Parliament and Council* (2009),[87] *Digital Rights Ireland*[88] and, most recently, *Schrems.*[89] These will now be explored in greater detail.

Ireland v. Parliament and Council The first of these cases, *Ireland v. Parliament and Council*, was a challenge to the legal basis on which the Data Retention Directive[90] was adopted, with the CJEU rejecting the argument that the Union legislator was not entitled to adopt this provision as an internal market measure. While the case is doubtless an important one in terms of the jurisprudence on internal market measures, it would be hard to say that it had implications for data protection rights as a topic in itself. At the same time, the fact that the action was dismissed may have given the wrong impression that the Directive itself was impregnable to future legal challenge. Many commentators may thus have overlooked the Court's express saver at the commencement of its discussion of the merits of the action:

> It must also be stated that the action brought by Ireland relates solely to the choice of legal basis and not to any possible infringement of fundamental rights arising from interference with the exercise of the right to privacy contained in Directive 2006/24.[91]

While the Court acknowledged that data retention is directly concerned with criminal justice and the prevention of terrorism,[92] it also stressed that this topic has significant implications for the internal market:

> It is also clear from the file that the obligations relating to data retention have significant economic implications for service providers in so far as they may involve substantial investment and operating costs.
>
> The evidence submitted to the Court shows, moreover, that the national measures adopted up to 2005 pursuant to Article 15(1) of Directive 2002/58 differed substantially, particularly in respect of the nature of the data retained and the periods of data retention. …
>
> In the light of that evidence, it is apparent that the differences between the various national rules adopted on the retention of data relating to electronic communications were liable to have a direct impact on the functioning of the internal market and that it was foreseeable that that impact would become more serious with the passage of time.

---

[87] Case C–301/06 *Ireland v. Parliament and Council* [2009] ECR I-00593.

[88] Joined cases C-293/12 and C-594/12 *Digital Rights Ireland and Seitlinger and Others* [2014] ECLI:EU:C:2014:238.

[89] Case C-362/14 *Schrems* [2015] ECLI:EU:C:2015:650.

[90] Directive 2006/24/EC of the European Parliament and of the Council of 15 March 2006 on the retention of data generated or processed in connection with the provision of publicly available electronic communications services or of public communications networks and amending Directive 2002/58/EC, [2006] OJ L 105/54.

[91] Case C-301/06 *Ireland v. Parliament and Council*, n. 87, at para. 57.

[92] Ireland had argued that the 'centre of gravity' of the measure related to the prevention of crime and the protection of national security. Cf. the later comments of the Court in *Digital Rights Ireland* (at para. 41): '…[t]he material objective of that directive is, therefore, to contribute to the fight against serious crime and thus, ultimately, to public security.'

> Such a situation justified the Community legislature in pursuing the objective of safeguarding the proper functioning of the internal market through the adoption of harmonised rules.[93]

While there was disappointment in official Irish circles that the objections to the legal basis of the Directive were rejected – it was, after all, the first time in which Ireland had challenged EU legislation on this basis – the Directive was duly transposed into domestic law. Certainly, few were prepared for what happened next.

Case C-293/12 *Digital Rights Ireland* Digital Rights Ireland Ltd. (DRI) is a company limited by guarantee, which focuses on data protection and data privacy. It sought to challenge in the Irish High Court a direction issued by the Garda (Police) Commissioner instructing telecommunications providers to retain telecommunications data. DRI further challenged the constitutionality of legislation which sought to authorise retention of such data.

Much of the judgment of the High Court is devoted to the question of whether a limited company had locus standi to challenge the validity of this legislation.[94] Following a review of the Irish constitutional case law on this topic, McKechnie J. granted DRI the right to pursue an *actio popularis* in relation to interference with constitutional rights to privacy and communications, but not in respect of grounds alleging an interference with marital privacy and the right to travel. Since, however, the state sought to justify the legislation by reference to the Data Retention Directive, McKechnie J. felt that he had no alternative but to make a reference on the validity of the Directive to the CJEU.

The decision of the CJEU in respect of the Art. 267 TFEU reference was that the Directive was invalid having regard to Arts. 7 and 8 of the Charter.[95] The Court stressed the fact that the Directive permitted the storage of data on an open-ended and undifferentiated basis, and that such interference was significant:

> It must be stated that the interference caused by Directive 2006/24 with the fundamental rights laid down in Articles 7 and 8 of the Charter is … wide-ranging, and it must be considered to be particularly serious. Furthermore … the fact that data are retained and subsequently used without the subscriber or registered user being informed is likely to generate in the minds of the persons concerned the feeling that their private lives are the subject of constant surveillance.

At the same time the Court observed that the essence of the rights was not affected, as under Art. 1(2) of the Directive, 'the acquisition of knowledge of the content of the electronic communications as such' is not permitted by the Directive. Nevertheless, given that the interference was significant, any interference had to be limited to that which was strictly necessary:

[93] Case C-301/06 *Ireland v. Parliament and Council*, n. 87, paras. 68–72.

[94] *Digital Rights Ireland v. Minister for Communications* [2010] IEHC 221, [2010] 3 IR 251.

[95] Although the plaintiff was also challenging the constitutionality of the legislation in the Irish courts, there appears to have been no reference to the Irish constitutional provisions in the Art. 267 reference itself.

> Consequently, the EU legislation in question must lay down clear and precise rules governing the scope and application of the measure in question and imposing minimum safeguards so that the persons whose data have been retained have sufficient guarantees to effectively protect their personal data against the risk of abuse and against any unlawful access and use of that data … .
>
> The need for such safeguards is all the greater where, as laid down in Directive 2006/24, personal data are subjected to automatic processing and where there is a significant risk of unlawful access to those data … .

So far as the proportionality of the measure was concerned, the Court noted that it applied to virtually all electronic communications, so that the measure applied to virtually the entirety of the European population. The Court also appears to have been struck by the fact that the Directive did not provide any measured exceptions:

> Directive 2006/24 affects, in a comprehensive manner, all persons using electronic communications services, but without the persons whose data are retained being, even indirectly, in a situation which is liable to give rise to criminal prosecutions. It therefore applies even to persons for whom there is no evidence capable of suggesting that their conduct might have a link, even an indirect or remote one, with serious crime. Furthermore, it does not provide for any exception, with the result that it applies even to persons whose communications are subject, according to rules of national law, to the obligation of professional secrecy.

The CJEU further found that the Directive does not require any relationship between the data of which retention is provided for and a threat to public security, e.g. by reference to a particular time period or a particular geographical zone, or a circle of particular persons likely to be involved in a serious crime. Additionally the Directive 'also fails to lay down any objective criterion by which to determine the limits of the access of the competent national authorities to the data and their subsequent use for the purposes of prevention, detection or criminal prosecutions concerning serious offences. Furthermore, Directive 2006/24 'does not contain substantive and procedural conditions relating to the access of the competent national authorities to the data and to their subsequent use'. 'Above all, the access by the competent national authorities to the data retained is not made dependent on a prior review carried out by a court or by an independent administrative body whose decision seeks to limit access to the data and their use to what is strictly necessary for the purpose of attaining the objective pursued …'. Nor did the measure lay down clear and precise rules regarding the time period during which the data is to be retained. It likewise was found not to have adequate safeguards against potential abuse. The Court further added that:

> The directive does not require the data in question to be retained within the European Union, with the result that it cannot be held that the control, explicitly required by Article 8 (3) of the Charter, by an independent authority of compliance with the requirements of protection and security, as referred to in the two previous paragraphs, is fully ensured. Such a control, carried out on the basis of EU law, is an essential component of the protection of individuals with regard to the processing of personal data … .

Given that the measure failed the proportionality test, it followed that the Directive had to be annulled. It may be significant that the Court did not address questions of retroactivity in its decision.

Schrems v. Data Protection Commissioner The third case, *Schrems v. Data Protection Commissioner*[96] arose in judicial review proceedings before the High Court in which the above-named applicant, an Austrian national, challenged a decision of the respondent Data Protection Commissioner (hereinafter Commissioner) not to investigate a particular complaint of his any further pursuant to Sect. 10(1)(b) of the Data Protection Act 1988 (hereinafter 1988 Act). All users in Europe of the major social network, Facebook, are required to sign a contract with Facebook Ireland Ltd. (Facebook Ireland). To that extent, therefore, Facebook Ireland is regulated by the Commissioner under the Irish Data Protection Acts. Facebook Ireland is a subsidiary of its US parent, Facebook Inc. (Facebook). Some or all data relating to Facebook subscribers residing within the EU/EEA is in fact transferred to and held on servers which are physically located within the United States.

The essence of Mr. Schrems' complaint of 25 June, 2013 to the Commissioner was that in the light of the revelations made from May 2013 onwards by Edward Snowden concerning the activities of the US National Security Agency (NSA), there was no meaningful protection in US law and practice in respect of data so transferred to the US so far as State surveillance was concerned.

The Commissioner rejected this complaint on two grounds. First, he considered that there was no evidence that Mr. Schrems' personal data had been accessed by the NSA (or other US security agencies) ('the *locus standi* objection'), so that the complaint was purely hypothetical and speculative. Secondly, the European Commission had determined in its decision of 26 July, 2000 (2000/520/EC) ('the Safe Harbour Decision') that the United States 'ensures an adequate level of [data] protection' in accordance with Art. 25(6) of Directive 95/46/EC (the 1995 Directive). The Commissioner noted that the Safe Harbour decision was a 'Community finding' for the purposes of Sect. 11(2)(a) of the 1988 Act, so that any question of the adequacy of data protection in that third country (in the present case, the United States) where the data is to be transferred was required by Irish law 'to be determined in accordance with that finding'. As this was the gist of the applicant's complaint – namely, that personal data was being transferred to a third country which did not in practice observe these standards – the Commissioner took the view that this question was foreclosed by the nature of the Safe Harbour Decision.

---

[96] [2014] IEHC 310, [2014] 2 ILRM 441 (Irish High Court), Case C-326/14 *Verein für Konsumenteninformation* [2015] ECLI:EU:C:2015:462 (pending before the CJEU). I should disclose that the author was the referring judge. Nothing in this commentary should be taken as reflecting one way or another on the merits of litigation which is currently pending before the Court of Justice.

The evidence and the findings of fact The High Court of Ireland found the following facts regarding the interception of personal data:

(a) Electronic surveillance and interception of communications in the manner provided by law serves necessary and indispensable objectives which are in the public interest, namely, the preservation of national security and the prevention of serious crime. The surveillance and interception of personal data transferred from the EU to the US by the US National Security Authority (and other similar agencies, both in the US and elsewhere) serves legitimate and necessary counter-terrorism objectives and goals.
(b) Nevertheless, the revelations made by Edward Snowden demonstrated a significant over-reach on the part of those authorities. While there is oversight on the part of the Foreign Intelligence Services Court in the US, this is done on an *ex parte* and secret basis. EU citizens have no effective right to be heard on the question of the interception and surveillance of their data and, furthermore, decisions taken to access such data are not conducted on the basis of EU law.
(c) While there may be some dispute regarding the scope and extent of some of these programmes, it was clear from the extensive exhibits contained in the affidavits filed in these proceedings that the accuracy of much of the Snowden revelations did not appear to be in dispute. The Court accordingly found that personal data transferred by companies such as Facebook Ireland to its parent company in the United States can thereafter be accessed by the National Security Authority (and other federal agencies such as the Federal Bureau of Investigation) in the course of a mass and indiscriminate surveillance and interception of such data. Indeed, in the wake of the Snowden revelations, the available evidence presently admitted of no other realistic conclusion.[97]
(d) Both Facebook and Facebook Ireland had self-certified pursuant to the Safe Harbour Decision.

National law So far as Irish national law is concerned, Sect. 11(1) of the 1988 Act precludes the transfer of personal data outside of the State, save where that foreign State 'ensures an adequate level of protection for the privacy and the fundamental rights and freedoms of data subjects in relation to the processing of personal data having regard to all the circumstances surrounding that transfer'. The Court then held that the accessing of private communications by the State authorities through interception or surveillance engages the constitutional right to privacy. Further, accessing by State authorities of private communications generated within the home – whether this involves the accessing of telephone calls, internet use or private mail – is also a clear interference with the inviolability of the dwelling as guaranteed by Art. 40.5 of the Constitution.[98]

The Court next held that the mere fact that these rights are thus engaged does not mean that the interception of communications by State authorities is necessarily or

[97] At paras. 10–13 of the judgment of the Irish High Court, [2014] 2 ILRM 441, 447–448.
[98] Paragraphs 47 and 48 of the judgment, [2014] 2 ILRM 441, 457–458.

always unlawful. The Preamble to the Constitution of Ireland envisages a 'true social order' where the 'dignity and freedom of the individual may be assured', so that both liberty and security are valued. Provided appropriate safeguards are in place, the Court ruled that in a modern society electronic surveillance and interception of communications is indispensable to the preservation of State security. It was accordingly plain that legislation of this general kind serves important – indeed, vital and indispensable – State goals and interests, drawing by analogy on the decision of the German Constitutional Court in the *Anti-Terrorism Database* case[99] and the comments of the Court of Justice in Case C-293/12 *Digital Rights Ireland.*

It further held that the importance of these constitutional rights is nonetheless such that the interference with these privacy interests must be in a manner provided for by law, and any such interference must also be proportionate. This is especially the case in respect of the interception and surveillance of communications within the home. While the term 'inviolable' in respect of the dwelling in Art. 40.5 of the Constitution does not literally mean what it says (i.e. the right is not absolute or incapable of being interfered with), the reference to inviolability in this context nonetheless conveys that the home enjoys the highest level of protection which might reasonably be afforded in a democratic society.[100]

The High Court then held that the mass and undifferentiated accessing of personal data generated perhaps especially within the home – such as e-mails, text messages, internet usage and telephone calls – would not pass any proportionality test or could not survive constitutional scrutiny on this ground alone. The potential for abuse in such cases would be enormous and might even give rise to the possibility that no facet of private or domestic life within the home would be immune from potential State scrutiny and observation. Such a state of affairs would be totally at odds with the basic premises and fundamental values of the Constitution: respect for human dignity and freedom of the individual (as per the Preamble to the Constitution); personal autonomy (Art. 40.3.1 and Art. 40.3.2); the inviolability of the dwelling (Art. 40.5) and protection of family life (Art. 41). Drawing on earlier Irish case law,[101] the Court noted that Art. 40.5 of the Constitution presupposes that 'in a free society the dwelling is set apart as a place of repose from the cares of the world' and assures 'the citizen that his or her privacy, person and security will be protected against all comers', save in a manner provided for by a law which respects the essence of that constitutional guarantee.

The Court then held that a dwelling could not in truth be a 'place of repose from the cares of the world' if, for example, the occupants of the dwelling could not send an e-mail or write a letter or even conduct a telephone conversation if they were not protected from 'the prospect of general or casual State surveillance of such communications on a mass and undifferentiated basis'. The Court observed:

---

[99] 24 April 2003 at paras. 106, 131 and 133, *passim*.

[100] At paras. 49–50 of the judgment, [2014] 2 ILRM 441, 457, 458.

[101] Such as *The People v. O'Brien* [2012] IEHC 68.

> That general protection for privacy, person and security in Article 40.5 [of the Constitution of Ireland] would thus be entirely compromised by the mass and undifferentiated surveillance by State authorities of conversations and communications which take place within the home. For such interception of communications of this nature to be constitutionally valid, it would, accordingly, be necessary to demonstrate that this interception of communications and the surveillance of individuals or groups of individuals was objectively justified in the interests of the suppression of crime and national security and, further, that any such interception was attended by appropriate and verifiable safeguards.[102]

The Court further held that if this matter were entirely governed by Irish law, then measured by these particular constitutional standards, at the very least a significant issue would arise as to whether the United States 'ensures an adequate level of protection for the privacy and the fundamental rights and freedoms' within the meaning of Sect. 11(1)(a) of the 1988 Act, such as would permit data transfers to that country. Moreover, given the (apparently) limited protection given to data subjects by contemporary US law and practice so far as State surveillance is concerned, this would indeed have been a matter which the Commissioner would have been obliged to investigate.

Accordingly, the Court found that if the matter were to be judged *solely* by reference to Irish constitutional law standards, the Commissioner could not properly have exercised his Sect. 10(1)(a) powers to conclude in a summary fashion that there was nothing further to investigate.

National law pre-empted by European Union law? The Safe Harbour Decision

The parties agreed, however, that the matter was only partially governed by Irish law and that, in reality, on this key issue of the adequacy of data protection law and practice in third countries, Irish law has been pre-empted by general EU law in this area.[103] On this point the Court stated:

> This brings us to the nub of the issue for the Commissioner. He is naturally bound by the terms of the 1995 Directive and by the 2000 Commission Decision. Furthermore, as the 2000 Decision amounts to a 'Community finding' regarding the adequacy of data protection in the country to which the data is to be transferred, s. 11(2)(a) of the 1988 Act (as amended) requires that the question of the adequacy of data protection in the country where the data is to be so transferred 'shall be determined in accordance with that finding'. In this respect, s. 11(2)(a) of the 1988 Act faithfully follows the provisions of Article 25(6) of the 1995 Directive.
>
> All of this means that the Commissioner cannot arrive at a finding inconsistent with that Community finding, so that if, for example, the Community finding is to the effect that a particular third party state has adequate and effective data protection laws, the Commissioner cannot conclude to the contrary. The Community finding in question was, as we have already seen, to the effect that the US does provide adequate data protection for

[102] Paragraph 55, [2014] 2 ILRM 441, 459.

[103] This is because Sect. 11(2)(a) of the 1988 Act (as substituted by Sect. 12 of the Data Protection (Amendment) Act 2003) effects a *renvoi* of this wider question in favour of EU law. Specifically, Sect. 11(2)(b) of the 1988 Act provides that the Commissioner must determine the question of the adequacy of protection in the third state 'in accordance' with a Community finding made by the European Commission pursuant to Art. 25(6) of the 1995 Directive.

data subjects in respect of data handled or processed by firms (such as Facebook Ireland and Facebook) which operate the Safe Harbour regime.

It follows, therefore, that if the Commissioner cannot look beyond the European Commission's Safe Harbour Decision of July 2000, then it is clear that the present application for judicial review must fail. This is because, at the risk of repetition, the Commission has decided that the US provides an adequate level of data protection and, as we have just seen, s. 11(2)(a) of the 1998 Act (which in turn follows the provisions of Article 25(6) of the 1995 Directive) ties the Commissioner to the Commission's finding. In those circumstances, any complaint to the Commissioner concerning the transfer of personal data by Facebook Ireland (or, indeed, Facebook) to the US on the ground that US data protection was inadequate would be doomed to fail.

This finding of the Commission is doubtless still true at the level of consumer protection, but, as we have just seen, much has happened in the interval since July 2000. The developments include the enhanced threat to national and international security posed by rogue States, terrorist groupings and organised crime, disclosures regarding mass and undifferentiated surveillance of personal data by the US security authorities, the advent of social media and, not least from a legal perspective, the enhanced protection for personal data now contained in Article 8 of the Charter.

While the applicant maintains that the Commissioner has not adhered to the requirements of EU law in holding that the complaint was unsustainable in law, the opposite is in truth the case. The Commissioner has rather demonstrated scrupulous steadfastness to the letter of the 1995 Directive and the 2000 Decision.

The applicant's objection is, in reality, to the terms of the Safe Harbour Regime itself rather than to the manner in which the Commissioner has actually applied the Safe Harbour Regime. There is, perhaps, much to be said for the argument that the Safe Harbour Regime has been overtaken by events. The Snowden revelations may be thought to have exposed gaping holes in contemporary US data protection practice and the subsequent entry into force of Article 8 of the Charter suggests that a re-evaluation of how the 1995 Directive and 2000 Decision should be interpreted in practice may be necessary. It must be again stressed, however, that neither the validity of the 1995 Directive nor the validity of the Commission's Safe Harbour decision have, as such, been challenged in these proceedings.

Although the validity of the 2000 Decision has not been directly challenged, the essential question which arises for consideration is whether, *as a matter of European Union law*, the Commissioner is nonetheless absolutely bound by that finding of the European Commission as manifested in the 2000 Decision in relation to the adequacy of data protection in the law and practice of the United States having regard in particular *to the subsequent entry into force of Article 8 of the Charter*, the provisions of Article 25(6) of the 1995 Directive notwithstanding. For the reasons which I have already stated, it seems to me that unless this question is answered in a manner which enables the Commissioner either to look behind that Community finding or otherwise disregard it, the applicant's complaint both before the Commissioner and in these judicial review proceedings must accordingly fail.[104]

[104] At paras. 64–70 of the judgment, [2014] 2 ILRM 441, 462–463.

Given that the critical issue in the present case was whether US law and practice afforded sufficient data protection and that no issue was ever raised in these proceedings concerning the actions of Facebook Ireland or Facebook[105] *as such*, the Court took the view that the real question was whether the Commissioner was bound by the earlier findings to this effect by the European Commission in the Safe Harbour Decision. In other words, the Court considered that this was really a complaint concerning *the terms* of that decision, rather than the manner in which the Commissioner *had applied it*.[106] While Art. 3(b) of the Safe Harbour Decision allows the national authorities to direct an entity to suspend data flows to that third country, this is in circumstances where the complaint is directed to *the conduct of that entity*. Here the real objection was not to the conduct of Facebook as such, but rather to the fact that the Commission has already determined that the US law and practice provides adequate data protection in circumstances where it is clear from the Snowden disclosures that personal data of EU citizens so transferred to the US can be accessed by the US authorities on a mass and undifferentiated basis.

In these circumstances the High Court found that it would be appropriate to refer to the Court of Justice the question whether, having regard in particular to the earlier findings of fact regarding the Snowden disclosures and the subsequent entry into force of Art. 7 and Art. 8 of the Charter and the recent judgment of this Court in *Digital Rights Ireland*, the Commissioner was bound by the earlier determination of the European Commission in the Safe Harbour Decision as to the adequacy of the data protection offered by US law and practice. The outcome of this reference is currently pending.[107]

2.5 Unpublished or Secret Legislation

2.5.1 The rules regarding the promulgation of legislation are contained in Art. 25 of the Constitution, which provides that Bills must be presented to the President for signature.[108] The critical provisions are Art. 25.4 paras. 1 and 2:

---

[105] Mr. Schrems has made other separate complaints to the Commissioner concerning Facebook, but none of these complaints arose for consideration in these judicial review proceedings.

[106] Paragraph 69 of the judgment, [2014] 2 ILRM 441, 463.

[107] In its judgment in C-362/14 *Schrems*, n. 89, delivered on 6 October 2015, the Court of Justice held (i) that the Data Protection Commissioner was not so bound and (ii) the Safe Harbour Decision was itself invalid.

[108] This is not a pure formality, as the President could elect to refer the Bill to the Supreme Court to test its constitutionality, having first consulted with the Council of State. The Council of State has met on 27 occasions for this purpose, and the relevant Bills have been referred on 15 occasions.

1. Every Bill shall become and be law as and from the day on which it is signed by the President under this Constitution, and shall, unless the contrary intention appears, come into operation on that day.
2. Every Bill signed by the President under this Constitution shall be promulgated by him as a law by the publication by his direction of a notice in the Iris Oifigiúil[109] stating that the Bill has become law.

These provisions do raise the possibility that a measure may become law before the public can access the text of the new legislation, although the difficulties thereby presented appear to be more theoretical than real. To date the Irish Supreme Court has been largely unsympathetic to arguments of this kind, citing the express language of Art. 25.4.[110] A curious variation of this problem emerged in *Cussens v. Brosnan*,[111] a VAT case where it emerged in the course of an appeal to the Supreme Court that the Irish Revenue Commissioners had withheld the text of a derogation by Ireland from the application of the VAT rules on the disposal of property and, just as remarkably, that the EU Commission had agreed to this. In the light of this admission, the Court gave the appellant leave to amend its pleading based on the emergence of this new fact.[112]

2.6 *Rights and General Principles of Law in the Context of Market Regulation: Property Rights, Legal Certainty, Non-retroactivity and Proportionality*

2.6.1 The question of the protection of property rights and legitimate expectations in the context of EU legislation has rarely arisen in the Irish courts. This is principally because insofar as such a measure interferes with property rights or other procedural entitlements, it will nonetheless be held to be 'necessitated' by the obligations of EU law for the purposes of Art. 29.4.6 of the Constitution and, hence, immune from constitutional review.

---

[109] I.e., the Official Gazette.

[110] *Minister for Justice and Equality v. Adach* [2010] IESC 33, [2010] 3 IR 402, *Minister for Justice v. Bailey* [2012] IESC16, [2012] 4 IR 1.

[111] [2015] IESC 45.

[112] As Laffoy J. commented in her judgment:
'Further, it is difficult to understand how a State body could consider that it had the entitlement to withhold the derogation, which, in reality, is a legal instrument which regulates the charging of VAT and … can be regarded as part of the law of the land, from a taxpayer's adviser, for example, from Mr. Brennan and other partners of Deloitte. It should have been furnished when it was sought in the context of this appeal in March 2012. While the Court was told, in the course of the submissions, that its withholding was not wilful, in that neither the respondent nor the European Commission was able to find it, there was no evidence to support that. Further, as counsel for the appellants emphasised, by letter dated 12th August, 2002 from the European Commission, Mr. Brennan was informed that the "Irish authorities have informed my services that they do not agree to the release of these documents".'

This was made clear by the Supreme Court's decision in *Maher v. Minister for Agriculture and Food.*[113] In that case the plaintiff farmers, who were not at that time milk producers themselves, had leased their milk quotas to other producers from which they derived an income. They challenged the constitutionality of a ministerial order which directed them to either sell back their quotas at par value[114] or else to resume milk production and cease the leasing of the quota. The Supreme Court held that the order was 'necessitated' by the obligations of the EU milk quota system and was, accordingly, immune from constitutional review. The Court added for good measure that milk quotas were creatures of EU law and as the Court of Justice had ruled that such quotas were not in themselves a species of property rights,[115] such quotas could not be regarded as a form of property rights for the purposes of Irish constitutional law.

The courts will not, however, interpret national legislation affecting fundamental rights in a manner which is *contra legem*, even if the ultimate consequence is that the national legislation is interpreted in a manner which is contrary to the intentions of the relevant EU directive.[116]

2.7 The ESM Treaty, Austerity Programmes and the Democratic, Rule-of-Law-Based State

2.7.1 Under the Treaty Establishing the European Stability Mechanism (ESM Treaty), Member States may be required to contribute funds to the ESM that in several countries amount potentially to a large proportion of the annual state budget. In Ireland, the liability of the Irish State under the ESM Treaty is 11.1454 billion EUR; the projected Irish Government expenditure for 2015 is 50 billion EUR, and thus the exposure represents some 22% of the Irish annual budget. The use of such funds is not subject to democratic control or judicial review, and the 85% majority rule means that smaller states have no say over the use of the funds. The constitutionality of the ratification of the ESM Treaty was, however, directly challenged in *Pringle v. Government of Ireland.*[117] Part of the challenge was to the validity of the ESM Treaty itself as a matter of EU law. This aspect of the proceedings ultimately resulted in a reference by the Supreme Court to the Court of Justice which, as is well known, sustained the validity of the treaty.[118] Independently of

[113] [2001] IESC 32, [2001] 2 IR 139.

[114] I.e. at a price lower than the prevailing market price.

[115] See e.g. Case 2/94 *Bostock* [1994] ECR I-00995.

[116] See e.g. *Albatross Feeds Ltd. v. Minister for Agriculture and Food* [2006] IESC 52, [2007] 1 IR 271.

[117] [2012] IESC 47, [2013] 3 IR 1.

[118] Case C-370/12 *Pringle* [2013] ECLI:EU:C:2012:756.

that decision, however, a majority of the Supreme Court upheld the constitutionality of the ratification of the ESM Treaty without a referendum.

The judgments of the Court are lengthy and complex and do not lend themselves to an easy summary. Both the majority judgments and the minority judgment spend much time on the implications of the earlier *Crotty* decision.[119] While the majority judges acknowledged the serious implications of the ESM Treaty, they considered that unlike Title III of the Single European Act which was at issue in *Crotty*, the ESM Treaty did not involve an abdication of or the fettering of the executive power of the State. They stressed that, on the contrary, ratification of the Treaty involved the exercise of the executive power of the State in the manner contemplated by Art. 29 of the Constitution. The dissenting judge, Hardiman J., dissented principally on the basis that the ESM Treaty

> involves a transfer of sovereignty to a degree that makes it incompatible with the Constitution when one applies the principles set out by this Court in *Crotty*, such that a referendum amending the Constitution is necessary to permit the State to ratify the ESM Treaty on behalf of Ireland.[120]

2.7.2 No significant constitutional issues have been raised with regard to the Banking Union.

2.7.3 Ireland was in an EU sponsored bailout from 2010 to 2013. This bailout proved necessary after Ireland had to spend enormous sums rescuing its banks at taxpayers' expense during 2008–2010, the costs of which threatened to overwhelm the financial stability of the state. Even prior to that period, there had been a series of fiscal retrenchments from the onset of the financial crisis in the mid-summer of 2008. During this period, from 2009 onwards, there were a series of emergency measures reducing public sector pay and other disbursements from public moneys through the Financial Emergency Measures in the Public Interest Acts. The courts have, moreover, almost always consistently rejected all challenges to executive or other decisions designed to give effect to the austerity and deficit reduction programme. Thus, the constitutionality of legislation affecting the pension payments of public servants with privately funded pensions[121] or effecting significant reductions in payments to pharmacists[122] or payments to police officers[123] has been upheld, even though by definition the legislative measures in question adversely affected

[119] *Crotty v. An Taoiseach* [1987] IR 713.

[120] In his dissent, Hardiman J. also drew attention to other potential implications of the Treaty for the budgetary process prescribed by the Constitution. For example, although Art. 17.2 provides that no money shall be appropriated save on a recommendation to the lower House, Dáil Éireann, by the Taoiseach, '[w]hat would be the position, having regard to Art. 17.2, of a future Government, Taoiseach, who did not wish to approve, or to recommend, an appropriation for payments to the ESM to Dáil Eireann?'

[121] *Unite the Union v. Minister for Finance* [2010] IEHC 354.

[122] *JJ Haire Ltd. v. Minister for Health and Children* [2009] IEHC 562, [2010] 2 IR 615.

[123] *Garda Representative Association v. Minister for Finance* [2010] IEHC 78.

contractual and other entitlements protected by the property provisions contained in Art. 40.3.2 and Art. 43 of the Constitution. The courts have likewise rejected all claims based on legitimate expectations in relation to changes to a teachers' early retirement scheme[124] or in sick pay benefits for public servants,[125] with the courts expressly citing the financial crisis as a justification.

There is, perhaps, only one case of this kind where a claimant has succeeded: *Dellway Investments Ltd. v. National Asset Management Agency.*[126] In that case the Supreme Court held that the principles of fair procedures were violated when the performing loans of the plaintiff company were transferred to the National Asset Management Agency (NAMA) without giving that company an opportunity to be heard on the matter. NAMA was the 'bad bank' established by the Oireachtas in the wake of the property and banking collapse designed to take major debtors off the books of the Irish banks, so that they could resume lending again in the ordinary way. The Court held that the transfer of these loans to NAMA in practice unambiguously signalled to the markets that there were serious solvency issues arising in respect of the company in question. It followed that the applicant company was entitled to be heard on this question prior to such transfer.

While the decision in *Dellway* was regarded as a major defeat for the Government, it is nonetheless significant that it was the first and only such reverse so far as the austerity programme was concerned. It is ever more significant perhaps that the decision was based on procedural grounds only, since there was no equivalent at all of the decision of the Portuguese Constitutional Court invalidating a budgetary measure adopted as part an austerity measure on proportionality or similar substantive grounds.

The High Court has also upheld the constitutionality of the legislation (Credit Institutions (Financial Support) Act 2008) giving effect to the banking sector guarantee in September 2008 which was at the heart of the financial crisis: see *Collins v. Minister for Finance.*[127] The Court held that the legislation contained sufficient principles and policies which enabled the courts to review decisions taken under the legislation and to ensure democratic accountability. The Court further rejected the argument that the appropriations clause in Art. 11 of the Constitution was violated by the 2008 Act because of the open-ended nature of the guarantee.[128]

---

124 *Curran v. Minister for Education* [2009] IEHC 378, [2009] 4 IR 300.

125 *Garda Representative Association v. Minister for Public Expenditure and Reform* [2014] IEHC 457.

126 [2011] IESC 14, [2011] 4 IR 1.

127 [2013] IEHC 530.

128 The Court said that it was sufficient for this purpose that:

'the appropriation must be for "*an object*, to an extent, and out of a *fund*, which the laws have prescribed." Applying that test to the present case, it can be said that the objects of the appropriation under the 2008 Act are clear and satisfy the requirements of Art. 17.2 [of the Constitution] Section 6(12) of the 2008 Act further provides that the payment comes from the Central Fund in the manner envisaged by Article 11. The *extent* of the payments are also clear. While, of course, the Oireachtas did not know precisely the sums which were at stake when enacting the 2008 Act, it

2.8 *Judicial Review of EU Measures: Access to Justice and the Standard of Review*

2.8.1 The number of Irish cases which have been the subject of Art. 267 TFEU references is not high, although the number has begun to rise steadily from a low base in recent years.[129] Since 2006, there has been only one instance where a reference has expressly sought the annulment of an EU measure, namely, *Digital Rights Ireland* (see Sect. 2.4).

2.8.2–2.8.3 So far as the domestic judicial review is concerned, the standard of review is mixed. There is vigorous judicial review of administrative decisions on grounds of fair procedures, adherence to procedural rules and vires. In this area the record of the Irish courts is very good indeed: one might almost regard it as exemplary. So far as substantive review is concerned, the record is more mixed; there is, to some extent, a culture of deference and unwillingness to intervene. This is especially true of specialist agencies such as planning bodies.[130] There is, however, some sign that this standard of review is regarded as too restrictive, so that a more elaborate review takes place in cases where the protection of fundamental rights is at stake.[131]

So far as domestic constitutional review is concerned, there have been some 94 declarations of unconstitutionality since 1937. While this is in some respects impressive, it might also be said that given the breadth and extent of the fundamental rights guarantees contained in the Constitution, the courts have too often looked away and not engaged sufficiently with major constitutional claims. Against that background, one cannot say from an Irish perspective that the standard of review performed by the Court of Justice in respect of proceedings against EU institutions in matters of economic regulation is lower than that which in practice prevails in ordinary constitutional and judicial review cases in Ireland.[132]

2.8.4 The Irish courts have not yet given any indication of a *Solange* style rebellion. This is perhaps because the question is to some degree pre-determined by the language of Art. 29.4.6 of the Constitution: if the matter is 'necessitated' by the obligations of EU law, then it is beyond the purview of constitutional review. The

---

laid down principles and policies in s. 2 and s. 6 of the 2008 Act which circumscribe the extent of the Minister's discretion to provide financial support.'

Article 17.2 of the Constitution provides that the Dáil may not vote for the appropriation of public money without a message signed by the Taoiseach for this purpose.

[129] The Court of Justice of the European Union, Annual report 2013, Luxembourg 2014, p. 107, puts the figure at 72.

[130] See most notably the leading decision in *O'Keeffe v. An Bord Pleanála* [1993] 1 IR 39.

[131] See e.g. *Holland v. Governor of Portlaoise Prison* [2004] IEHC 208, [2004] 2 IR 573; *Clinton v. An Bord Pleanála* [2007] IESC 19, [2007] 4 IR 701; *Meadows v. Minister for Justice and Equality* [2010] IESC 3, [2010] 2 IR 701 and *Efe v. Minister for Justice and Equality* [2011] IEHC 414, [2011] 2 IR 798.

[132] For relevant case law, see Chalmers et al. 2006, pp. 436–437.

Irish courts have, by and large, taken an accommodating view of what is 'necessitated'[133] by the obligations of Union law. While there remains uncertainty as to the extent to which discretionary decisions taken within the purview of EU law can be described as 'necessitated' for this purpose, Treaty obligations, decisions of the Court of Justice and the method of implementation of EU legislative measures can all be regarded as 'necessitated' obligations required by EU law.

2.9 Other Constitutional Rights and Principles

2.9.1 The other major constitutional issue which has arisen is the method of implementation of EU directives. The Irish courts have, by and large, facilitated the implementation of EU legislative measures by means of ministerial orders made under the European Communities (Amendment) Act 1973, with the Supreme Court reasoning that the practical necessity of transposing such statutory instruments in this fashion means that this method of implementation is itself 'necessitated' and, hence, immune from constitutional review by reason of Art. 29.4.6 of the Constitution.[134] Following two further decisions which invalidated statutory instruments that were found to have by-passed the prohibition on the creation of indictable offences by means of statutory instruments,[135] the European Communities Act 2007 now expressly permits a statutory instrument to give effect to EU legislative requirements and to create an indictable offence for this purpose.[136] This is further discussed in Sect. 1.4.1 above.

2.10 Common Constitutional Traditions

2.10.1 Much of the contemporary Irish historical constitutional scholarship has stressed the extent to which many of the substantive provisions have drawn not only on the US Constitution and the UK common law constitutional historical heritage,[137] but also on a variety of continental constitutions, most notably the Weimar Constitution of 1919.[138] A good example is provided by Art. 40.5 of the

[133] Most notably in cases such as *Meagher v. Minister for Agriculture and Food* [1994] 1 IR 329. See generally Barrett (2013), pp. 154–155.

[134] *Meagher v. Minister for Agriculture and Food* [1994] 1 IR 329.

[135] *Kennedy* v. *Ireland* [2005] IESC 36, [2007] 2 IR 45, *Quinn v. Ireland* [2007] IESC 16, [2007] 3 IR 395.

[136] Provided that the maximum penalty is now greater than five years imprisonment.

[137] See generally, Keane 1992, p. 25; Jaconelli 1992; O'Donnell 2014, p. 139.

[138] See generally, Kelly 1983; Hogan 2014, p. 155.

Constitution which provides: 'The dwelling of every citizen is inviolable and shall not be forcibly entered save in accordance with law.'
This has a direct counterpart in Art. 13 of the German Basic Law, which in turn had a corresponding provision in Art. 115 of the (1919) Weimar Constitution. The latter, however, also drew on earlier sources, such as Art. 3 of the French Constitution of 1848, which provided that the 'residence of every person dwelling in French territory' was 'inviolable'.

It is indeed striking that there has been little comparative analysis of similar constitutional provisions of this kind, of which many unexplored examples abound. As Besselink and others have noted, the references in the case law of the Court of Justice and, for that matter, of the European Court of Human Rights to national constitutions is often perfunctory.[139] Two reasons may be advanced for this. The first is quasi-legal in nature, since it suits the two European Courts to fashion a new homogenised European jurisprudence in matters of human rights which, while acknowledging the original national sources, seeks to carve out a new jurisprudence which is divorced from and independent of national case law and traditions. The second reason is that it is now almost forgotten that the European standards were (originally) designed to set minimum benchmarks. Thus, for example, the drafters of the ECHR deliberately rejected arguments which had been advanced by, *inter alia*, the French delegation that Art. 8(1) should protect the 'inviolability' of the dwelling and the 'natural rights deriving from marriage and paternity and those pertaining to the family'. The compromise which was arrived at was that Art. 8(1) should simply 'respect' those rights, leaving each state free to have higher domestic constitutional standards.[140]

2.10.2 There are in this context practical mechanisms for rendering the 'common constitutional traditions' a more direct and relevant source in EU law. In the *Schrems* data protection reference, the Irish High Court drew attention to the manner in which the Irish courts had protected the inviolability of the dwelling and suggested that, drafting differences notwithstanding, Art. 7(1) of the Charter might well be interpreted in a similar fashion.

2.11 Article 53 of the Charter and the Issue of Stricter Constitutional Standards

2.11.1 It is, perhaps, not altogether surprising that Art. 53 of the Charter was interpreted in a restrictive fashion by the Court of Justice in *Melloni*. In effect, Member States are not permitted to have higher constitutional standards where this would jeopardise the uniform application of EU law. Not, perhaps, for the first time,

[139] Besselink 2012, pp. 137–138.
[140] Hogan 2014, pp. 167.

the wording of the Charter is apt to mislead. As thus interpreted, Art. 53 of the Charter permits Member States to have their own national constitutional standards and to apply them to those cases where either the Charter or, for that matter, EU law is not engaged. It would nonetheless have to be admitted that any other interpretation of Art. 53 would potentially jeopardise the uniform application of EU law.

There has, however, been little discussion in Ireland on whether the Court of Justice should properly set the level of Charter rights at the level of the ECHR, or whether there are areas where there may be a case for increasing the standard to match that provided under the Constitution. This is mainly because it is recognised that the ECHR is the only common template among the Member States which would justify this approach.

2.12 Democratic Debate on Constitutional Rights and Values

2.12.1 Fair Trials International has noted that the adoption of the European Arrest Warrant Framework Decision was marked by 'the lack of public engagement in the area of defence rights and the almost total absence of political debate on the subject' (cf. the Questionnaire). This was certainly true in Ireland as much as elsewhere in the EU. The elaborate nature of the safeguards and protections contained in the 2003 Act is largely due to the fact that the Minister for Justice at the time[141] was a very prominent lawyer who was greatly interested in the entire EAW process and its implications for the administration of criminal justice. There has been even less debate on the question of the EU Data Retention Directive. Unlike in other jurisdictions – such as e.g. Germany – data protection is regarded as an exotic topic which excites few outside of a cadre of specialists.

There is little doubt but that, as the Irish *Meagher* and *Maher* case law shows, the need for the speedy and effective transposition of EU directives and the supremacy of EU law dilutes the opportunity for democratic deliberation, constitutional review and accommodation of important constitutional issues. In *Meagher* the Supreme Court upheld the constitutionality of a procedure whereby a fixed time limit contained in earlier legislation was amended by ministerial order. The Court reasoned that in the circumstances of the substantive prosecution at issue in that case,[142] it was necessary for the time limit[143] to be extended to ensure an effective

141 Michael McDowell S.C. Mr. McDowell was a former Attorney General who later held the office of Tánaiste (Deputy Prime Minister).

142 The applicant had been prosecuted for the possession of illegal animal growth promoting substances which Member States were required by a series of directives to make illegal.

143 The time limit was extended from six months (in legislation) by two months (by ministerial order).

prosecution system for these offences.[144] This system of amending legislation by ministerial order was accordingly deemed to be 'necessitated' to give effect to European Union obligations and was accordingly immune from constitutional challenge by reason of Art. 29.4.6 of the Constitution.[145]

Other examples can be given where the decisions of the Court of Justice or the European Court of Human Rights have also effectively lessened or weakened the protection of domestic fundamental rights provided for in Irish constitutional law. One example from the sphere of immigration law and family life is the 'insurmountable obstacles' line of case law from the ECtHR where that Court has held that there is, generally speaking, no objection on Art. 8 grounds to the deportation of a spouse to that spouse's country of origin where it is reasonable to expect the other spouse to join him or her.[146] This test has proved very influential with the Irish courts, even though the practical effect of this decision may be that non-national parents are in effect obliged to take their Irish citizen children back with them to their country of origin.[147] This test has been applied even though Art. 8 ECHR refers merely to 'respect' for family life, whereas Art. 41.1.1 of the Constitution guarantees the 'inalienable and imprescriptible rights' of the family. Some later judgments have dissented from the proposition that the 'insurmountable obstacles' test is the appropriate test to apply in view of the higher standard of protection contained in Irish constitutional law, 'as some weight must be given to the even more emphatic description of family rights contained in Article 41' as compared with Art. 8 ECHR.[148]

In other cases, however, the Court of Justice has shown the way. Thus, for example, the Court's own decisions in *Chen*[149] and *Ruiz-Zambrano*[150] have illustrated how the right of European citizenship contained in Art. 20 TFEU will serve to protect the (third country) parents of minor children who are citizens of the

[144] As Blayney J. put it ([1994] 1 IR 329, 360:
'The relevant directives here were binding on the State from the moment they were adopted, "as to the result to be achieved." One result to be achieved clearly was the creation of effective sanctions for the enforcement of the measures contained in the directives. So the State was bound to introduce effective measures, and if this necessitated adopting a measure which impliedly amended an existing statute, that measure would prevail over the statute because it was in substance a measure of Community law. It is really only in form that it is part of the domestic statute.'

[145] The reasoning of the Irish Supreme Court in *Meagher* has met with almost universal criticism in the academic literature. See e.g. the comments of Fahey 2010 at 50 describing the decision as 'an unfortunate case of the Irish judiciary demonstrating yet again that they are excessively pragmatic in this area of the law'.

[146] See, e.g., *Boultif v. Switzerland,* no. 54273/00, ECHR 2001-IX; *Üner v. the Netherlands* [GC], no. 46410/99, ECHR 2006-XII.

[147] See, e.g., *Alli v. Minister for Justice, Equality and Law Reform* [2009] IEHC 595, [2010] 4 IR 45.

[148] See, e.g., *AO v. Minister for Justice* [2012] IESC 79, *EA v. Minister for Justice* [2012] IEHC 371.

[149] Case C-200/02 *Chen* [2004] ECR I-09925.

[150] Case C-34/09 *Ruiz-Zambrano* [2011] ECR I-01177.

Member State in question from deportation where this would have the 'effect of depriving citizens of the Union of the genuine enjoyment of the substance of the rights conferred by virtue of their status as citizens of the Union'. A majority of the Irish Supreme Court had previously reached exactly the opposite conclusion in the context of the operation of the rights of citizenship conferred by Art. 2 and Art. 9 of the Constitution.[151] That Court has now – tacitly at least – acknowledged that its earlier decision was wrong and that it must be re-considered in the light of *Chen* and *Zambrano*.[152]

3 Constitutional Issues in Global Governance

3.1 Constitutional Rules on International Organisations and the Ratification of Treaties

3.1.1–3.1.4 International relations are regulated in Art. 29 of the Constitution, where the relevant sections provide as follows:

> 1 Ireland affirms its devotion to the ideal of peace and friendly co-operation amongst nations founded on international justice and morality. …
>
> 3 Ireland accepts the generally recognised principles of international law as its rule of conduct in its relations with other States. …
>
> 5 1° Every international agreement to which the State becomes a party shall be laid before Dáil Éireann.
>
> 2° The State shall not be bound by any international agreement involving a charge upon public funds unless the terms of the agreement shall have been approved by Dáil Éireann.
>
> 3° This section shall not apply to agreements or conventions of a technical and administrative character.

As we have already noted, where an international treaty involves a significant derogation from national sovereignty or materially affects the international operation of executive, legislative or judicial powers, a referendum will generally be required to effect constitutional change. This has been the basis of the various constitutional amendments dealing with EU Treaty change, but it also explains the basis for the constitutional amendment dealing with the Belfast Agreement in respect of Northern Ireland and the ratification of membership of the International Criminal Court. The relevant provisions include the following:

> 7 1° The State may consent to be bound by the British-Irish Agreement done at Belfast on the 10th day of April, 1998, hereinafter called the Agreement. …
>
> 9 The State may ratify the Rome Statute of the International Criminal Court done at Rome on the 17th day of July, 1998.

[151] *AO and DL v. Minister for Justice* [2003] 1 IR 1.

[152] *Okunade v. Minister for Justice* [2012] IESC 49, [2012] 3 IR 152.

Where an international treaty involves a charge on public funds, it must be laid before Dáil Éireann (cf. Art. 29.5.2 above) and the courts will not give effect to any international treaty where this constitutional requirement has not been complied with. For example, a ministerial order giving effect to an Irish-US extradition treaty was found unconstitutional, as the treaty provided for a charge on public funds and it had not received the prior approval of Dáil Éireann.[153]

3.2 The Position of International Law in National Law

3.2.1–3.2.2 Article 29 of the Constitution commits Ireland to the classic position of the dualist state, since Art. 29.6 provides that an international agreement has force in domestic law only to the extent that such is provided by the Oireachtas itself:

> No international agreement shall be part of the domestic law of the State save as may be determined by the Oireachtas.

In recent times both the Supreme Court and the Court of Appeal have stressed that the effect of this provision is that international agreements do not have, as it were, direct effect in Irish law unless the Oireachtas has clearly indicated to the contrary.[154]

Beyond the rules outlined above and in the preceding section, the Irish courts have nonetheless faithfully given priority to international treaty obligations which have been incorporated into EU legislative instruments. If, as nowadays is often the case, these treaty obligations have been subsumed into an EU legislative instrument, then this will have the effect that, by virtue of Art. 29.4.6 of the Constitution, the treaty (as thus subsumed into EU law) is beyond challenge on domestic law grounds. This can be seen in cases involving the European Arrest Warrant,[155] but perhaps a better example can be found in one aspect of the *Bosphorus Airways* litigation.

At the height of the Yugoslav wars, economic sanctions were imposed by means of Council Regulation 990/93/EEC. These sanctions in turn reflected the terms of a UN Security Council resolution to the same effect. Acting pursuant to the sanctions Regulation, the Irish authorities had impounded an airplane owned by Yugoslav Airways but which had been the subject of a dry lease to Bosphorus. The airplane in

---

[153] *The State (Gilliland) v. Governor of Mountjoy Prison* [1987] IR 201.

[154] See, e.g., *McD. v. L.* [2009] IESC 81, [2010] 2 IR 199 (European Convention on Human Rights), *Sweeney v. Governor of Loughan House Open Prison* [2014] IESC 42, [2014] 2 ILRM 401 (European Convention on the Transfer of Sentenced Persons); *McCoy v. Shillelagh Quarries Ltd.* [2015] IECA 28 (Aarhus Convention outside the scope of EU law).

[155] This unhappiness is most notably visible in the judgments of McKechnie J. and MacMenamin J. in *Minister for Justice and Equality v. Ostrowski* [2013] IESC 24.

question had never returned to Yugoslavia, but had been principally utilised for the purpose of charter flights between Turkey and the rest of Europe. In the High Court Murphy J. stressed that the lease in question was *bona fide* and did not represent an attempt to circumvent the sanctions in these regulations. Accordingly, he declined to hold that the 1993 Regulation should apply to the situation presented by this case:

> As long as the position is that no citizen of Serbia or Montenegro has any use or control over the aircraft in question or the opportunity to receive any income derived from it, then it would seem to me that the regulations have achieved their purpose fully and the impounding of the aircraft would constituted a wholly unwarranted interference in the business of Bosphorus.[156]

The state appealed to the Supreme Court, which in turn made a reference under Art. 267 TFEU (then Art. 177) to the Court of Justice. That Court, however, saw no real difficulty in the manner by which the sanctions operated. It stated that all sanctions regimes might impact on innocent third parties. It continued:

> Moreover, the importance of the aims pursued by the regulation at issue is such as to justify negative consequences, even of a substantial nature, for some operators….. the aim pursued by the sanctions assumes especial importance, which is, in particular, in terms of Regulation No 990/93 and more especially the eighth recital in the preamble thereto, to dissuade the Federal Republic of Yugoslavia from 'further violating the integrity and security of the Republic of Bosnia-Herzegovina and to induce the Bosnian Serb party to cooperate in the restoration of peace in this Republic.
>
> As compared with an objective of general interest so fundamental for the international community, which consists in putting an end to the state of war in the region and to the massive violations of human rights and humanitarian international law in the Republic of Bosnia-Herzegovina, the impounding of the aircraft in question, which is owned by an undertaking based in or operating from the Federal Republic of Yugoslavia, cannot be regarded as inappropriate or disproportionate.[157]

While *Bosphorus Airways* may properly be regarded as a special – almost unique – case so far as Ireland is concerned, it may nonetheless be thought to illustrate how the decisions of global institutions such as the UN see justice through the prism of a global governance and are, perhaps, less sensitive to the appeals of individuals affected by such measures. No one doubted the grave and terrible humanitarian consequences of the Bosnian War, but it might be thought that the Court of Justice made undeservedly little of the argument that the operation of the sanctions regime had a disproportionate effect on what the Irish court regarded as a *bona fide* leasing arrangement.

---

[156] *Bosphorus Airways v. Minister for Transport* [1994] 2 ILRM 550, 560, *per* Murphy J.

[157] Case C-84/95 *Bosphorus* [1996] ECR I-03953.

3.3–3.4 *Democratic Control and Judicial Review*

See Sects. 3.1 and 3.2.

3.5 *IMF Bailout Programme*

3.5.1–3.5.2 When the bail-out package was announced in December 2010, the issue arose as to whether the agreement with the IMF was an international agreement which involved a charge on public funds for the purposes of Art. 29.5.2 of the Constitution. If it was, Art. 29.5.2 would require that the agreement receive the prior approval of Dáil Éireann (the lower House of Parliament). Although the IMF denied that the agreement was an international agreement for this purpose on the basis that it was a simply a 'letter of intent' to enter into a conditional assistance programme, it awaited the formal approval of the Dáil[158] before the bail-out package was agreed with the Irish Government.

References

Besselink L. (2012) General Report. In: Laffranque J. (ed.) The Protection of Fundamental Rights Post-Lisbon, Reports of the XXV FIDE Congress Tallinn 2012, Vol. 1. Tartu University Press, Tallinn, pp. 63–139.

Bradley S.T. (1987) The Referendum on the Single European Act. E.L. Rev. 12:301 et seq.

Casey J.P. (2000) Constitutional Law in Ireland. Sweet & Maxwell, Dublin.

Chalmers D., Hadjiemmanuil C., Monti G., Tomkins A. (2006) European Union law: text and materials. Cambridge University Press, Cambridge.

Chubb B. (1974) Cabinet Government in Ireland. Institute of Public Administration, Dublin.

Fahey E. (2010) EU Law in Ireland. Clarus Press, Dublin.

Farrell R., Hanrahan A. (2011) The European Arrest Warrant in Ireland. Clarus Press, Dublin.

Foley B. (2010) The BUPA Ireland Case and Constitutional Litigation. Irish Jurist 45:230 et seq.

Geoghegan H. (2014) Crotty put to sleep by Pringle. In: Bradley K., Travers N., Whelan A. (eds.) Of Courts and Constitutions: Liber Amicorum in Honour of Nial Fennelly. Hart, Oxford, pp. 233 et seq.

Hogan G. (1987) The Supreme Court and the Single European Act. Irish Jurist 22:55 et seq.

Hogan G. (1997) The Constitution, Property Rights and Proportionality. Irish Jurist 32:373 et seq.

Hogan G. (2000) The British-Irish Agreement and the Irish Constitution. E.L. Rev. 6:1 et seq.

Hogan G. (2012) The Origins of the Irish Constitution 1928–1941. Royal Irish Academy, Dublin.

Hogan G. (2014) The Influence of the Continental Constitutional Tradition on the Drafting of the Constitution. In: Ruane B., Barniville D., O'Callaghan J. (eds.) Law and Government: A Tribute to Rory Brady. Round Hall, Dublin.

Jaconelli J. (1992) Human Rights and Irish Home Rule. Irish Jurist 25–27:181 et seq.

Keane R. (1992) Fundamental Rights In Irish Law: A Note on the Historical Background. In: O'Reilly J. (ed.) Human Rights and Constitutional Law: Essays in Honour of Brian Walsh. Round Hall, Dublin, pp. 25 et seq.

[158] 725 *Dáil Debates*, Col. 337 (15 December 2010).

Keane R. (2014) Reconciling Ireland's Sovereignty with Membership of the European Union – the Lessons of Crotty and Pringle. In: Ruane B., Barniville D., O'Callaghan J. (eds.) Law and Government: A Tribute to Rory Brady, Round Hall, Dublin.

Kelly J.M. (1983) Equality before the Law in Three European Jurisdictions. Irish Jurist 18:259 et seq.

Kelly J.M. (2003) The Irish Constitution, Fourth edn., Tottel, Dublin.

Kenny D. (2014) Proportionality, Burden of Proof and Some Signs of Reconsideration. Irish Jurist 49:141 et seq.

Kiernan F., Brittain S., Donnelly C. (2012) Ireland. In: Laffranque J. (ed.) The Protection of Fundamental Rights Post-Lisbon, Reports of the XXV FIDE Congress Tallinn 2012, Vol. 1. Tartu University Press, Tallinn, pp. 561–580.

O'Donnell D. (2014) The Most Curious Forerunner. In: Ruane B., Barniville D., O'Callaghan J. (eds.) Law and Government: A Tribute to Rory Brady. Round Hall, Dublin.

Temple Lang J. (1987) The Irish Court Case which delayed the Single European Act. CML Rev. 24:709 et seq.

Tomkin A. (2004) Implementing Community Legislation in to National Law: the Demands of a New Legal Order. Judicial Studies Institute Journal (2):130 et seq.

Walsh D.P.J. (2009) The European Arrest Warrant in Ireland: Surrendering Our Standards to a European Criminal Law Area. In Bacik I.C., Heffernan L. (eds.) Criminal Law and Procedure: Current Issues and Emerging Trends. First Law, Dublin, pp. 5–34.

Permissions

All chapters in this book were first published in NCEGGDRRL, by Springer Nature; hereby published with permission under the Creative Commons Attribution License or equivalent. Every chapter published in this book has been scrutinized by our experts. Their significance has been extensively debated. The topics covered herein carry significant findings which will fuel the growth of the discipline. They may even be implemented as practical applications or may be referred to as a beginning point for another development.

The contributors of this book come from diverse backgrounds, making this book a truly international effort. This book will bring forth new frontiers with its revolutionizing research information and detailed analysis of the nascent developments around the world.

We would like to thank all the contributing authors for lending their expertise to make the book truly unique. They have played a crucial role in the development of this book. Without their invaluable contributions this book wouldn't have been possible. They have made vital efforts to compile up to date information on the varied aspects of this subject to make this book a valuable addition to the collection of many professionals and students.

This book was conceptualized with the vision of imparting up-to-date information and advanced data in this field. To ensure the same, a matchless editorial board was set up. Every individual on the board went through rigorous rounds of assessment to prove their worth. After which they invested a large part of their time researching and compiling the most relevant data for our readers.

The editorial board has been involved in producing this book since its inception. They have spent rigorous hours researching and exploring the diverse topics which have resulted in the successful publishing of this book. They have passed on their knowledge of decades through this book. To expedite this challenging task, the publisher supported the team at every step. A small team of assistant editors was also appointed to further simplify the editing procedure and attain best results for the readers.

Apart from the editorial board, the designing team has also invested a significant amount of their time in understanding the subject and creating the most relevant covers. They scrutinized every image to scout for the most suitable representation of the subject and create an appropriate cover for the book.

The publishing team has been an ardent support to the editorial, designing and production team. Their endless efforts to recruit the best for this project, has resulted in the accomplishment of this book. They are a veteran in the field of academics and their pool of knowledge is as vast as their experience in printing. Their expertise and guidance has proved useful at every step. Their uncompromising quality standards have made this book an exceptional effort. Their encouragement from time to time has been an inspiration for everyone.

The publisher and the editorial board hope that this book will prove to be a valuable piece of knowledge for researchers, students, practitioners and scholars across the globe.

List of Contributors

Anneli Albi
Law School, University of Kent, Canterbury, UK

Samo Bardutzky
University of Ljubljana, Ljubljana, Slovenia

Nóra Chronowski
Hungarian Academy of Sciences, Budapest, Hungary
National University of Public Service, Budapest, Hungary

Márton Varju
Hungarian Academy of Sciences, Budapest, Hungary

Petra Bárd
Eötvös Loránd University Faculty of Law, Budapest, Hungary
Central European University, Budapest, Hungary

Gábor Sulyok
Hungarian Academy of Sciences, Budapest, Hungary
Széchenyi István University, Győr, Hungary

Xenophon Contiades
Panteion University, Athens, Greece

Charalambos Papacharalambous
Law Department, University of Cyprus, Nicosia, Cyprus

Christos Papastylianos
School of Law, University of Nicosia, Nicosia, Cyprus

Joan Solanes Mullor and Aida Torres Pérez
Pompeu Fabra University, Barcelona, Spain

Gerard Hogan
European Court of Justice, Luxembourg, Luxembourg

Index

www.ingramcontent.com/pod-product-compliance
Lightning Source LLC
LaVergne TN
LVHW051046220926
848485LV00001BA/21
9781639872176